The College of William and
Mary in the Civil War

The College of William and Mary in the Civil War

Sean M. Heuvel *and*
Lisa L. Heuvel

McFarland & Company, Inc., Publishers
Jefferson, North Carolina, and London

ISBN 978-0-7864-7309-0
softcover : acid free paper ∞

LIBRARY OF CONGRESS CATALOGUING DATA ARE AVAILABLE

BRITISH LIBRARY CATALOGUING DATA ARE AVAILABLE

© 2013 Sean M. Heuvel and Lisa L. Heuvel. All rights reserved

No part of this book may be reproduced or transmitted in any form or by any means, electronic or mechanical, including photocopying or recording, or by any information storage and retrieval system, without permission in writing from the publisher.

On the cover: A sketch by David E. Cronin, depicting the April 9, 1863, Confederate raid on Williamsburg, which resulted in heavy skirmishing on the William and Mary campus (collection of the New-York Historical Society)

Manufactured in the United States of America

*McFarland & Company, Inc., Publishers
Box 611, Jefferson, North Carolina 28640
www.mcfarlandpub.com*

To the memory of Benjamin Stoddert Ewell, whose vision of William and Mary carried it through what were arguably the College's most calamitous years.

Contents

Acknowledgments	ix
Preface	1
Introduction	9
1. Memories of Grandeur	15
2. On the Eve of War	33
3. A Bitter Demise	49
4. The College's Ambitious Sons	67
5. Warrior Scholars	85
6. The Old Guard at War	105
7. One Faithful Heart	133
Epilogue: The Old College Moves Forward	159
Military Service Table	169
Appendix A: The Civil War Service of William and Mary Students, 1861–1865	170
Appendix B: The Civil War Service of William and Mary Faculty, 1861–1865	173
Appendix C: The Civil War Service of William and Mary Alumni, 1861–1865	174
Chapter Notes	187
Bibliography	205
Index	215

Acknowledgments

For the authors, William and Mary is our alma mater almost six times over, with three degrees (B.A., M.A., Ed.D.) for one of us and two with a third in progress (B.A., M.Ed., Ph.D.) for the other. Both of us have written previously about William and Mary's history in the Civil War era and Benjamin Stoddert Ewell's leadership. This book originated in a master's thesis on the College's underrepresented faculty, students, and alumni who marched off to war, and their postwar fates. It grew into a larger exploration of largely forgotten aspects of the College's Civil War history. We also chose to explore this in the context of William and Mary's master narrative, which centers on it's distinguished colonial history and alumni. Although those contributions to the formation of our nation are justly celebrated, they have eclipsed significant people and events of the mid-to-late 19th century deserving recognition for their parts in preserving that heritage and moving it forward into the 20th century. Further, William and Mary maintained its iconic status largely through the efforts of Benjamin Ewell, other College leaders, and friends determined to rebuild and restore the College following the major fires of 1859 and 1862.

We acknowledge those individuals as well as Robert E. Lee and other Confederate veteran officers who, like Benjamin Ewell, took leadership roles in struggling colleges and universities throughout the South. Others also deserve recognition: the College was helped and hindered by those above the Mason-Dixon Line. There were Northerners who supported the College even after the war had hardened sentiments against the South: merchant princes in New York, members of Congress, publishing executives, university officials, and donors in major cities such as Philadelphia, Baltimore, and New York City.

In essence, the College of William and Mary is a case study in tradition caught in the crossfire of changing values. For both of us, the process of exploring the College's largely forgotten Civil War history was an enriching and fulfilling experience. For helping us pursue this intellectual journey, we are grateful to a number of scholars who supported our project from its earliest stages. Dr. Robert Kenzer of the University of Richmond encouraged the beginnings of this research as a master's thesis project. His support and enthusiasm for the topic were what initially encouraged us to envision this research as culminating in a possible book. Dr. Jonathan White of Christopher Newport University was also incredibly helpful in suggesting sources, providing leads for further research, and providing encouragement through all stages of this research.

As we researched this intriguing subject, we were helped immeasurably by the staffs and collections of the Earl Gregg Swem Library at William and Mary, the New York Historical Society, and the John D. Rockefeller Library at the Colonial Williamsburg Foundation. Specifically, Swem Library's university archivist, Amy Schindler, played a major role in supporting the project and providing key images. The New-York Historical Society's Robert Delap and the Colonial Williamsburg Foundation's Marianne Martin were also very helpful in tracking down important images for use in the book. Further, Kate Egner Gruber and Drew Gruber of the Colonial Williamsburg Foundation provided valuable feedback on early drafts of the manuscript and played vital roles in facilitating and encouraging our research.

We both gratefully acknowledge our spouses, Johannes J. Heuvel, Jr., and Katey Cunningham Heuvel, who is an alumna of the College and mother of Sean M. Heuvel, Jr. Their support and patience played vital roles in allowing us to finish this book in a timely manner. We are also grateful to our extended families and friends for their support. Most of all, we are thankful to those forerunners who preserved William and Mary's history for future generations, even in its darkest hours.

Preface

Like many other institutions of higher learning in the shattered South, The College of William and Mary in Virginia suffered from the Civil War and military occupation. Over the years, campus tradition and historical accounts chronicled how one man fought for it before, during, and after the war: Benjamin S. Ewell (1810–1894), its beloved president and protector. Yet, standing in the shadows are his contemporaries: the College's wartime students, faculty and alumni who went to war, almost all on the Confederate side. Outside of a 1914 memorial, the majority of these soldiers and officers go unmentioned in College histories; some, like Lt. Gen. Winfield Scott, are prominent figures, others much less so. Bringing their lives and wartime records to light adds another dimension to William and Mary's history, as does placing it at the center of related themes: the history of higher education in the South, William and Mary's evolution as an iconic representation of American heritage, and the support it received from Northern as well as Southern sources in the 19th century.

The College of William and Mary was founded in 1693 by royal charter. Its history mirrors America's saga of growth and conflict over more than four centuries, including military occupation during the American Revolution and the Civil War. This book examines the South's oldest higher education institution through the political and wartime service of its students, faculty, and alumni. They represented the College honorably, yet much of their story disappeared over time. Of the well-researched histories of the College and Williamsburg that include the Civil War era, none to date have traced how the William and Mary community collectively answered the call to military service, or what happened to those who did. Therefore, this expanded study asks, "Who served in the Civil War, and what happened to them?"

That question became part of a larger exploration. We had to understand what happened to the College before, during, and after the war, because its narrative has developed in a distinctive way, shaping the attitudes of its constituencies and the general public. In surveying that history, we asked, are there reasons for what has been remembered and what remains less known about this Civil War chapter and its aftermath in William and Mary's institutional history?

This book was written to answer those questions at a fitting time. The Civil War Sesquicentennial has been the catalyst for research and commemoration of the war, but equally, for a re-examination of how the past is interpreted. Many individuals merit inclusion in this book and appear within its pages for their military service as members of the College community, but William and Mary itself predominates through the historical development of a body of fact, belief, and tradition that forms its identity. This is important to consider, because a substantial number of its faculty, students, and alumni reconnected to the College after the war ended. Benjamin Ewell, its president, returned to take up the task of bringing it back into operation, and some faculty members resumed their teaching responsibilities.

From William and Mary's former students and alumni came the advocates who would help support it during the coming decades. Members of this postwar generation also served their alma mater. Confederate alumni included Col. William Lamb and Maj. Gen. William B. Taliaferro, who were Board of Visitors members in 1867 and 1870, respectively. The College's own came back for ceremonial events: The first post–Civil War alumni reunion took place in 1875. In 1894, Confederate veterans joined townspeople, faculty, students, other alumni, and Board members in escorting Benjamin Ewell's body to the Wren Chapel. After the funeral service, they gathered at the little cemetery Ewell established in 1859, to watch him interred near his mother and sister.[1] In 1895, E.J. Harvie, former inspector-general of the Army of Tennessee and a member of Gen. Joseph E. Johnston's staff, mourned Benjamin Ewell as one who knew him. Harvie wrote of that occasion: "His death was felt all over the State, and in Williamsburg, where he was loved, honored and looked up to, tears from old and young fell without restraint at the grave where their President was buried."[2] He would not be forgotten by the alumni in that era and they took action for the future, erecting a tablet in his memory that was unveiled in the College Chapel on June 21, 1899.

Although the Revolutionary era was not in living memory for people like Harvie, many knew of the College's illustrious past through one of its greatest advocates. As Lester's 1883 *History of the United States* noted, "William and Mary College has been well claimed by President Ewell to hold the same rank to the South, as an educator of our eminent national men, that Harvard and Yale do to the North."³ William and Mary's iconic status and prestige evolved in large part from its colonial origins. Three presidents of the United States — Thomas Jefferson, James Monroe, and John Tyler — studied at William and Mary, and a fourth, George Washington, was the institution's first chancellor. Declaration of Independence signer George Wythe was its first professor of law and police, and John Marshall, later the first Chief Justice of the United States, was a student. The College's historic firsts include the establishment of the Phi Beta Kappa Society in 1776; Benjamin Ewell would help to revive the College chapter.

William and Mary's impressive heritage was central to President Ewell's promoting the recognition of its national significance, and he would do so unceasingly during his tenure. Ewell was the school's interim president for part of 1848, a faculty member, and its sixteenth president from 1854 until 1888. Legendary in the William and Mary narrative for his commitment, Ewell disseminated its heritage through multiple channels. He reached out to influential figures in all spheres of society, chronicled its history, and lobbied for its survival in the halls of Congress. Historical records indicate that Northern businessmen, leaders, and institutions also supported William and Mary in specific times of need; the actions of many in the North and South saved this "Spartan among American universities," as President Warren G. Harding called it in 1921. Thanks to them, it endured despite the extraordinary challenges of the College's most desperate era.

Benjamin Ewell's efforts at the College are all the more compelling because of issues in his personal life, and that is acknowledged in this work. He sought to secure student enrollment, to raise funds, and later, to assist in William and Mary's post–Civil War recovery. Ewell and alumni such as former president John Tyler (1790–1862) and Gov. Henry A. Wise (1806–1876) strove to save the College from periodic calls for closure or removal from Williamsburg. Benjamin Ewell's strategies for survival included reaching out to the general public for support, plus writing and lecturing extensively on William and Mary's importance to America. Ewell's return to a deserted campus to ring the College bell during its darkest times is legendary for fulfilling William and Mary's continued existence under the ancient royal charter. In fact, the aging president and his tenant farmer Malachi Gardiner did so at the beginning of each semester through most of the 1880s. Largely overlooked until now has been Ewell's significant military service during the Civil War, which receives greater attention here. Over time, Ewell's dedication to the College eclipsed his role as a Confederate officer. This book explores all those at the College who faced similar crossroads as the war began, many leaving campus for military service and lives transformed by the conflict. It examines William and Mary's Civil War history through the lenses of social history and the history of higher education and also traces the evolution of its public persona into the early 20th century, comparing that to today's College.

As authors and alumni, we have both written previously about our alma mater's history in the Civil War era and Benjamin Ewell's leadership. Over the past several years, our research has evolved as we completed magazine articles, academic papers, and conference presentations on this topic. However, the genesis of this book came from Sean's graduate work for a M.A. in history at the University of Richmond, where his 2005 thesis was on the Civil War service and postwar fates of the College's students, faculty, and alumni. Since then, additional research has yielded important parts of that story, but there is always more to learn.

The Civil War service of William and Mary students, faculty, and alumni was determined from a variety of sources. Student and faculty wartime service was relatively easy to trace because of the small number of people involved — just over seventy. Working off the list of students and faculty members present on the Civil War commemorative tablet in the Wren Building was a starting point. Primary and secondary sources were also gathered from four university archives, from the Library of Congress, and from the Virginia Historical Society, in addition to published works and academic papers. All of those sources combined to present a fairly complete picture of student and faculty Civil War service.

Researching the College's alumni Civil War service was an entirely different matter. Despite their importance to the College, the alumni were the most challenging group to study for a variety of reasons. It was relatively easy to find outside information on alumni who held high-profile positions during the war (i.e., generals, colonels, legislators). Learning about the lesser-known individuals who served as enlisted men or junior officers was much more difficult. There was also the issue of sheer numbers: only a few dozen students and a handful of faculty were concentrated on the campus by the dawn of the conflict. However, there were hundreds of William and Mary graduates scattered all over the country just prior to the war.

Evidence suggests that by the late antebellum era, the College's alumni base was more geographically diverse than ever before. While most William and Mary alumni lived in Virginia, there were graduates living in such far-flung places as Texas, Illinois, and California in the years preceding the war. Since College records only listed the name and place of origin (usually in Virginia) for each alumnus, it is difficult to track individuals who moved elsewhere after leaving William and Mary. To compound the problem, the College only attempted to identify Confederate Army veterans in its late 19th-century alumni rosters, obscuring the service of graduates who were Union Army veterans or non-military public officials.

Several other obstacles made determining alumni military and political service difficult. First, because of challenges in gathering information during the postwar years, the College identified at most only half of its alumni with Confederate Army service in its published catalogues, leaving many other veterans unlabeled. However, careful research uncovered many of the unlisted veterans, who are identified for the first time here by cross-listing individuals and their places of origin with published regimental records and government databases. For instance, the Confederate Army service of an alumnus listed in College matriculation records as "John G. Williams from Orange County, Virginia," could be determined by examining regimental rosters of units formed in that section of the state. In general, that approach was only effective if the alumnus in question had a unique name, or moved back to his place of origin after leaving William and Mary, or both. Conversely, for alumni who possessed common names (e.g., "Robert Smith") or moved elsewhere following graduation, their military service was nearly impossible to determine, since it could not be said with certainty that we had the correct "Robert Smith" in question.

The format of the College's matriculation records also made it extremely difficult to determine how many alumni served in the Union Army. Since the vast majority were native Virginians, most went on to align with the Confederate cause. Yet, sprinkled among each graduating class during the antebellum era were alumni from such states as Illinois, Massachusetts, Pennsylvania, and New York, thus offering a possibility that some served in the Union Army. Unfortunately, College records only listed the state of origin for out-of-state students, unlike in-state students, who had their home city or county listed. Knowing only his state of origin made it very difficult to determine the Union Army service of an alumnus. Despite these research challenges, the following chapters contain the most comprehensive overview of William and Mary student, faculty, and alumni Civil War service ever attempted.

The traumatic effects of war and occupation on Williamsburg and the College contributed to the lack of information about William and Mary faculty, students, and alumni in that era. While acknowledging that, we sought a better understanding of why the College's institutional narrative, traditions, and public persona came to be transmitted within a narrow range regarding the Civil War, with a much broader focus on the College's colonial history. As noted, the Civil War military service of even illustrious alumni has been obscure, with the war itself defined by one incident (the 1862 firing of the main college building by Union soldiers) and one individual, Benjamin Ewell (but not his Civil War service).

How and why has the College's history been transmitted over time with some aspects achieving enduring prominence and others not? Exploring this question led us to discussion — and sometimes debate — about social history and public memory, particularly when accounts about the Civil War era split along Northern-Southern lines. Northern accounts of Civil War events and people in Williamsburg added significantly to the study, as did College documentation of support William and Mary received from Northern donors, businesses, and institutions of higher learning before, after, and even during after the war. Comparing multiple accounts of historical events and individuals was another research avenue, particularly with the well-known and highly contested fire of 1862. We considered the effects of war and military occupation as a factor, and also the establishment of the Colonial Williamsburg Foundation in 1926, which created an enduring emphasis on Williamsburg's colonial history in the public imagination.

One of the most challenging components of research and writing was in the synthesis of information and scholarship as we discovered an alternative interpretation of William and Mary's Civil War history. As with the content on military and political service, information on the 19th-century College and its societal context came from primary source collections and research papers at the Colonial Williamsburg Foundation, official records and the papers of Benjamin Ewell at The College of William and Mary, academic papers, and published works on related events, people, and places. Specific sources are cited in the bibliography and acknowledgments. Of the published scholarship written within the last quarter-century, the works of Carol K. Dubbs (1999, 2002), Susan Godson, Ludwell H. Johnson, Richard B. Sherman, Thad W. Tate, and Helen C. Walker (1993), and Wilford Kale (2007) have contributed a comprehensive overview of William and Mary's history. Among College of William and Mary theses and dissertations, those by Ruby Osbourne (1981), Anne Chapman (1984), David Sacks (1984), and Russell T. Smith (1980) pointed to ways in which the College master narrative has emphasized or omitted critical historical details. Comparing them to earlier scholarship by College presidents Benjamin Ewell and Lyon G. Tyler (1902, 1906), the work of J.E. Morpurgo (1976), and Parke Rouse (1973) also has suggested how William and Mary's colonial heritage was emphasized to promote and preserve it long before John D. Rockefeller and the Rev. Dr. W.A.R Goodwin envisioned the restoration of Williamsburg.

The work of Colonial Williamsburg Foundation researchers and historian Carson O. Hudson contributed to our understanding of how oral accounts and early 20th-century research defined Civil War Williamsburg in specific ways. Scholarship by higher education and Civil War historians such as Peter Carmichael (2005), James McPherson (1988), Robert Pace 2004), John Thelin (2004), and Michael David Cohen (2012) led to consideration of unexplored aspects of the College's history in Southern and national contexts. From these and many other sources, evidence emerged of biographical omissions in the College's Civil War saga. Some historical elements additionally have faded from William and Mary's history, which is embedded within a strongly Southern and colonial context. Understanding how that saga has evolved in institutional memory and public consciousness is critical and helps to explain why the contributions of so many faculty, alumni, and students disappeared for so many years.

This work begins with William and Mary's 17th-century origins as the catalyst for its iconic public persona. The Introduction articulates the book's premise that William and Mary's focus on selected historical events and personages has been deliberate, and operates within sociologist Burton Clark's theory of the *organizational saga* as an educational institution. Chapter 1 discusses William and Mary's institutional development up to the Civil War, focusing on its history prior to 1861. In the 19th century, "the Alma Mater of a Nation" was at the mercy of forces beyond its control: changing times, major destruction, and invasion. However like the mythological phoenix that so often has represented it, William and Mary would rise again from the ashes. Chapter 2 delves into the Civil War's immense impact on the College and Williamsburg, particularly through the Union forces there in wartime, using additional Northern perspectives to enhance well-known eyewitness accounts and historical analysis of how Federal occupation affected the College and local residents. Chapter 3 picks up on events in 1862, highlighting the deep divides separating Unionists from Southern loyalists and critical differences in how both sides perceived the realities of war. This chapter also goes further into the mythicized account of the College fire of 1862, which becomes a defining moment in North-South relationships during and after the war.

Moving away from the examination of wartime events on or near the William and Mary campus, several of the book's later chapters explore the military and political Civil War service of the College's students, faculty, and alumni. Chapter 4 provides a thorough examination of the military service of William and Mary's wartime students, highlighting some. It discusses the regiments in which students served, in what battles they fought, casualty information, and how alumni fared after the war.

Chapter 5 explores the Civil War service of the College's seven wartime faculty members, each of whom went on to active service in the Confederate government or armed forces. The chapter also examines these individuals' postwar fates, noting that while some died shortly after the war, others went on to make important contributions to American higher education. Chapter 6 examines the wartime service of the College's alumni within both the military and political realms. There is a special focus on Union and Confederate William and Mary graduates who held high-level wartime positions and played significant roles in shaping the conflict's outcome, such as U.S. Sen. John J. Crittenden, Union Lt. Gen. Winfield Scott, and Confederate diplomat James Murray Mason.

Returning to the William and Mary campus, Chapter 7 centers on one of the College's most iconic leaders, Benjamin Stoddert Ewell. It places his efforts to preserve William and Mary within the larger context of wartime losses suffered by other Virginia colleges, attempts by Southern scholars to bring a new interpretation to the South's defeat, and heroic strategies by Ewell and other William and Mary supporters to revive the College. To do so not only meant effecting reconciliation between the vanquished and the victors; it also meant negotiating a new mission for "Their Majesties' Royall Colledge" that was more inclusive socioeconomically, but still reflected the inherent racial bias of the period.

As the Epilogue points out, College advocates grappled with its postwar transition into the New South and a new century. The College's colonial heritage, preserved with such persistence, is still deeply embedded today in its traditions and identity. Looking through the lens of the Civil War Sesquicentennial does not diminish William and Mary's venerable saga of triumphs, tragedies, and endurance. Instead, it enhances that saga by opening it to new perspectives.

Introduction

In studying William and Mary's history and image as they have been portrayed since the mid-19th century, we found a parallel to sociologist Burton Clark's concept of an "organizational saga," wherein a school or other organization develops a defining body of traditions.[1] Clark further contended that in some cases, a school's mission is so transformative that it achieves "legendary and even heroic features."[2] A collective understanding evolves from specific aspects of an institution's history and accomplishments; this emotionally based interpretation goes beyond historical fact. As these defining beliefs develop, participants' pride and loyalty to the institution grow stronger, manifesting as a saga shared by students, faculty, alumni, and outside supporters.[3] So what aspects of William and Mary are presented publicly and within the William and Mary community? Heroic endurance is a recurring theme: William and Mary has risen phoenix-like from the ashes of three major fires that gutted the Wren Building in 1705, 1859, and 1862, and has overcome the effects of two wartime occupations.

William and Mary ranks second to Harvard (1636) as America's oldest college in actual operation, but traces its origins to the "College of Henricus," which was planned for the Virginia colony beginning in 1619 and ended by the native uprising of 1622. Within the College community and in its public persona, William and Mary's historical narrative boasts extraordinary "firsts" among American colleges. Among these, it was the first to receive its charter from the Crown (1693); the first to receive a coat of arms from the College of Heralds (1694); the first to have a full faculty (1729); the first to establish an intercollegiate fraternity (1776); and the first to have an Honor System, to have an elective system of studies, and to become a university (all 1779).[4] The College proudly affirms that it is the "Alma Mater of a Nation," numbering Thomas Jefferson, James Monroe, and John Tyler among its illustrious alumni.

The College's defining history and traditions are reinforced for students at events such as the Yule Log ceremony, Commencement, Charter Day, and Senior Day, when graduating seniors are permitted to ring the College bell. Prospective students and website visitors may discover that this colonial college has endured invasion, fires, and destitution, and are introduced to its historic list of "firsts." At some point in virtual or on-site visits, they may learn that Union soldiers set fire to the Wren Building during the campus's Federal occupation and that William and Mary's royal charter was upheld in its darkest days through President Benjamin Ewell's dedication. Yet the College's colonial heritage is at the forefront within its community of students, faculty, and alumni, as well as in the identity it projects. Using Burton Clark's lens, William and Mary's body of traditions, its identity, and its organizational saga all proudly affirm its ties to British and American colonial history. The academic year begins with the Opening Convocation at the Wren Building, in which freshmen are welcomed by other members of the College community. In February, Charter Day celebrates the 1693 granting of the royal charter. This observance is rooted in 1859 and 1893 commemorations; with a few gaps, it has been observed annually since 1923.[5]

There also have been a series of royal visits over the years: Queen Elizabeth II and Philip, Duke of Edinburgh, in 1957, for the 350th commemoration of Jamestown's founding; Charles, Prince of Wales, in 1981 and 1993; Queen Elizabeth and Philip again in 2007, for Jamestown's quadri centennial, and in 2012, a return visit by the Queen. Margaret, the Lady Thatcher, became the College's 21st chancellor in 1993, visiting campus six times while she held that position.

As alumni authors and as students of American higher education history along with Virginia history, we appreciate the uniqueness of this historical connection. However, we perceived an imbalance in the information gap about contributions made by College students, faculty, and alumni during and after the Civil War, particularly when some are notable figures. William and Mary alumni who were active in this period included Lt. Gen. Winfield Scott (commander of all U.S. forces during the Mexican War and in the early stages of the Civil War), John J. Crittenden (U.S. attorney general, U.S. senator, and governor of Kentucky), and Edmund Ruffin, the Southern rights activist remembered for firing the first shot at Fort Sumter. A host of governors, congressmen, and policy makers on both sides of the Mason-Dixon Line called William and Mary their alma mater, and their names, along with those of faculty members and students serving in the Civil War, are listed within this book, their service honored.

Although the College's total number of enlisted soldiers and officers was relatively small, their cumulative achievements would be noteworthy at institutions and locales where Civil War history predominates. As competent men of learning, William and Mary faculty, like President Benjamin Ewell, were called on to serve on the staffs of CSA General Joseph E. Johnston, Richard S. Ewell, Lafayette McClaws, and Alexander R. Lawton. Of the five faculty members who served, the four survivors all remained in higher education after the war. Each returned for some years to the College. Among them, former professor Edward Joynes was instrumental in establishing three Southern institutions of higher learning, and was later known for his support of public education.

All of these individuals and more figure in this book's chapters as a response to their omission in the College's modern narrative. In fairness to that omission, it has required over seven years of research to document the names and service of those found: information remains elusive for others' military service, but may yet be located. Until the publication of this work, outside of College records any recognition of individuals' Civil War service was limited to the tablet mentioned in the Wren Building and a related memorial service, the Sunset Ceremony. The Virginia Alpha Chapter of Phi Beta Kappa annually met at Benjamin Ewell's graveside on Alumni Day to recognize the anniversary of his death, June 16. After a lapse of over four decades, Dr. Davis Y. Paschall brought back the tradition in 1961 for his presidential inauguration as the Sunset Parade, moving the ceremony to October and honoring alumni who died during the past year.[6]

We have drawn on prior research and our own to address the traces of Civil War history at William and Mary, and why so few landmarks or signs are on the William and Mary campus—or in Williamsburg. The city has been visually, culturally, and economically connected for almost a century to the modern Colonial Williamsburg Foundation, the world's largest living history museum. The Foundation is internationally known for its impressive museum and research resources, and for restoration and re-creation of buildings and gardens that once graced Virginia's colonial capital. Later chapters discuss the evolution of Colonial Williamsburg from its establishment in 1926, reawakening the town to its colonial history and removing signs of 19th- and 20th-century life within Historic Area boundaries.

Visitors will not find a museum dedicated to the Battle of Williamsburg. However, this de-emphasis of the Civil War era has been reversed somewhat in recent years, with Colonial Williamsburg adding tours of important landmarks in the occupation of Williamsburg. Civil War Trail signs and highway markers help visitors to retrace the Peninsula Campaign

(1862) and locations of the Battle of Williamsburg (May 5, 1862). There are still existing redoubts from Maj. Gen. John B. Magruder's line of Confederate defenses, built across the James River–York River peninsula in 1861-62. A small United Daughters of the Confederacy park marks part of the battlefield site, and the City of Williamsburg built Redoubt Park, protecting Redoubts One and Two for visitors to see. This park is adjacent to the same Quarterpath Road where J.E.B. Stuart once rode with his men. A motel in the vicinity was once named for Fort Magruder; for years, its lobby has displayed paintings, maps, and exhibit cases of artifacts found on site, and Redoubt Six is visible in its garden patio area. A few miles away is Magruder Elementary School, and the Civil War Trust has acquired a portion of woods where the battle took place.

On Jamestown Island, where the Virginia colony took hold in 1607, military leaders from the 17th century, Revolutionary War, and Civil War all took advantage of the site's strategic location on the James River. Seeing the benefits of clear visibility eastward toward the Chesapeake Bay, Confederates built five earthworks on the island as part of their Richmond defenses. One of two forts, Fort Pocahontas, is partially visible; the section that once covered the 17th-century James Fort has been removed in archeological excavations. Historian David F. Riggs observed that several of the defenses are hidden in the island's marshes, "much as Jamestown's Civil War history has been overshadowed by the dynamic role it played in founding a nation."[7]

Rigg's 1999 comparison is just as valid today for the Historic Triangle of Jamestown, Williamsburg, and Yorktown, which collectively mark the rise and fall of British power in the American colonies. Recognition of that part of our national history, and The College of William and Mary's role in it, is nothing new: Benjamin Ewell, John Tyler, and other prominent 19th-century supporters invoked that role in order to protect the College from being moved to another location, to attract funding, and protect it from harm or closure. William and Mary's place in colonial history was reinforced throughout the 20th century and continues today, but as the Epilogue notes, the Civil War Sesquicentennial has attracted attention to that lesser-known part of the College's past. Exhibits, recent archeological discoveries on the campus, and other related events are returning it to public memory. At the same time, Civil War historians and enthusiasts are seeking out this past, not only looking for new information but also searching for new significance in previous interpretations.

Emerging research such as Michael Cohen's 2012 work on the consequences of the Civil War on higher education in the North and South can build on previous histories, "connecting the dots" in new ways. Seminal works by scholars like Roger Geiger (2000), Robert M. Pace (2004), Joseph Stetar (1985), Michael Sugrue (2000), and John Thelin (1976) contributed significantly to our understanding of how American higher education was affected before, during, and after the Civil War. When compared to lay and academic works on specific colleges and universities, or to historical research, there has been much less research published on this era. However, the 150th anniversary of the Civil War has generated more attention through related publications and activities such as conferences, exhibits, and reenactments.

Because this book focuses on one institution, we have framed it within a broader context to explain why and how this institution has been defined. Our work draws on military history, social history, and higher education history to consider a specific hypothesis: Although the Civil War certainly affected The College of William and Mary and brought about significant contributions by its community, the College's identity, history, and traditions give preference to its colonial history. Benjamin Ewell and other 19th-century supporters promoted that history in order to help the College survive, and other factors such as the Williamsburg Restoration maintained real and symbolic colonial references.

The relationship of the College's history to its institutional saga is a critical element in this book, as is William and Mary's role in Southern higher education before and after the 1860s. To that, we add acknowledgment of William and Mary's Civil War volunteers, placing them once more within public and institutional memory.

CHAPTER 1

Memories of Grandeur

At William and Mary; three buildings symbolize the intertwining of its traditions, mission, and history. They *are* the College, in brick and mortar, standing as silent witnesses to American history in the making. Behind them stretches the rest of campus in an archeological timeline of the school's development as a modern university. William and Mary is ranked one of the nation's top "public ivies" today, in addition to being the second of nine colleges founded before the American Revolution.

Flanked by the early 18th-century President's House and the Brafferton, the Sir Christopher Wren Building is the oldest college building in the nation (constructed 1695–1700).[1] It faces east toward the restored streets and buildings of the Colonial Williamsburg Foundation's living history museum. Westward on a small peninsula, English colonists in 1607 staked a claim to Virginia and the New World, naming it "Jamestown" to honor King James I, and marking the beginning of permanent English settlement in the New World. In 1693, William and Mary was named for the monarchs who established it with their royal charter. "Their Majesties' Royall College" is deeply rooted in its British heritage, but its faculty and alumni include those who debated, legislated, and fought to secure independence from Great Britain.

Less than a century later, most of William and Mary's faculty and students again left campus to fight for a cause. The campus they left behind became contested ground between Confederate and Union forces from 1861 to 1865, but finding that Civil War past on campus can be elusive. Neither the Wren Building, the Brafferton nor the President's House retain their mid–19th century appearance, having been restored and maintained as colonial-era Georgian structures. The walk westward from the Wren Building now has tree-lined brick pathways, academic buildings and dormitories constructed in the last two centuries, blending Colonial Revival and more recent architectural styles. Yet there are still landmarks of the

Civil War era. Near modern-day Richmond Road, a small brick-walled cemetery contains President Benjamin Stoddard Ewell's grave. Ewell Hall is not far from the Wren Building, where a memorial tablet dedicated to Ewell is among those displayed in its chapel.

When members of the College community and visitors enter the Wren Building's front doors, they pass war memorial tablets, one erected by the Board of Visitors and alumni in 1914. It is dedicated: "To the memory of the professors and the students who left the College of William and Mary in May 1861 and in patriotic devotion fought in defense of the Confederate States of America." Although the memorial names them, there are no details of military service, or the names of hundreds of alumni who served the Confederacy. Also missing is the name of one student from Baltimore who fought for the Union side.

These individuals represent many more from Northern and Southern schools who faced serious new realities in 1861. Older beliefs and loyalties took precedence as students on both sides headed for home and enlistment. Students faced transformational leaps in maturity and decision-making because of the war. In the postwar years, these soldier-veterans, including those from William and Mary, helped create long-lasting social, political, and educational change in America. In fact, the College rising from the ashes of the Civil War no longer educated sons of Virginia's elite in the post-bellum South. William and Mary became part of a more democratic society, a process forged through difficult times and controversy. Yet its heritage has remained a source of pride within the College community. Traditions maintained across

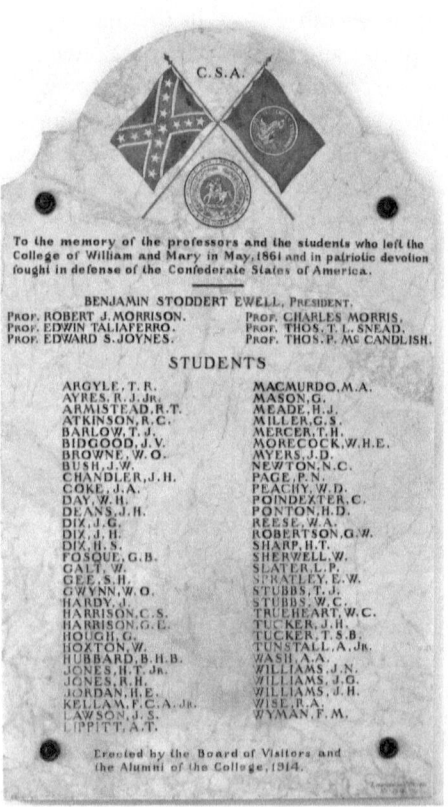

The Wren Building plaque commemorating the Civil War service of the College's students and faculty (collection of the authors, photograph by Kelly J. Mihalcoe).

generations mainly tie to William and Mary's colonial past, with passing mention of a disastrous 1862 fire set by "drunken Union soldiers" and Benjamin Ewell's service to the College as president before and after the Civil War. The full story is richer and more complex.

By 1861, the College already had faced numerous highs and lows in its 168-year existence, including the departure of many faculty members and students during the Revolutionary War and devastating fires in 1705 and 1859. This venerable institution had educated some of America's leading statesmen, but by the dawn of the Civil War it had trouble just staying open. What led to such change, and how did its origins and development affect William and Mary's history in the Civil War era? These are critical factors in understanding that period, as is identifying what led members of the College's community to support secession and to serve in the impending war.

The Civil War ravaged William and Mary through the immense damage from fire and vandalism and its resulting postwar desolation. Despite these misfortunes, this school so deeply intertwined with America's beginnings did not fade away. The College's sixteenth president, Benjamin Ewell (serving from 1854 to 1888), would not allow that to happen, just as the first president, James Blair (serving from 1693 to 1743), ceaselessly lobbied for its establishment. At that point in the late 1600s, William and Mary's heroic saga had just begun.

There was a missionary aspect to English colonization in the New World, with education viewed as a strategic tool for assimilation and conversion of native peoples. In 1619, Virginia governor Sir George Yeardley carried instructions for "the building and planting of a college" that was in part a university and in part a missionary effort "for the training up of the Children of those Infidels in true Religion moral virtue and Civility and for other godly uses."[2] The Virginia Company of London had raised funds and endowed 10,000 acres below modern-day Richmond on the north bank of the James, near the colony's second settlement of Henrico (also called Henricus). With one hundred workmen from England on site and the appointment of a rector, the school seemed on its way to gaining a faculty and students. However, it became a historical footnote with the 1622 destruction of the "citie of Henricus" during native attacks on outlying English settlements that were intended to push back against such expansion.[3] The need for colonial education was still clear, but Virginia's financial mismanagement had reached crisis proportions; accordingly, King James I took control by declaring Virginia a royal colony in 1624. The Virginia General Assembly initiated another attempt to establish a university by passing a land purchase act in 1661, but this new effort stalled.

Three decades later, momentum seemed to build again. Virginia clergy and colonial administrators believed in reinforcing English mores through the education of native and Anglo-Virginian youths, training Anglican ministers, and converting indigenous people to Christianity. Robert Beverly's 1705 *History and Present State of Virginia* noted that Council President Nathaniel Bacon and his council took up the matter, the first known reference to William and Mary's founding:

> During that Gentleman's Presidency, which began Anno 1689, the Project of a College was first agreed upon. The Contrivers drew up their Scheme, and presented it to the President and Council. This was by them approved and referr'd to the next Assembly. But Col. Bacon's Administration being very short, and no Assembly call'd all the while, this pious Design cou'd proceed no further.[4]

Led by the Rev. James Blair, Virginia's Church of England clergy members proposed a plan with grammar, philosophy, and divinity schools in July 1690. By 1691, Blair had secured the political support from colonial leaders to launch his campaign in England. Success finally came through a combination of factors: the colony's rapid population growth, nearby Middle Plantation's attractiveness as a site, and the prospect of a bequest from English natural philosopher Robert Boyle's estate. But most of all, the new college was secured by the tenacious Scottish minister who set his sights on securing funds from private donors as well as the crown. James Blair successfully approached executors of Robert Boyle's estate with persuasive plans for educating native youths as Christian clergymen and missionaries to their people. Blair also pressed for royal support. On February 8, 1693, King William III and Queen Mary II of England established the College via royal charter, the only one ever granted to an American institution by British monarchs.[5] William and Mary took its rightful place with Harvard College (established 1636) as the earliest Anglo-American colonial colleges in operation. The new institution became a reality, and there were signs of permanence: a coat of arms granted in 1694, and bricks laid ceremonially for the main building's foundation in 1695. As president, Blair raised money for the school and focused on the continuing construction of its first building, which would open in 1700.

In 1699, President Blair joined Governor Frances Nicholson in a strategy of persuasion to move Virginia's capital from Jamestown. Middle Plantation had the potential to become a thriving seat of government and other societal institutions, if its advocates could convince their peers. On May Day, 1699, Blair and Nicholson saw to it that five young students of William and Mary's Grammar School gave speeches before the colony's leaders that successfully highlighted the importance of education — more specifically, a Virginia education — and the benefits of making Middle Plantation the new site of the capital.[6] Middle Plantation was later renamed Williamsburg in honor of William III. Due to the new town's shortage of facilities, this move prompted the General Assembly to meet and often board on the College's campus for several years thereafter.[7]

In its early years, William and Mary served primarily as a grammar school for young boys. At any given time, there were about thirty individuals enrolled on the campus. Once these boys reached the age of sixteen, they had to pass an examination with the faculty before proceeding to advanced study at the College. There were three levels of study at the time, including the grammar school itself, a school of natural and moral philosophy, and a school of divinity to prepare students for service in the church.[8] A catastrophic fire in 1705 consumed the College's main building and thus stalled the institution's growth. Consequently, William and Mary did not expand to include students of traditional college age until about 1717. A separate Indian school was established during this period and housed in the Brafferton building in 1723. It had a conflicted history and few students, closing for good in 1779.

By the mid–18th century, William and Mary had matured into a well-respected institution. Prominent Tidewater families, including the Harrisons, Randolphs, and Tuckers, regularly sent their sons to study in Williamsburg. In 1747, the young land surveyor George Washington

The College as it appeared circa 1732. From Lyon G. Tyler, *The College of William and Mary in Virginia: Its History and Work, 1693–1907* (Richmond: Whittet & Shepperson, 1907), 24.

obtained his professional license from the College, which resulted in his first government appointment as surveyor for Culpeper County, Virginia. Thomas Jefferson attended in the early 1760s before going on to study law under the tutelage of George Wythe.[9] Thanks to its bright students and rigorous curriculum, the College contributed to Williamsburg's advancement as the colony's cultural and intellectual center. During this time, a typical William and Mary student could expect eight hours of daily study in the philosophy school, with rigorous study from seven to eleven o'clock in the morning and from two to six o'clock in the afternoon. Most students boarded on campus and often developed close bonds with the faculty members who served as mentors and tutors. Although much of the students' attention was devoted to academics, student behavior such as horseplay, practical jokes, and fights were relatively common: in the 1760s, a son of William Byrd III was nearly expelled for inciting a student riot.[10]

By 1770, 120 college students were enrolled, with eighty-five boarding on the campus. Seventy more students attended the Indian and grammar schools. Encouraged by this growth, College leaders began planning the construction of new campus facilities. William and Mary's accomplishments continued in 1776, when a group of its students created Phi Beta Kappa, America's first intercollegiate Greek-letter fraternity.[11] Although there were constant feuds between the faculty and board members as well as occasional financial problems, this was in many respects a golden era for the College.

However, William and Mary's prospects quickly soured with the outbreak of the American Revolution. As would happen again in 1861, enrollment dropped quickly as students and faculty went off to war, leaving the College with only eighteen students (along with thirty grammar school students) by 1777. Overall, thirty students and three professors would join the Continental Army.[12] The Rev. James Madison also led a new military company at William and Mary in 1775, but classes continued with significant occurrences such as the founding of Phi Beta Kappa.[13] After six years as president, John Camm — Anglican minister, faculty member, and Loyalist — was forced to withdraw. Madison was his successor (1777–1812).[14] In some cases, parents refused to enroll their children at the College, in apparent retribution for William and Mary's close ties to the British Crown. Consequently, the College's annual income fell from over 5,000 pounds in the early 1770s to only 712 pounds in 1777. In response to this crisis, Gov. Thomas Jefferson pushed a major reorganization for William and Mary through the General Assembly in 1779, overhauling its curriculum and weakening its ties to Great Britain.[15] There was hope that these changes would bring stability back to the College. For a time they appeared to work.

However, outside factors further eroded William and Mary's precarious position, eliminating any possibility for rapid recovery. Wartime considerations motivated Virginia legislators to move the capital from Williamsburg to Richmond in 1780.[16] This move dealt a near-fatal blow to the College, as much of its success to date was due to its proximity to supportive government officials. The political hustle and energy of earlier days quickly disappeared as Williamsburg was reduced to a dusty, nearly forgotten town. As state and College leaders recognized this problem, they attempted for several years to move William and Mary to Richmond. However, influential alumni who vowed to keep the campus in its original location stopped them every time. Although the College was permitted to stay in Williamsburg, it would face hard times for years to come.[17]

As William and Mary struggled into the first decades of the 19th century, its reputation had lost much of its luster. By the early 1800s, elite Virginia planters sent their sons to Princeton, Columbia, or even England to finish their education. The less affluent were content with the local academies and a few years at William and Mary, then Virginia's sole collegiate institution.[18] Although William and Mary was the South's only higher education institution before the Revolutionary War, that standing was about to topple, along with the entrenchment of the classical curriculum.[19] In his earlier political career, Thomas Jefferson believed that he could mold his alma mater into a flagship institution of higher education. However, when he tried to institute reforms as governor and as a member of the Board of Visitors, Jefferson encountered many problems with the College's curriculum, governance, and infrastructure. Although it was not the full reform he hoped for, Jefferson participated in William and Mary's 1779 reorganization as a university providing secular training to sons of the gentry.[20] Retaining his vision for an ideal university, Jefferson later would set out to create such an institution in his native Charlottesville. The afterglow from reorganization of the College and solid leadership by its presidents lasted for several years, but faded in the mid-1810s when Jefferson and others pushed for establishment of a university "to be called The University of Virginia" in a "central and healthy part of the Commonwealth," as opposed to Williamsburg's location and climate.[21] After years of lobbying, the General Assembly finally authorized the creation of the University of Virginia in 1819.[22] At the time, officials at William and Mary felt that all had been lost. A nearly 50 percent decline in enrollment in 1818 left the College with only fifty students, and helped fuel this sentiment. Enrollment dropped even further to just thirty-five students by 1824. The popular perception during these years was that William and Mary was well past its prime. In an 1823 letter, Jefferson wrote, "It is now much reduced by ill management of it's [sic] funds, and less resorted to on account of climate."[23]

Visitors to the campus often took note of its neglected appearance, with broken windowpanes and decrepit buildings. Consequently, even the College's alumni sometimes advised their sons to obtain their education elsewhere. One distinguished alumnus told his son that William and Mary was "a declining institution about to relinquish its flickering blaze."[24] Many students on campus also noticed this rapid deterioration, but were nevertheless still attracted to the College's storied history. In a November 6, 1823, letter to his sister, William H. Garland wrote:

> There is nothing here [on campus] that would interest you in the least, unless you would be amused with falling walls and decaying houses. This spot, on which so many noble actions have been performed, now presents nothing to engage the imagination, but the recollection of what it once was. From day to day there revolves one lifeless monotony. The regular tolling of the College bell and the students attending to its call, presents the most animated scene that I have witnessed since I have arrived at this place.
>
> Which to you would be very uninteresting; but to me, who compose one of the number, it affords considerable pleasure. To be seated under that roof and surrounded by those walls, where knowledge has for so long a time reigned, and where learning first erected her crest, in this state, and to listen to the voice of science and the expounding of philosophy, I find not only agreeable and amusing but also instructive.[25]

Meanwhile, the College's Board of Visitors was actively discussing the school's removal from Williamsburg to Richmond in a lengthy controversy that embroiled the General Assembly, the press, and citizens of Williamsburg. President John Augustine Smith (1814–1826) pursued the removal with many of the board and faculty members. In contrast, Rector John Tyler and his two brothers-in-law (one on the board and one on the faculty) stood with townspeople to keep the College in place.[26] Thomas Jefferson, Joseph Cabell, and others supporting the University of Virginia also had reason to keep William and Mary from regaining the connection to power and influence it had enjoyed when Williamsburg was the capital of Virginia. The stakes escalated in 1825 when Thomas Jefferson prepared a substitute bill recommending that the College be discontinued and dissolved and its resources distributed among ten colleges statewide, including the College of Williamsburg, which would replace William and Mary.[27] However, Jefferson's substitute bill was not introduced on the floor of the General Assembly. The petition for removal crafted by William and Mary's leadership was defeated in early 1825, possibly as a strategic move by allies to prevent its dissolution under Jefferson's plan.[28] According to historian Lyon G. Tyler, Ewell's successor as president, the defeat also was influenced by Rector John Tyler's speech in the legislature against removal.[29]

Despite declining enrollments and increased competition, the College lingered on into the mid–19th century. In the 1830s and 1840s, William and Mary's fortunes improved under a series of effective presidents who focused on attracting quality faculty members and improving the overall appearance of the campus. One of the newly arrived faculty members in this period, Benjamin Ewell, was destined to lead it for almost half a century, through times of progress, disaster, and transformation. In 1848, William and Mary was in a state of turmoil, riven by power struggles between the faculty and Board of Visitors that erupted in the wake of President Thomas Roderick Dew's death from pneumonia on August 6, 1846. Friction continued during the pro tem presidency of Robert Saunders, professor of mathematics, and after his formal appointment to that post, which he held from October 12, 1847, to July 13, 1848. When Professor George F. Holmes resigned in January 1848, his letter to the Board of Visitors cited "no conceivable possibility of unanimity among the Professors, or of cordiality between the Faculty as a Body and its Students," making it impossible to fulfill his duties without risking misunderstanding or suspicion from factions within the faculty, students, or visitors.[30]

When the Board of Visitors approached Benjamin Ewell to become professor of mathematics and acting president, his academic background and reputation as a popular professor were certainly factors. Ewell held the Cincinnati professorship of mathematics and military science at Washington College in Lexington, Virginia, having taught previously at Hampden-Sydney College and West Point. Ewell also had work experience outside military service and academe. An 1832 West Point graduate, he applied his engineering skills from 1836 to 1839 as principal assistant engineer for construction of the Baltimore and Susquehanna Railroad. In 1839, the twenty-nine-year-old Ewell also mar-

William and Mary's Civil War–era president, Col. Benjamin S. Ewell, CSA. From Lyon G. Tyler, *The Making of the Union: Contribution of The College of William and Mary in Virginia* (Richmond: Whittet & Shepperson, 1899), 6.

ried lively Julia McIlvaine, eleven years younger than her husband and a Pennsylvania doctor's daughter. The Ewells' life together was turbulent, marked by long separations, family tensions, and discord. Julia had not accompanied her husband to Williamsburg. Instead, she stayed with her parents in York, Pennsylvania, arrived at Williamsburg in September 1850, and returned to her parents in late 1851. In related moves, Benjamin and Julia's daughter Elizabeth ("Lizzy") had lived with his parents in Prince William County, and after Julia's departure, Ewell's mother Elizabeth and Lizzy created a new family nucleus in the President's House, with his sister Rebecca also taking a hand in providing a stable home life for her niece.[31] The memoirs of one of his colleagues (the embittered Silas Totten, whose motivations are discussed in Chapter 2), imply that Julia's problems stemmed from her unhappy marriage to Ewell, who was Totten's nemesis. Other period accounts allude to Julia's bouts of violent, aberrant behavior, presenting multiple views of what clearly was a family tragedy. Anne Chapman's 1984 Ph.D. dissertation on Benjamin Ewell documents the deterioration of their marriage — and the aftermath. The couple's paths diverged with Julia's departure from Williamsburg; Lizzy maintained lifelong bonds with her parents.

As difficult as Ewell's personal life had become, there were also serious issues facing him at William and Mary. The campus buildings were in a major state of disrepair, and the earlier argument for removing the College had resurfaced in 1847. Friction concerning the College's finances and general appearance closed all but the law classes on campus for a year. Pressures for removal would mount again in 1848 and 1865, as William and Mary struggled to survive.

The student enrollment fluctuated markedly during these years, from a high of 140 in 1839 to a low of twenty-one in 1849. However, on average the student body regularly numbered between fifty and one hundred students. Problems persisted in this period, but even so, William and Mary appeared to be moving toward greater stability.[32]

Upon becoming president again in 1854, Benjamin Ewell worked hard to revitalize the College further. He published William and Mary's first catalogue in 1855 and oversaw a comprehensive renovation of the College Building in 1856 and 1857. The Phi Beta Kappa Society, which had fallen dormant at the College for many years, was also reorganized during this period. President Ewell's popularity with the students and faculty was apparent, and many affectionately referred to him as "Old Buck."[33] His relations with the Board of Visitors were less agreeable: he clashed with them over a proposed reorganization of the school, reaching the brink of resigning the presidency and actually doing so in 1858. For one of several times in his College career, Ewell saw the advantage of restoring William and Mary's ties to the Episcopal Church. He supported hiring the Rev. Robert Barnwell of South Carolina, who declined. Ewell stepped back into his presidential role, albeit with the understanding that it was temporary.

President Ewell's leadership mettle was tested further when the newly renovated College Building caught fire in 1859, gutting the entire structure. The accident was doubly unfortunate in its timing: The 166th anniversary of William and Mary's founding was imminent, with a major celebration planned.[34] Many historical artifacts, including a George Washington letter, rare books and manuscripts presented by heads of state, chapel tablets, and a pre–Revolutionary War scientific apparatus collection, were lost in the early morning blaze on February 8.

Professor Robert J. Morrison was living in part of the President's House and heard cries that the College was on fire. Seeing flames coming from the library and laboratory in the building's north wing, Morrison hastily dressed and headed toward the conflagration. He wrote of the scene:

> I had not reached the College when I met President Ewell, who had just returned from the second floor of the Building, where he had been to rescue the students who were sleeping in the dormitories. All the students were fortunately saved, though several of them for a short time were in peril. Three or four of them lost their effects. I urged Mr. Ewell, who was not half dressed, to go to his chamber for warmer clothing, as the weather was cold and damp, but he said, "I must first go with him to the basement under the Laboratory, to discover, if possible, the origin of the fire."[35]

Although the fire was first assumed to be laboratory-related, it was later connected to a worker cutting wood by candlelight, in the cellar under the laboratory.[36]

Alumnus St. George Tucker wrote to Professor Morrison the day after the fire, mourning "such an awful loss."[37] When he wrote those words, the time span between the end of the Revolutionary War and that point was less than eighty years. Tucker had succeeded George Wythe as the College's second law professor and had become a judge of the Supreme Court of Virginia. He expressed what anyone reading the roster of Founding Fathers connected to the College might write, looking at such loss from a historical perspective:

> At any time, the destruction of almost the only link which binds Virginia to her golden age, would have awakened emotions of the deepest sorrow; but more particularly now, as I have been fully identifying myself with her destiny, and projecting myself into her early history, does the deepest regret penetrate my soul.[38]

The campus community and townspeople rallied. Donations of money poured in to rebuild the damaged structure, and the College opened once more on October 13, 1859. The institution's 166th anniversary had been celebrated as planned despite the destruction, with a stirring speech by now–Chancellor John Tyler. The former president would hold that position until his death in 1862. Part of Tyler's address was included in the *Historical Sketch of the College of William and Mary, in Virginia*, published as part of the 1870 William and Mary catalogue. According to that account, Tyler expounded on the College's history in his address but also looked to the present: "If her catalogue closed with the names of those who belong to the dead generations, might not William and Mary take her place among her sister Universities proudly and rightfully? But it bears the names of living generations, who add to her renown."[39] Many considered this resurrection to be the College's finest hour.[40] Exactly a year from the date of the fire, Ewell reported to the faculty, "In all the essentials of its building, furniture, apparatus, and library, the College is now in a better condition than it was on that day."[41] In many ways, the College's physical renewal was evidence of its continuing evolution. Although it was acknowledged as preserving the heritage of a nation, Southern culture and Virginia history, William and Mary's Anglican establishment, its British royal heritage, and its classical curriculum were subsumed by its becoming a university for modern times, albeit one with a strong Southern tradition.

In 1860, the College's prospects seemed bright. Serious challenges had been overcome, yet a greater threat was brewing on its campus and others throughout the South. Beginning in the 1850s, students and faculty could not, and increasingly did not, ignore the growing national divide. As Michael David Cohen pointed out, no one could ignore it at colleges east of the Rocky Mountains: campus debates over sectional conflict came first, and enlistment followed later on most campuses.[42] Issues raised by Congressional battles over slavery, John Brown's raid on Harpers Ferry, and the 1860 presidential election of Abraham Lincoln drew political lines in the sand on campuses, just as they would do with families, communities, and states. The crisis intensified when South Carolina, followed by six other Southern states, seceded from the Union. Never in American history had educational institutions in the South experienced such widespread turmoil, confusion, unrest, and hysteria.[43] They mirrored the dissention developing throughout the nation.

Hope of compromise faltered despite the efforts of leaders like John Tyler. The former U.S. president came forward in February 1861 to call for a peace conference in Washington, D.C., of which he said, "The eyes of the whole country are turned to this assembly, in expectation and hope."[44] Tyler chaired the month-long effort to avoid secession and war, but representatives' arguments overpowered any hope of peace.[45] Virginia seceded in April 1861, and Tyler himself became a member of the Confederate Congress shortly thereafter.

Virginia's heritage, resources, and strategic location were valuable assets in the power struggle underway. Virginia and her sister states in the Upper South ranked high in population, industry, and agriculture, and Virginia led in those categories throughout the South.[46] As historian James McPherson has pointed out, the Commonwealth also boasted exceptional military talent in Robert E. Lee, Thomas J. "Stonewall" Jackson, Joseph E. Johnston, J.E.B. Stuart, and Ambrose Powell Hill.[47] Another noted Civil War historian, James I. Robertson, Jr., wrote, "Without Virginia, the Confederacy could not hope to win a war. With Virginia, the young nation had a chance."[48] Many, expecting that the war would end in a year or so, participated with a rush of enthusiasm in parades and enlistments across eastern parts of the state. However, residents in the western counties had stronger pro–Union sentiments, propelling their eventual secession from Virginia.[49] Meanwhile, Williamsburg and the College were drawn increasingly into the conflict, with Southern loyalists leading the way. Williamsburg's strategic location on the James–York peninsula was between Richmond, which became the Confederate capital, and Union-held Fort Monroe. This made it an important post for both sides, held at times by each, and subject to all the outcomes of occupation.

In 1861, some somberly envisioned what could lie ahead for Virginia, the South, and the nation. Overzealous and naïve students at most Southern colleges generally promoted secession, while hesitant faculty members, many of whom had been trained in the North, urged caution and restraint.[50] This pattern was evident at William and Mary, where President Ewell spent much of his time maintaining order on a campus where students were increasingly distracted by the prospect of war. Although Ewell had devoted his life to higher education, military matters were nothing new to this former U.S. Army officer. Descending from an old Virginia family, Ewell had several relatives who had fought in the American Revolution—a few even went on to marry relatives of George Washington. Further, his maternal grandfather, Benjamin Stoddert, had served as the nation's first Secretary of the Navy (1798–1801) under President John Adams. However, despite his deep Southern roots, Ewell bitterly opposed secession.[51] Although Ewell, like Lee and Jackson, later joined the Confederate Army to defend his native state of Virginia, he hoped until the very end that disunion could be avoided. However, his sentiments were in the minority in Williamsburg, with its large population of Confederate sympathizers.[52]

By all accounts, most William and Mary students joined their Williamsburg neighbors in supporting secession.[53] Their presentation of the petition to President Ewell to create a student militia company in January 1861 represented the first step in a process that led most of them to the Confederate Army. According to student Richard A. Wise, the company uniform was to consist of homespun pantaloons and a red flannel shirt and fatigue cap. Furthermore, the students were to be armed with Bowie knives and double-barreled shotguns or rifles. Despite student zeal for this unit, it was intended for training purposes only and not as a permanent organization. Following Virginia's secession, most students eventually went home to join formal Confederate regiments at the outbreak of the war.[54]

Although Ewell could only acquiesce to the creation of this militia unit, he still demonstrated his Unionist and antiwar sentiments. Student William Reynolds wrote that the company never advanced past its first meeting and "it was the general impression among the students that President Ewell had got himself appointed captain for the express purpose of preventing the company from ever being organized."[55] Ewell also had Reynolds, one of the few staunch Unionists on campus, deliver the traditional oration commemorating George Washington's birthday that Febru-

A ca. 1860 depiction of the College of William and Mary by Lefevre James Cranstone (Colonial Williamsburg Foundation; museum purchase).

ary. The speech was intended to denounce secession and make a strong appeal for the preservation of the Union. When Reynolds expressed fear that the topic could enrage the pro-secession audience, Ewell told him that he would personally stand behind the contents of the address. However, despite their best efforts, the appeal appeared to fall on deaf ears. By mid–April, upon hearing the news of Virginia's secession by a vote of eighty-eight to fifty-five, zealous William and Mary students quickly hoisted a pro-secession flag up a pole on the College yard.[56]

Meanwhile, similar student activity was taking place on college campuses across Virginia. As early as December 1860, students at Washington College in Lexington had hoisted a secessionist flag on their campus, and continued doing so through spring 1861. Students at Roanoke College and Virginia Military Institute soon followed their lead on their own campuses. Meanwhile, students from the University of Virginia, Hampden-Sydney College, and others also joined William and Mary in forming their own student militia companies to prepare themselves in the event of war. Faculty members at all of these institutions had trouble trying to maintain order and stop the "war-fever" that was spreading around their campuses.[57] The students' eagerness to support secession raises many questions for modern historians. What motivated them to support disunion so enthusiastically? Why were they so willing to risk their lives to support this growing rebellion? What was college life like at the time, and did that have any influence on their actions? Before analyzing the roles that William and Mary students played in the Civil War, it is useful to understand what motivated them to fight. It is therefore important to examine the dynamics of college life as well as college students in the late-antebellum South.

In many ways, academic life at William and Mary in 1861 resembled that of colonial times. As in earlier years, students were required to demonstrate fundamental knowledge of Latin, Greek, and mathematics before entering the College, a standard common among most Southern higher education institutions. Due to the varying quality of preparatory education across the country, most colleges also required oral examinations for matriculation. Upon entry to William and Mary, students faced a challenging and demanding curriculum. Recitation was the primary teaching method at most colleges: instructors assigned long book passages to students, who were then expected to demonstrate knowledge of each sentence and were often tested to gauge comprehension. Instructors often required students to prepare and present speeches on various topics.[58] Although curricula would evolve into a liberal arts framework in later decades, Southern colleges were still entrenched in classical education.

Along with the academic regimen, William and Mary student life had changed little since the 18th century. Late-antebellum era students joined their predecessors in playing practical jokes, engaging in rowdy behavior, and pursuing romance with Williamsburg's young ladies when they were not studying. College laws promoted "correct habits" and prohibited drinking, partying, missing prayers or recitations, or distracting other students during study hours.[59] More refined pursuits included membership in literary societies and other student organizations. These activities were also common at other Southern colleges. Although many students "sowed their wild oats" in college, they also took their studies seriously. In the mid–19th century, a college education was considered essential for success by most of the elite. Although few professions required such training, advanced education was highly desirable in the finest social circles. This was especially evident in the South, where social standing was critical to enjoying good fortune and influence. College students in the late-antebellum South were raised to believe that they had to conform to society's expectations. Obtaining a college education would help them meet that goal.[60]

While some elements of college life were tied to earlier times, other concepts were more specific to the mid–19th century. These help explain the mindset of Southern college students prior to the Civil War. One was the concept of Southern honor. Honor in the South, according to historian Peter Bardaglio, was "that constellation of ideas and values in which one's self-worth rested on the degree of respect commanded from others in the community."[61] In a region steeped in hierarchy and tradition, it was crucial for male Southerners to display duty, respect, and honesty in order to be considered "honorable men." According to historian Bertram Wyatt-Brown, honor had always been an important regional trait. It gained added importance in the late-antebellum period, when the South felt increasingly isolated from the rest of the nation over the issue of slavery. In their way of thinking, honor was a distinctive trait that made Southerners feel superior to their Northern neighbors.[62] Honor was satisfied on Southern campuses through challenges and duels between students, but not with the approval of college policy makers. For instance, the laws of the College of William and Mary were explicit on dueling. No student could send or accept a challenge, act as principal, convey such a challenge, or act as second. Students were banned from possessing or using firearms.[63] Similarly, historian Michael Sugrue has written that violence was "an important trope of cultural expression" among males in pre-secessionist South Carolina.[64] For college students, the maintenance of honor signaled patrician status and governed interactions between gentlemen, while preserving the hierarchy of Southern culture.[65]

William and Mary students in the mid–19th century, like other students throughout the South, grew up in an environment immersed in this code of honor.[66] It provides one explanation for their enthusiastic support for secession and the Confederacy as a whole. Faced with a threat of civil war, they felt an obligation and duty to defend their homeland. To them, refraining from this course of action would indicate cowardice and bring about charges of disloyalty. For Southerners of this generation, dishonor was not an option. Thus, even if they privately felt fear and uncertainty, William and Mary students put on a public persona of bravery and determination to meet the mounting crisis.

Other factors help explain the mindset of these William and Mary students and their colleagues at other Southern colleges. For one, it is important to remember that these individuals came of age in a period of national political crisis. Born in the early 1840s, they grew up in an environment of heightened political tension and regional rivalry over the issue of slavery. No period of American history had produced more chaos and divisiveness, and the developing national tension possibly deepened their regional ties and loyalties.[67] As historian Peter Carmichael has asserted, this era of turmoil did not necessarily turn these students into radical Southern nationalists. Rather, they felt comfortable in an eclectic mix that reflected their diverse attachments to their local environs, the state, the region, and the nation. In fact, upon analyzing a group of Virginia college students in the 1850s, Carmichael discovered that they developed a Southern perspective solely in response to internal issues and debates relating exclusively to Virginia.[68] Therefore, this was not the only factor responsible for creating enthusiasm for secession among students at William and Mary and other Southern colleges.

Virginia students were profoundly influenced by a growing perception: that the Commonwealth was quickly losing its place of prominence in the Union. These students grew up in an era of political conflict and simultaneously were raised in a time of growing technological progress. Telegraphs, manufacturing, and railroads were transforming society, particularly in the North. Many young Virginians subsequently campaigned for statewide economic and political progress. Visions of prosperity beckoned a cadre of ambitious young men seeking material wealth and social influence.[69]

Many Virginia students were therefore critical of older leaders who seemed oblivious to needed change, revering the past while allowing the state to stagnate. As the Civil War approached, progressive students throughout the Commonwealth saw a way through the impasse. They argued that by leaving the Union, Virginia would free itself from the abolitionist and domineering North, and help to lead a new Southern nation.[70] Williamsburg had been at the center of colonial influence and power in the 18th century; through its faculty and alumni, the College had helped to form the new nation politically and intellectually. Since the Revolution, the town and the College had experienced much less dynamic times. Now, once again, there was a cause to champion and deeply felt principles at stake.

However, when moderate Virginia politicians hesitated to join the seceding Southern states, students at William and Mary and other state colleges felt even more betrayed. This action confirmed their belief that Virginia's leadership was decrepit, morally bankrupt, and out of touch with reality. It strengthened the students' resolve for secession, as they believed that it would cleanse the Commonwealth of these ineffective officials. For their part, Virginia Unionists accused the students of silliness and immaturity, both seen as synonyms for weakness. This further goaded the young Virginians to organize for the Confederacy and, if necessary, to demonstrate their valor on the battlefield. Overall, by supporting secession, they believed they could redeem their native state and prove their masculinity and honor.[71]

On the William and Mary campus, peer pressure also played a role in driving support for disunion. According to William Reynolds, students and faculty expressed a diverse range of opinions over the issue of secession. He also recalled that there were a number of pro–Union students on the campus at one point. Over time, however, "a great many yielded to the pressure and went over to the other side."[72] This pattern was likely present on other Southern college campuses as well. All of these factors intensified college students' support for the rebellion throughout the region. Yet, while students could advocate secession from the relative security of the William and Mary campus in early 1861, the day was rapidly approaching when their commitment to "the cause" would be tested on the battlefield. As they would soon discover, this test — so far removed from the classroom — would last for four long years.

Chapter 2

On the Eve of War

As the new nation emerged after the Revolutionary War, William and Mary's Church of England heritage was a colonial relic compared to the emerging secularism exemplified by the University of Virginia. Even so, the College was not trapped in the past; its students were shifting from the previous generation's views of Southern identity and intellectualism. As was true at other institutions of higher learning, William and Mary's faculty and curriculum also faced change.

The Civil War interrupted a steady flow of ideas and interactions in higher education. The exchange of students from Northern states attending Southern schools halted and vice versa, although some held lingering affection for students and alumni on the opposing side. War also interrupted the financial support that Northern donors, particularly those in New York, had provided for the College's renewal after the 1859 fire. Perhaps the most long-lasting outcome has been the not-so-peaceful coexistence of differing historical narratives. The interpretation of events such as the Federal occupation of the campus or the fire of 1862 is not as clear as it might seem from some sources, with persistent variations in shades of gray — and blue. The North and South were destined to clash violently over physical resources, power, and moral authority; each side would lay claim to the nation's identity, its history, and some might say its soul.

After Virginia's fitful secession process, its citizens realized that they were entering a wartime way of life, but few could envision what would happen on the home front. Longtime Williamsburg residents knew what an earlier generation had experienced during the American Revolution: families, friends, and neighbors were torn apart by divided loyalties and many experienced the uncertainties of the 1781 British invasion. During that time, the French occupied the William and Mary campus, using the President's House and later the Wren Building as hospitals for their wounded. That war left its mark in the suspension of classes and extensive fire damage to the President's House, requiring French reparation and over four years to repair.[1] Thus, William and Mary was no stranger to the effects of war or to the sacrifices war demanded.[2]

The vivid signs of America's war for independence faded over time in Williamsburg and life moved on. Campus visitors in the mid–19th century saw none of the formal gardens familiar to 18th-century residents, but there were other reminders of the colonial past. According to period illustrations of the campus, the pre–Revolutionary statue of Lord Botetourt looked eastward from the College yard. It stood squarely in the grassy yard, complemented by young trees lining the existing dirt path to the Wren Building. Framed porches fronted the Georgian-style President's House and Brafferton while smaller frame buildings served as faculty housing.[3] Shortly after the 1859 fire, a large brick structure located behind the Brafferton was purchased for student housing and for faculty lectures, and came to be called the College Hotel.[4]

The Board of Visitors had voted unanimously to rebuild the damaged Wren Building immediately. Silas Totten (1804–1873), the College's professor of belles lettres and moral philosophy (1849–1859), had criticized it as "uncouth and ill proportioned" in his campaign to see the remaining

The Italianate version of the Wren Building, which stood from roughly 1860 to 1862 (University Archives Photograph Collection, Special Collections Research Center, Swem Library, College of William and Mary).

walls razed and replaced with a totally new building.[5] When completed, the painted structure had a strikingly different appearance "relieved by two towers of the Italian style of Architecture," one tower containing the College bell and the other functioning — at least in theory — as an observatory.[6] After this short-lived third form of the College building was destroyed in the 1862 fire, President Ewell reported to the Visitors, "It would be advisable ... to take down the towers as there are some serious cracks in their comparatively thin walls. This is not to be regretted for they were not of the slightest use and were not ornamental."[7] In his memoirs, Professor Silas Totten recalled recommending at the time that firewalls be placed between the towers and the Wren Building's walls, but to no avail.[8]

William and Mary's visible changes reflected societal transitions. Peter Carmichael has observed that Southern youth born between 1831 and 1843 were the last generation to grow up with slavery as a legal and cultural norm.[9] Change and tradition were at odds: many young Virginians attending college were impatient with outmoded thinking and pushed for progress, yet supported the institution of slavery as part of the Southern culture. Historian Samuel Eliot Morison has noted how war altered the North and the South in different ways.[10] Higher education institutions in both regions felt the effects in the late 1850s, as the political climate changed. From that time on, colleges and universities were at different points on the timeline, ranging from suspension or status quo to innovation. Higher education historian John F. Thelin noted that between 1860 and 1890, curricula actually expanded in some colleges and universities, particularly in the fields of teacher education, applied sciences, engineering and agriculture, while other programs were established through the milestone 1862 Morrill Land Grant Act.[11]

During the first half of the 19th century, Southern states had expanded educational opportunities through denominational colleges like Virginia's Hampden-Sydney College (Presbyterian), Richmond College (Baptist), and Randolph-Macon College and Emory and Henry College (Methodist).[12] Those colleges reflected the significantly stronger position of those three denominations in founding institutions of higher learning, although other faiths also had schools.[13] Southern universities such as the University of Alabama, the University of Mississippi, and the University of Virginia were growing in academic achievement and civic favor. An average of 200 students annually attended "Mr. Jefferson's university" in the mid–19th century, and its enrollment passed that of Harvard and Yale during 1859–60.[14] More than 600 students were enrolled at the University of Virginia for the 1860–61 academic year, of which 263 were from out of state. Nine of those were from Delaware, California, Massachusetts, and Pennsylvania, sixty-two from Alabama and Louisiana, and thirty from Maryland.[15] William and Mary's inability to compete with the University of Virginia on a level playing field is indicated by enrollment figures for 1855–56: whereas the University of Virginia had 645 students, William and Mary had sixty-six enrolled.[16] During the 1850s, William and Mary's smallest enrollment was twenty students during the 1849–50 session, while the largest enrollments came during the 1853–54 and 1854–55 sessions, at eighty-two students.[17] Most William and Mary students were Virginians or were from other Southern states.[18] The College was variously perceived as a secular or non-secular school, receiving no substantial support from church *or* state. Faculty member Silas Totten noted, "The University of Virginia was swallowing up everything."[19]

In comparison, students from twelve Southern states attended the colleges of Harvard, Princeton, and Yale in the decades from 1820 to 1860. From these states south of the Mason-Dixon Line, including Texas and the pro–Southern border state of Missouri, there were 193 students at Harvard during that forty-year period, a total of 250 at Yale, and 206 at the College of New Jersey (Princeton).[20] During that time, thirty-three Virginia students went to Harvard, thirty-seven to Yale, and sixty to Princeton. Back at William and Mary, there was, according to the 1859–60 College catalogue, a competent faculty covering six departments: Edwin Taliaferro, A.M., professor of Latin, Latin literature, and the Romance languages; Edward S. Joynes, A.M., professor of Greek, Greek literature, and German; the Rev. Silas Totten, D.D., professor of moral and intellectual philosophy, and belles lettres; Robert J. Morrison, professor of history, political economy, and constitutional law; and President Benjamin S. Ewell, professor of chemistry and natural philosophy. Mathematics was taught by Ewell and by Adjunct Professor Thomas T.L. Snead.[21] In that eventful year, forty-seven students' names were listed as enrolled, including one from Alabama, one from Delaware, and two from North Carolina. The list was replete with Williamsburg names such as Armistead, Coke, and Tucker. The list reads like a map of the Commonwealth of Virginia, including the Tidewater areas of Williamsburg, James City, Gloucester, Norfolk, Onancock, Surry, Hampton, Kilmarnock, Yorktown, and Warwick, with more students from Richmond, Petersburg, King George, Prince William, and other counties. President Ewell apparently challenged the Williamsburg area's reputation as being unhealthy and rife with malarial-type disease. The 1858–59 William and Mary catalogue argued persuasively that mild outbreaks, controlled by medicine, only occurred in August and September, and that Richmond actually was hotter in comparison. The College catalogue contained this inviting description: "The city of Williamsburg, in which the College is located, has a population of nearly two thousand, and has long been celebrated for the elegant hospitality of its inhabitants, making it a more agreeable residence for the student." The catalogue further stated, "Few places in the South can boast a more salubrious climate than this during the College session." With a final burst of statistics, the argument concludes, "During the present century only six deaths have occurred among the students of the College; and two of these were from drowning."[22]

At William and Mary, the record suggests differences in how faculty members and members of the Board of Visitors acted in relation to their political views in the years leading up to the Civil War. For instance, pro–Unionists like Totten and Ewell apparently did not bring their sentiments into instruction or interactions with students: A correspondent wrote in the February 27, 1852, *Richmond Daily Republican* that there were "both Whigs and Democrats in the faculty, but politics are not taught directly or indirectly."[23] Conversely, members of the Board of Visitors and others connected with the College were known to be far more forthcoming in their views, as were outsiders connected to it. The New York philanthropist-merchant Alexander Turney Stewart (ca. 1802–1876), was successfully approached for funds after William and Mary's disastrous 1859 fire by William T. Vest, a prominent Williamsburg merchant. Stewart's letter to Vest, written on September 28, 1859, was recorded in the October 17 faculty minutes that year. He donated five hundred dollars to purchase books in ancient languages for the library, hoping that the College would arise "phoenix-like" and that it would "never omit the opportunity to instill into the youthful mind of its students, that the Union of the United States must be preserved in all time to come."[24]

Despite Stewart's hopes, others closer to the College and to the South voiced opposing views of what students should do, particularly as political tensions mounted. On December 23, 1859, the *Richmond Daily Dispatch* recorded Board of Visitors member Henry A. Wise's remarks to university students returning by train to Virginia, after John Brown's raid on Harpers Ferry. Wise, who was later Virginia's governor, stated:

> Let us employ our own teachers, especially that they may teach our own doctrines. Let us dress in the wool raised on our own pastures. Let us eat the flour from our own mills, and if we can't eat that, why let us go back to our old accustomed corn bread.[25]

Sentiments about the war generated strong reactions at William and Mary and other Southern schools, some centering on the faculty and officials. William and Mary professor Silas Totten, later the second president of the

University of Iowa, wrote in his memoirs that his Northern birth factored in his not being appointed president of the College. He reported that an anonymous attack in a Richmond newspaper charged him with admiring abolitionist sentiments, but that the "charge was indignantly denied by the faculty and students and I do not believe anyone believed it for a moment."[26]

Born in New York, Silas Totten was a Union College graduate, ordained Episcopal minister and president of Trinity College in Connecticut, which provides some context for his words and actions as a member of the William and Mary faculty. Totten felt that charges made against him in the May 27, 1853, *Richmond Examiner*, a secessionist paper, swayed those supporting his advancement to president in favor of Benjamin Ewell: "One of the Visitors, also, told me after the election of Prof. Ewell, that I would have been chosen had there not been a fear of this prejudice on the part of the majority of the Visitors."[27]

Totten felt that although Ewell was popular with students, his West Point College background did not provide him sufficient credentials to evaluate instruction outside of mathematics and physics. Such frustrations probably heightened Totten's criticisms of Ewell and the College administration; it must have galled him to be passed over as a Yankee despite his academic credentials and experience. In fact, Totten's own son Robert was a student during the 1858–59 College session.[28] However, sectionalism was growing in Virginia and the nation. Years later, Totten reflected that had he stayed on at William and Mary, he might have lost everything in the war, concluding, "God was thus taking care of me and mine though I knew it not."[29]

Rev. Silas Totten, Ll.D.—1860 (Library of Congress).

Although Totten did not become president, William and Mary students had vigorously defended his reputation in an angry local environment, responding to the *Examiner* editor, "We have never heard fall from him one single expression or witnessed a single act of his calculated to produce an impression that he was in the slightest or remotest manner tainted with the heresy and crime of abolitionism." They also wrote, "We have not [sic] hesitation in saying, he is able, he is kind, he is amiable, and good tempered, and his whole conduct stamps him as a good man and a Christian."[30] Northerners at two other Southern universities were not so fortunate. At the University of North Carolina, alumnus and faculty member Benjamin Sherwood Hendrick, who had been appointed in 1854, was the subject of a newspaper attack that, after he published a defense explaining his opposition to slavery, ultimately resulted in his expulsion.[31] At Wake Forest, John B. White, a Brown University graduate and former Wake Forest professor, served as president from 1849 to 1853. He was compelled to resign despite faculty and student support, first accepting the presidency of a girls' seminary in Tennessee and then the presidency of Almira College in Illinois (1855–1864).[32] University of Mississippi president Frederick A.P. Barnard, a Yale graduate, became president of the University of Mississippi in 1856 and its chancellor in 1861; he left during the war because of his pro-abolitionist beliefs and became president of New York's Columbia University in 1864.[33]

By William and Mary's 1860–61 session, there had been some changes. President Ewell and Professors Taliaferro, Joynes, and Snead held the same teaching positions, but Silas Totten was gone, leaving no one in charge of moral philosophy and political economy. Thomas P. McCandlish was assistant professor of ancient languages and mathematics, and Charles Morris was now professor of law. Edwin Taliaferro had taken on the additional responsibility of librarian, and William R. Garrett was master of the grammar school and its thirty-nine students.[34] Although many of the sixty-three students listed still reflected a strong Virginia focus, one was from "Washington City," two from Baltimore, and one from Vicksburg, Mississippi.[35]

Doubts about Williamsburg's unhealthy climate remained and were debated in this extract credited to an address by the late John Tyler, who asked rhetorically:

> Is there an absentee who has been stricken down by climatic disease? What is his name and from whence did he come? Where are to be found the memorials of the dead? In what spot of earth do they sleep their last sleep? Accidents which happen everywhere may have sometimes occurred here; but I doubt very much whether in all that time

[the previous fifty years] a single young man has perished by disease incident to the climate and originating here.³⁶

By this time, the College had rebounded dramatically from the devastation of the 1859 fire. The Catalogue boasted that the new library, "which already numbers between four and five thousand volumes, has been selected with great care, and consists of the most valuable works of reference necessary to illustrate the various departments of instruction, as well as a valuable collection of miscellaneous literature."³⁷

Students at two of William and Mary's sister schools to the north, Harvard and Princeton, experienced the war in strikingly different ways. At Harvard, most Southern students left to enlist in 1861. Notwithstanding pro–Union activities on campus such as the establishment of a cadet corps and military drills on the lawns, Harvard student life and classes continued. According to the Harvard College catalogues, 896 students were enrolled in 1860–61, 833 in 1861–62, 814 in 1862–63, and 822 in 1863–64.³⁸ Although many enlisted early on, many decided to finish their educations first. Arguably having the most celebrity status in his class, Abraham Lincoln's eldest son Robert entered Harvard for the 1860–61 school year. Like many of the students, he continued his studies, took an active part in campus traditions like the Hasty Pudding Club, and traveled.³⁹ Of course, parental and presidential concerns played a hand in that decision, mostly because of Mary Todd Lincoln's fears for his safety.⁴⁰ After his graduation, Robert Todd Lincoln attended Harvard Law School for four months and then joined Lt. Gen. Ulysses S. Grant's staff from February 1865 until the end of the war.⁴¹ In total, 1,568 Harvard men enlisted between 1861 and 1865, with 1,311 fighting for the Federal forces and 257 for the Confederacy. A total of 138 on the Union side and sixty-four on the Southern side died or were killed during the war.⁴²

At Princeton, the divided loyalties between Northern and Southern students did not replace established friendships. The Southerners' place in the Princeton community was recognized and valued, although the number of students from Southern states had decreased by the 1860s with a third from slave-holding states.⁴³ The *Princeton Standard* forecast in 1862 that

> the expected absence of students from the States, which are waging war to overthrow the Union, will greatly increase the interest of the free States in this institution. We know that not a few parents at the North and West have heretofore withheld their sons from this college because of the predominating influence of Southern students here.⁴⁴

Incoming student Thomas W. Hunt recalled that in June 1861 he saw a group of seniors "assembled at the east end of Nassau Hall, bidding each other an affectionate farewell" as they prepared to fight on opposing sides.⁴⁵

Princeton students' affection and tolerance for Southern peers were not extended to Northern students holding Southern sympathies, and there was public support for students who were punished for attacking them. Conversely, the outside community frowned on faculty members' continuing affection for Southern students as disloyal to the Northern cause, even though the College demonstrated pro–Union sentiments.[46] Princeton contributed generals and other officers to both sides of the conflict, and President John Maclean and the campus community retained feelings for Southern Princetonians. Princeton Memorial Room in Nassau Hall memorialized its students from both the Union and the Confederacy.[47] In comparison to these sentiments, William and Mary later memorialized alumni who served in the Confederate Army, and Harvard honored Union alumni in its Memorial Hall.

In 1861, such memorials were far off, but William and Mary's Civil War involvement had already begun. That spring, with the College in the strategic collision path of Confederate and Union forces, both President Ewell and the faculty had taken what steps they could to protect the College and prepare for war. With the April 12 Confederate attack on Fort Sumter and Virginia's April 17 secession from the Union, conflict was no longer unavoidable. May 10 brought the decision to suspend the College's 1861 exercises. Ewell attended that May faculty meeting along with Professors Robert J. Morrison and Edward S. Joynes.[48] In the face of imminent war and Ewell's acceptance of military service, the College records and keys were transferred to Professor Morrison. Morrison took responsibility for College property for as long as he could remain, and with Ewell, formed a committee to secure the library and scientific apparatus.[49]

Benjamin Ewell, Robert J. Morrison, and Edward S. Joynes resolved that "a certified copy of the above two resolutions be sent to the chancellor of the College" (ex–President John Tyler, who held that post until 1862). They resolved to confer three degrees to "the late students of this College": H.B. Hubbard of Lancaster and Charles Shirley Harrison of Brandon (Prince George), the degrees of bachelor of arts; John D. Myers of Lexington, the degree of bachelor of philosophy. Ewell, Morrison, and Joynes also resolved that "Professor Morrison be requested to ascertain and prepare for record hereafter a list of those students of this College who have enlisted or may enlist, during this crisis, in the defense of this State of the South."[50] What Ewell and the faculty members could not prepare for, even if they entertained fears, was how terribly the newly refurbished Wren Building would be scarred by 1862. There would be similar fiery destruction on other Southern campuses, including the University of Alabama and Virginia Military Academy.

As the war commenced, the Confederates proceeded to dig in their heels in Williamsburg and elsewhere on the Virginia Peninsula, building defensive lines. Their strategy was to protect Virginia and Richmond, the Confederacy's new capital as of May 29, 1861, from invasion. Military hospitals and makeshift medical treatment centers were established in homes, churches, and larger structures such as the College's Wren Building and the Female Academy (a school located at the eastern end of Main Street [Duke of Gloucester Street] on the Capitol site) with more space for the sick and wounded. Throughout the South, Confederate forces and those who treated them faced huge gaps in medical knowledge and resources from the beginning, since an estimated 90 percent of today's medical knowledge was unknown at the time.[51] Despite the odds against recovery, surgeons and citizens did what they could to combat epidemic diseases, illness, and combat injuries.

The Wren Building saw substantial use as a Confederate barracks and as a hospital, to the point that in September 1861, the William and Mary faculty resolved to hire a local attorney to determine how much Virginia military authorities and the Confederate States should pay for damages and rent due from their extended occupation of the College premises. In that meeting, the faculty still held the hope that the College might reopen by January 1, 1862, with Professors Morrison and Taliaferro appointed to find out how soon Confederate forces would vacate the College building, or alternatively, if the school could reopen in some other building.[52] However, the winter of 1861–62 saw no evacuation of the campus. Instead, something much more ominous was on the horizon: Maj. Gen. George B. McClellan's plan to land more than 100,000 Federal soldiers at Fort Monroe and then march seventy miles to Richmond. Through spring, McClellan's troops would engage the defending Confederate generals and forces in their path at Yorktown and Williamsburg.[53] President Ewell had protected the College for years. Now, tasked with Williamsburg's protection as a Confederate Army officer, he planned the defense works along the town's eastern side.

Over time, the campus's 18th-century Georgian structures had endured the vicissitudes of fashion and expediency. During the Revolutionary War, the Wren Building, the Brafferton, and the President's House served to heal or quarter the military, and they were spared severe damage by friend and foe. Respect for the College's heritage and traditions persisted in the 19th century despite internal dissention, calls for change, and criticisms through the years that it was too tied to its past. Deference for William and Mary's place in history crossed the Mason-Dixon Line, as evidenced by Northern donors contributing to College after the 1859 fire.

Twice, in May 1859 and again in July 1860, Prof. Robert Morrison was charged with visiting New York and Philadelphia (adding Baltimore in 1860) to solicit donations for the library. Despite growing national dissension, over fifty New York businesses and "public spirited individuals" donated books and money, as did Columbia University and the United States Military Academy. Even in December 1860, Professors Taliaferro and Joynes reported to the faculty that B. Westermann & Co. in New York City had donated "books selected by them" with a value of fifty dollars.[54] It was evident that times had changed, for at the donors' request, a resolution in the faculty minutes would be the only acknowledgment.[55]

In the months to come, procuring books for the College library and continuing the College's post-1859 fire restoration would become moot points. Instead, William and Mary's remaining community members struggled to maintain it on a bare-bones level. Between the May 1861 closing of the College and the end of the war, members of the faculty and the Board of Visitors held several meetings. According to the July 5, 1865, report made by President Ewell to the Board and Governors of the College, board members met in Richmond in fall 1861.[56] The faculty and President Ewell met sporadically in September 1861, and from January through March of 1862.

President Ewell and Professors Morris, Morrison, and Taliaferro resolved on September 28, 1861, as previously mentioned, to seek recompense for College damages from Confederate use, through the appointment of Williamsburg attorney William S. Peachy.[57] By September 30, they had a sadder duty: to pass resolutions on the "irreparable loss of Professor Morrison," as a "calamity to the College of which he was so bright an ornament and to the country of which he was so faithful and able a servant."[58] On January 18, 1862, they mourned the death of John Tyler, Ll.D., rector of the Board of Visitors and chancellor of the College. Tyler's passing from a sudden illness was reported in the faculty minutes as depriving William and Mary of "one of its truest and most zealous friends," who had watched over it in both adversity and prosperity.[59] By October 4, 1862, the faculty meeting held in Richmond transferred bursar's duties from Tazewell Taylor of Norfolk to President Ewell.

Just as the president and faculty adjusted to the College's changing governance and finances, the campus continued its inexorable transition from peacetime to wartime use. Alumnus John S. Charles later provided a detailed picture of how the College looked on the eve of war. Charles was a local student who attended William and Mary and then lived in the Brafferton while the College was closed, helping President Ewell to protect it from vandals. In his recollections of 1861 Williamsburg, Charles said that outside of the Wren Building, the Brafferton, and the President's House, the Old Steward's House was the only building on the campus, located where Jefferson Hall now stands. The two-story structure with dormer windows was used for faculty housing once the College Hotel was constructed, and like many other frame buildings, it disappeared during the war, broken up and used primarily as construction materials for officers' quarters and other buildings at Fort Magruder.[60]

When the war began, the campus had been enclosed in a picket fence that kept roaming cattle and horses at bay, with a gate for vehicles. Looking down Main Street, at each corner of the campus were massive live oak trees; Charles recalled "Old Buck" (President Ewell, whom Charles also called "the noblest Roman of them all") keeping young boys from climbing them to harvest the edible acorns in more peaceful times. Charles portrayed a much different College after Federal occupation began:

> In order to afford protection against frequent Confederate raids, the windows and doors of the College, opening to the north and westward were bricked up, with port holes in them for small arms. Deep ditches were dug from North, East, and the South East corners of the College, extending some distance beyond the "Stage Road" [Richmond Road], and the "Mill Road" [Jamestown Road]. In these ditches were placed vertically big logs ten feet long, and three feet in the ground. These logs were fitted with portholes so as to guard against Cavalry raids down the two roads. Some distance in rear of College and extending in a curved line far beyond the "Mill and the Stage Roads" was constructed an abatis consisting of tops of big oak and beech trees with sharpened limbs set in the ground, standing westward and all entangled with wire. These were there when the War ended.[61]

The soldiers of the 15th Virginia arriving from Richmond slept in the Wren Building, which apparently was as yet undamaged. One soldier later recalled, "We certainly rubbed our heads against its honored walls and slept upon its carpeted floors," and another described sleeping in the College library with "some of my favorite authors for a pillow."[62] Fleeing the Union forces marching toward them from Fort Monroe, Hampton citizens took refuge in campus buildings as they did elsewhere in Williamsburg.[63]

In February 1933, eighty-eight-year-old Victoria King Lee recalled Williamsburg in 1861. Born in Hampton, Virginia, she moved with her family to Williamsburg for safety, as her father Dr. John C. King was a Confederate surgeon. Although just a teen-age girl at the time, Lee herself helped in the war effort and later married and settled in Williamsburg. She noted that in 1861, Williamsburg was "overrun with refugees from the lower end of the Peninsula. Many of these unfortunate people were housed in the Main Building of the College, which was later used as a hospital."[64] Lee recalled "baking biscuits and fry meat" with other townspeople to hand out to Confederate soldiers under Gen. Joseph E. Johnston's command, and that as he passed, he reined in his horse, waved in their direction and said, "That's what we're fighting for, men."[65] When General McClellan's army passed through afterwards, Lee recalled, "It was one of the most beautiful sights I have ever seen — countless thousands of blue-clad troops, all in new uniforms, they were several days passing through Williamsburg. I saw part of this army when it returned from the vicinity of Richmond — it didn't look so splendid then."[66]

In late June 1861, the Wren Building was used as a military hospital primarily for soldiers from the newly arrived 10th Georgia Volunteers suffering from measles, mumps, and other diseases.[67] The "strange metamorphosis" of that structure from "the peaceful abode of science and learning into a veritable chamber of horrors" continued after the Battle of Williamsburg on May 5, 1862, described by a Confederate soldier who took refuge there from rain and darkness:

> Wounded, dying and dead — here, there, everywhere — halls, recitation rooms, dormitories — all were crowded with bloody bodies! Here a ghastly face lay dead, and by its side a wounded comrade writhing, and moaning. In one of the large rooms three surgeons were busy at low tables, sawing off, or binding up limbs of poor fellows who lay upon the tables in such a way that the ghastly hue of their distorted faces showed all the more horribly from the flickering glare of the tallow candles at each corner.... As I ascended the stairway my foot struck some object, and a man passing at that moment with a light from one of the rooms showed me a pile of legs and arms that had been amputated and thrown upon the landing of the stairway, that being the only place unoccupied by the wounded.[68]

Already transformed by war, William and Mary's iconic Wren Building was more vulnerable once Confederate forces withdrew toward Richmond after the battle.

Elsewhere on campus, Mrs. Virginia Southall and her family were living in the President's House, the Brafferton saw use as a Federal headquarters, and the Wren Building was used as a depot for commissary stores.[69] Additionally, some rooms were set aside for Union courts-martial, according to Charles H. Buttz, a commissioned officer of the 11th Pennsylvania Cavalry who participated in those legal proceedings in August and September 1862.[70] During the war's later stages, the Wren Building Chapel vaults served at least once as a secret Confederate mail drop for scouts.[71] As a Federal outpost, Williamsburg — and within it, the College —

James Taylor drawing (Acc.2011.12) of the Wren Building from August 17, 1862 (Special Collections Research Center, Earl Gregg Swem Library, College of William and Mary).

was at the mercy of Federal forces and a succession of military governors dispensing degrees of harsh or considerate treatment.

The wartime presence of Union forces increased significantly after May 1861. The College and Williamsburg became contested zones where residents' resistance and a series of strikes by Confederate forces under Brig. Gen. Henry A. Wise escalated the threat of violence and destruction. The specific Union troops that arrived became another factor in that scenario. The 65th Pennsylvania Regiment, also known as the 5th Pennsylvania Cavalry or the Cameron Dragoons, was transferred that month to the Yorktown–Williamsburg area. Most of this regiment was stationed at Fort Monroe, except for two companies (I and K) scouting as a rear guard as McClellan's army advanced on Richmond.[72] The 5th Pennsylvania assumed guard duty responsibilities for Williamsburg, with its colonel, David Campbell, assuming command as military governor and taking over the Brafferton building on campus.

The 5th Pennsylvania Cavalry has been categorized by two modern historians as either the most inept, or at least one of the most inept, Civil War regiments on either side, due to issues such as the quality of its leadership and the constant flux of inexperienced replacements due to death and disease within Tidewater Virginia. The 5th Pennsylvania troopers earned a reputation for drinking and brawling, particularly in ethnic clashes between the German-American and Irish regimental members.[73] In hindsight, one can only imagine the expectations, misunderstandings, and festering irritations as weeks of encampment on the Peninsula turned into months and years. The diary of Elisha Hunt Rhodes (1842–1917) of the 2nd Rhode Island Volunteers conveys his feelings while camped near Yorktown on August 24, 1862, months after the Battle of Williamsburg:

> Sunday night again and I fear we are no nearer the end of the war than we were when we first landed at Fortress Monroe five months ago. But then we have learned some things, I now I hope we shall go ahead and capture Richmond.... It looks now as if our Corps (Keyes 4th) would remain on the Peninsular [sic], as most of the other troops have been sent away.[74]

Wondering how long the war might last was not the only issue for Northerners assigned to the region. One Philadelphia regimental history reported that "the relatively large mortality list of officers and men who succumbed to disease was the inevitable result of almost constant campaigning in the malarial tidewater lowlands of Virginia and North Carolina."[75] Of a total enrollment of 3,000 officers and men, six officers and 210 men died from diseases or in Southern prisons between the 5th Pennsylvania Cavalry's mustering in at Philadelphia and Pittsburgh, and its staggered mustering out in May, June, and August of 1865. Overall, one officer and seventy-six men from the regiment were killed or died from wounds during the war.[76]

For their part, Williamsburg residents complained about property damage, thievery, and nighttime fires. They again endured the influx and departure of General McClellan's army after the Seven Days' Battles fought near Richmond between June 25 and July 1, 1862. As difficult as those days were in the early part of the war, worse days lay ahead both for Williamsburg and for the College.

Chapter 3

A Bitter Demise

William and Mary was on the front lines after the Battle of Williamsburg on May 5, 1862. The engagement was inconclusive; following the Confederates' withdrawal from Williamsburg, Union forces occupying the campus found that the furthest extent of their control was just west of the College. At that moment, the outcome of the war was in doubt. The North had scored a significant victory at the bloody Battle of Shiloh (April 6–7). Robert E. Lee was not yet commanding the Confederate forces. Northern leaders hoped that General McClellan and his Army of the Potomac could take Richmond in the ongoing Peninsula campaign, but that did not happen. By June, Lee would be commander-in-chief of the Army of Northern Virginia, mounting a successful offense to protect the capital of the Confederacy. Lt. Gen. Ulysses S. Grant would not take Richmond for another three years.

Williamsburg's strategic location made it an appealing target for Confederate raids. Following General McClellan's departure in May 1862, the town became a military outpost surrounded by a thin picket line composed of companies of the 5th Pennsylvania. There were more infantry and artillery units located at nearby Fort Magruder, with the main forces stationed along General Magruder's former defense line and earthwork fortifications two miles from the fort. Williamsburg still had vestiges of its colonial appearance in homes, streets, and prominent features such as the College, the Powder Magazine, and Bruton Parish Church, although the colonial capitol building was gone. Southeast of the College grounds was the Eastern Lunatic Asylum with close to 300 patients. At the College end of Main Street, two roads (now Jamestown and Richmond Roads) formed a "V," one merging southwest into the road to Jamestown and the other northwest into the road to Richmond. Union officer David Edward Cronin noted, "About a half mile from town both roads disappeared in a vast forest that stretched across the rolling lands of the Penninsula [*sic*], and broken only by plantation clearings, this forest continued as far north as the Chickahominy [River]."

In 1862 and later in the war, Williamsburg was a hotbed of overt and covert operations on both sides, connected by telegraph lines to the War Department in Washington from Fort Magruder. At times the closest Union outpost to Richmond, the town was within scouting and skirmish range for the Confederates. They kept ongoing surveillance with the help of Confederate loyalists in town and observation posts in tall pines outside the town. Messages and news were transmitted through signals, civilian assistance, and apparently in secret mail pickups. A May 1862 report to the *New York Times* from the camp of the 1st Brigade, Hooker's Division revealed the correspondent's sense of frustration as the Stars and Stripes flew over "William and Mary's College," with reports of guns, muskets, and even cannon hidden from view, and the few remaining white women residents expecting the worst: "No indignities whatever are offered the towns-people, and we hear of a few instances of returning reason and loyalty. But upon the whole, Williamsburgh [sic] is the most rabid secession neighborhood we have yet visited."[1]

By the end of August 1862, a combined force of close to 1,500 Federal

The Battle of Williamsburg, which was fought on May 5, 1862 (Library of Congress).

troops was stationed in Williamsburg, composed of some artillery and cavalry units, a battalion from New York, and the 5th Pennsylvania Cavalry, rejoined by its other two units under Maj. Gen. George B. McClellan's command.[2] On the evening of September 8, the Wren Building was set on fire, but local residents formed a bucket brigade and saved it — only for the moment, as it turned out. Cronin noted in his history that "members of the Fifth Pennsylvania Cavalry had begun to regard the building as an outpost of the enemy.... They claimed that the Confederate sharpshooters frequently used it as a shelter in skirmishes, firing from the upper windows and roof, and killing and wounding a number of their comrades."[3] That day's fire may have contributed to a surprise Confederate attack on September 9, which preceded a second, more destructive fire set afterwards. Early that morning, Confederate cavalrymen under Lt. Col. William P. Shingler rushed Williamsburg's Union forces. They passed Union picket lines on Stage Road, routing thirty-three sleeping members of the 5th Pennsylvania from the College. Some of the Federals abandoned their posts and fled toward Yorktown. The skirmish became known locally as "Shingler's Raid." This raid and its aftermath provoked four decades of controversy about the September 9 fire.

For a few hours that morning, Williamsburg was back in Confederate possession, causing shock and confusion to the Federal forces. "It [the 5th Pennsylvania] was attacked by a superior force and suffered a loss of six killed, fifteen wounded, and thirty-three captured, Col. Campbell [David Campbell, military governor of Williamsburg, June–Sept. 1862] among the latter," according to a report from Maj. Gen. John A. Dix to Maj. Gen. Henry W. Halleck.[4] Some 500 Confederates rode east from the College on Main Street. Part of the cavalry headed toward the main encampment at Fort Magruder, setting fires, cutting telegraph wires, and taking captives.

A smaller force rode hard for the Vest Mansion (now known as the Palmer House, on Williamsburg's Duke of Gloucester Street). Military commanders in charge of Williamsburg, including Colonel Campbell, occupied the well-appointed home. This military governor was already unpopular, having arrested several town residents, one being a practicing physician, and they were promptly returned by Campbell's superiors in Norfolk. All these citizens were friends of Confederate Brig. Gen. Henry A. Wise, who commanded 1,800 infantry and cavalry, as well as an artillery battery on the Peninsula; Campbell's action possibly may have spurred Wise's decision to order the September 9 skirmish, and his capture, as retaliation.[5] As a 1938 history put it, Campbell was unpopular with the townsfolk for "what might be delicately described as his lack of tact," and although General Wise had to retire strategically once the Federals came back in force, "to the joy of Williamsburg he took the provost marshal with him."[6]

David Edward Cronin's description of wartime Williamsburg includes the incidents described above, and his original manuscript and illustrations are the collection of the New-York Historical Society. Formerly a captain in Troop C, 1st New York Mounted Rifles, Cronin was later a brevet major and provost marshal of Williamsburg. Between 1908 and 1910, he wrote a history of its 1862–1865 occupation. As one of a succession of military governors and provost marshals in charge of the town, he took particular interest in documenting their active service against the backdrop of the Vest Mansion. The spacious brick residence became the headquarters for numerous military leaders, including Confederate generals Joseph E. Johnston and John Bankhead Magruder, as well as Union Maj. Gen. George B. McClellan. Provost marshals then took the mansion as their headquarters during Williamsburg's years under Federal martial law.

Maj. David E. Cronin, USA (image from the David E. Cronin Papers, MS 670.9; Digital ID #86718d; collection of the New-York Historical Society).

An accomplished artist who trained in Europe, Cronin used a pseudonym to work as a staff artist for *Harper's Weekly* from 1861 to 1865, and later became a journalist and accomplished illustrator. In writing his history of Williamsburg's military occupation, Cronin used source material he collected during and after the war. These included his pen-and-ink sketches of Williamsburg and the reports and dispatches taken from the Official War Records of 1905.[7] The text's preface stated his desire to "present correct glimpses of partisan warfare with its wanton wastes and relentless retaliations" and to "divert the material of superfluous boasts and belittling allusions so apt to creep into the stories of old soldiers in whatever cause."[8] Cronin openly stated that the reports of rival commanders written in the field immediately after an event could "flatly contradict each other" in the details, even bordering on the romantic.[9]

In his history, Cronin recounted that a Confederate officer and several soldiers in the advance group found Colonel Campbell asleep in his bed, despite the sounds of gunfire less than a mile away. Ordered at gunpoint to surrender, rise, and dress himself, Campbell was about to be taken away when General Wise arrived and ordered him back inside to his office. Cronin wrote that, adding to the captive's humiliation, Wise sat in Campbell's own chair to ask questions: "The General's first question was singular but explainable when it is remembered that Wise had near relatives in Philadelphia and the social consequence of the prisoner might be considered in the importance of his capture. 'To what family of the Campbell's in Philadelphia, do you belong?' he asked. 'To no family on the face of the Earth just now,' was the Colonel's bitter response."[10]

Campbell and approximately one hundred captives were taken to Richmond for imprisonment.[11] The Confederates' possession of Williamsburg lasted a few hours, ending ten minutes past ten o'clock on the morning of September 9.[12] Most residents were glad for the Federals' temporary upset; however, there was reason to dread what it would cost them, the town, and the College. Accounts generally agree that with the victorious Confederates gone and Union reinforcements arriving, things soon got out of hand. Caught by surprise in the raid, the 5th Pennsylvania regiment was dishonored by its lack of preparedness and organization during the attack.

In the days afterwards, military correspondence from the Union Army's general-in-chief, Maj. Gen. Henry W. Halleck, referred to the accused "cowards of Williamsburg": those regimental members who fled or headed toward Yorktown.[13] A series of reports and orders exchanged between Maj. Gen. John A. Dix, commanding officer of the Department of Virginia, and General Halleck, general-in-chief at Fort Monroe, indicates the initial shock, then outrage at what happened to Federal forces in Williamsburg. The day of the Wren Building fire, General Dix reported that Col. Campbell was attacked and beaten, and that some of his men had acted "with proper spirit," while others had either acted in a cowardly manner or been imprisoned along with the colonel.[14]

The next day, at 6:30 P.M., General Dix penned a fuller report specifying that in addition to the capture of Colonel Campbell, two majors, five other officers and twenty-nine men, seven were killed and thirteen wounded. About 430 soldiers of the 5th Pennsylvania remained in Williamsburg after the Confederate force got away. According to Dix, two Confederate prisoners confirmed that the attacking force consisted of no more than 300 Georgians, South Carolinians, and Virginians. Dix added, "One of the majors ran away, and if a court cannot be found who has courage to shoot him, he should be [banned from] the service. I will report on his case especially."[15] On September 10 and 11, General Halleck sent two messages to Dix ordering a court-martial and stating that should that not be possible, he would request that the president cashier Major Wilson and all the others whom the Confederate raiders drove toward Yorktown.[16] Halleck then asked of Dix, "What is the object of holding Williamsburg? Why not withdraw the garrison to Yorktown?"[17] Dix answered those questions in another dispatch on September 12. Dix wrote that he could not hold the town with 500 cavalry and would now withdraw, but had hoped his troops "might do something to retrieve the character of the regiment."[18]

By September 25, a general court-martial was convened in which Maj. Jacob P. Wilson was arraigned and tried on three charges: for misbehavior before the enemy, speaking words inducing others to abandon their posts, and cowardice while stationed with his regiment "on or about September 9, 1862."[19] Wilson was found not guilty and allowed to return to duty.[20] Although the report stated that he could be tried for misconduct in another court, if that was not advisable, "it is only for the reason that so many others are as deeply involved as himself in the general delinquency."[21] Of the regiment, it was said, "It can never regain its standing until this stain on its character is effaced by worthier conduct in the face of the enemy."[22] Colonel Campbell was found responsible along with the other principal officers for the regiment's lack of discipline and organization.[23] After being held in Libby Prison for several weeks, Campbell was exchanged and dismissed on October 13 for "incompetency and gross neglect of duty" in the "disgraceful defeat" at Williamsburg. Majors Edward Boteler, William C. Heuser, and Jacob P. Wilson were discharged the same day.[24] However, Campbell's resignation (dated to October 13, 1862) was accepted after the dismissal was revoked on September 10, 1863. A dry goods merchant before the war, Campbell lived until 1888, working as an insurance agent in Pennsylvania.[25] A Pennsylvania regimental history written in 1869 summarized the entire Confederate raiding incident as the result of inferior numbers and weaponry, omitting details of what happened on the campus and at the Vest Mansion.[26]

People recounted various versions of Colonel Campbell's actions and other events connected to the September 9 fire that gutted the Wren Building. As noted, Cronin's account states that Campbell was in bed in Williamsburg when the Confederates struck the morning of September 9, being then taken captive. Following Shingler's raid the morning of September 9, a number of 5th Pennsylvania cavalrymen were reported to have broken into supply stores of alcohol, becoming intoxicated. Amid the chaos and disorder, a young Union captain, Diodate C. Hannahs, was under orders to restore military discipline in Williamsburg. James L. Slater, who was ten years old in 1862, shared his memories of that day in 1895. Slater claimed to distinctly recall that an intoxicated Union soldier had sought out and shot Captain Hannahs of the 6th New York Cavalry, and then again threatened the wounded officer as he lay in Slater's home, where he'd been carried:

> While he [Hannahs] lay in bed, the solder came in again, and drew a pistol on him again, and said, "D—, you, you shot my horse, and I will shoot you in bed." The captain said that he was not one of his men, the Sixth New York, but the Fifth Pennsylvania. Next morning about midday the captain died in my mother's arms. The troops of the Fifth Pennsylvania threatened me if I told on their comrade, and though the solder was arrested, nothing could be proved on him.
>
> Later in the evening I was at the College gate searching, at the captain's request, for the captain's first lieutenant, when I saw the College on fire. Going home, I met one of the Fifth Pennsylvania Cavalry, who was cursing and saying, "I burned that d—d College, and I intend to burn this d—d town." I was young then, but I remember these events vividly.[27]

An older witness, James Griffin, said he witnessed Hannahs' shooting from the house across the street (owned by merchant John Deneufville). Griffin saw Hannahs' horse outside, a boy holding it, and young James Slater standing nearby. He also saw a soldier ride up, calling on the boy holding the horse to call Hannahs out. Griffin heard but did not see the fatal shot to Hannahs' throat, but next saw Virginia Slater take the injured officer into her home to nurse him.[28] Federal authorities took the accused soldier's punishment to the point of confining him and scheduling his court-martial, but he was released for lack of evidence.[29]

Later Northern accounts, such as the 1913 history of the Philadelphia Regiments published by the City of Philadelphia, a Yale College obituary of Diodate (i.e., Deiday) Cushman Hannahs, Class of 1859, and the notification of his funeral service in the *New York Times*, do not describe the College's burning or the circumstances under which he was shot.[30] Hannahs' death was summarized or implied in regimental histories as occurring in action. One such account described the event this way:

The enemy having retired before the approach of our forces, Capt. Hannahs' company was detached to reestablish the picket line in an advanced position. While employed on this service he was mortally wounded, by a ball through the right lung, and died the following morning.[31]

The General City News section of the *New York Times* ran this announcement on September 14, 1862, four days after Hannahs passed away in Williamsburg:

> THE ROLL OF HONOR.—It is a sad duty to record the end of another promising life. DIODATE C. HANNAHS, in his twenty-fourth year, Captain of Co. F, Sixth New York Volunteer Cavalry, was killed while on duty at Williamsburgh [sic], Va., on the 9th inst. A native of Brooklyn, well known and beloved theres [sic] a graduate of Yale College, where his name will be long remembered, a student in the law-office of Messrs. EVARTS, SOUTHMAYD & CHOATE, of this city, which he left to fight his country's battles, and a gallant officer of our New-York Cavalry—he leaves behind him, though young, a name which will be loved and honored by all who have ever known him. The funeral services will take place at the South Presbyterian Church, Clinton-Street, corner Amity, Brooklyn to-day, at 3 P.M.[32]

Captain Hannahs' life, cut short in Williamsburg, suggests another side to the war there—as a war of words between North and South. A promising young lawyer born into a prominent New York family, the facts surrounding his cause of death were laid out as murder by Williamsburg witnesses and omitted in a number of Northern accounts, including military histories, Yale records, and newspaper obituaries. Despite that, resident Virginia Slater's nursing of the dying Hannahs in her home stands as a humanitarian gesture across enemy lines, one of several documented in Williamsburg as contradictory accounts.

The most extensive account of Hannahs' life and death, and another account of the September 9 Wren Building fire, comes from Edward Pascal McKinney's book about the Civil War, published in 1922. *Life in Tent and Field: 1861–1865* also contains McKinney's observations of the war and describes his career as a military officer. At the time of Shingler's September 9 raid, Diodate Hannahs had been detached from the New York regiment and was serving on Maj. Gen. Erasmus D. Keyes's staff at Yorktown. Edward McKinney, then a first lieutenant, was the co-commander of Company F in Hannahs' place, according to McKinney's memoirs. One of Hannahs' fellow New Yorkers and a member of Yale's Class of 1861, McKinney asked for assignment to duty with Hannahs' company. In his 1922 biography, he wrote, "Captain Hannahs was a graduate of Yale College, of winning address and superior refinement of manners. We were acquainted in college and became most intimate friends."³³

Both McKinney and Hannahs received wartime praise from their classmates in the Triennial Meeting of the Yale Class of 1861, with McKinney honored as a faithful friend to his brother officer, one who eschewed promotion and honors in his subsequent military service. At that Yale meeting, speaker James Lanhan Harmar paid tribute to fallen comrades and those like McKinney who were still in service:

> Like all the three years' soldiers of the army, McKinney's life has been full of vicissitude and adventure, I have heard Bulkley [Milton Bulkey, Class of 1861] tell how one dark and rainy night, as they lay at one of the landings on the Peninsula, he saw a trooper tenderly bearing a sick and helpless officer through the camp, to place him on board one of the transports, that was to carry the wounded home. The trooper was McKinney, and the sick man, his friend, Capt. Diodate Hannahs. In spite of the orders, that only wounded could be received, these Yale men soon placed their friend on board. With this act of friendship done, McKinney prepared to leave.
>
> [However], In the stillness and the shadow of that last night, McKinney never left his dying friend. In his arms he quietly passed away; and he who had been his companion and faithful friend in life, was faithful even unto the end.³⁴

Rising to the rank of major, McKinney served as Maj. Gen. Philip Sheridan's commissary officer. After the war, he returned to New York and became a partner in a large grocery firm, writing *Life in Tent and Field, 1861–1865*. McKinney's writings and actions suggest why the September 9, 1862, Wren Building fire remained intensely controversial, even though his friend Hannahs' death was a brief moment in Civil War history. Northern accounts differed significantly from those of Williamsburg residents in both cases, indicating much different perceptions of culpability. That a Union soldier was accused by Southerners of killing a Union officer might be dismissed as confusion over just another wartime casualty. On the other hand, responsibility for the Wren Building's fiery destruction was contested, in part due to William and Mary's symbolic place in America's founding—a legacy that Benjamin Ewell continually reinforced after the war while seeking restitution for damage from Congress.

In later years, McKinney challenged two contemporary testimonies on the burning of the College and argued how that evidence related to Federal compensation and Southern enmity toward the North. McKinney was acquainted with the College's history and Williamsburg's colonial past. He wrote that Williamsburg was "known to the world as the seat of William and Mary College, the oldest college in America, next to Harvard."³⁵

He listed the colonial leaders and presidents among the College's alumni, then described its location between Richmond and "Fortress Monroe." Further, McKinney outlined the events of September 9 through 11, 1862: the raid by Confederates, the burning of the Wren Building, and the assassination of Capt. Hannahs in Williamsburg.

After the dawn attack on Saturday, September 9, McKinney described being sent to Williamsburg later, after Hannahs had already arrived with the 6th New York Cavalry to restore order and reorganize what was left of the 5th Pennsylvania. In seeking Hannahs, as his orders from General Keyes required, McKinney noted seeing the smoking ruins of the Main (Wren) Building.[36] He made no mention of ten-year-old James Slater or others relaying the message about his wounded friend, but described in similar fashion how Hannahs lay mortally wounded from a downward bullet that passed from his throat to his lung, leaving him mute and hemorrhaging, and tended by the "lady of the house," Slater's mother, Virginia.

McKinney remained by Hannahs' side until evening, returning to Yorktown and General Keyes to report and gain permission to go back after midnight, a twenty-four-mile round trip. Where Slater recalls Hannahs dying in his mother's arms, McKinney recalled, "He died in my arms about an hour after my return."[37] The next day, McKinney sought a coffin for his friend's body and investigated the calamities of the previous two days. Here his account differs from those of Slater and Griffin, with no mention of threats from 5th Pennsylvania Cavalry soldiers:

> Captain Hannahs, after establishing a new picket line, stopped at a little restaurant kept by a colored man, and left his horse in charge of a Negro boy. Some man took the horse from the boy and mounted, and when Captain Hannahs rushed out and seized the reins, shot him with a revolver. One or two of the inhabitants of Williamsburg saw the shooting and claimed it was done by a man in Federal uniform. A man of the Fifth Pennsylvania Cavalry was arrested and held for some time, and finally discharged for want of identification and lack of evidence. The murderer may or may not have been a Federal soldier.
> General Keyes sent an ambulance from Yorktown for Captain Hannahs, and sent his body, his orderly and horse, under my charge, to his home in Brooklyn, where he was buried with military honors.[38]

McKinney, as mentioned, had seen the devastation on campus as he rode into Williamsburg. In later life he questioned whether the prevailing story was true: that disgruntled Union soldiers set the fire while intoxicated and stood in a line, their sabers drawn, to bar townspeople from trying to extinguish it.

John Charles had no such doubts. Charles, who died in 1930 at almost

3. A Bitter Demise

A depiction of Williamsburg during the Union Army's occupation (Library of Congress).

seventy-nine years old, remembered that fire on September 9 in connection with a barn fire at the farm of Henley T. Jones, which extended north and west from the intersection of Stage Road [Richmond Road] and Boundary Street to the bordering woods. Charles claimed:

> The barn and its contents were destroyed by fire by Union soldiers on the same day that the College was burned. These soldiers were smarting under defeat by Colonel Shingler's Cavalry and also fired by a liberal supply of "The Rosy" [wine]. These were the same patriots who burned Old William and Mary on that same day and then hilariously rejoiced over their heroic work.[39]

An intriguing account of the fire comes from a later biographical entry for Maj. George Croghan McClelland, who graduated from West Point in 1843 and was a classmate of Ulysses S. Grant. McClelland served as a captain for two years with the 5th Pennsylvania. This history erroneously dates the raid to 1863, not 1862, and notes that McClelland's "distinguished services won the commendation of Generals Keyes and Peck."[40] In this version, McClelland was on guard with his company of about fifty men seven miles from Williamsburg when the rest of their regiment "came riding past at top speed."[41] The commanding officer — who must have been Maj. Wilson, since McClelland heard then that Colonel Campbell and the regiment's lieutenant colonel had been taken prisoner — called out to McClelland's company to "run for their lives."[42] However, Captain McClelland and his men fired and then charged the Confederate force (what this account refers to as about 600 South Carolina cavalrymen), turning them back toward Williamsburg and following in pursuit to retake the town. Thus, McClelland and his men may have been those who General Dix referred to as behaving "with proper spirit." This local 1919 Pennsylvania county history continued with what was apparently an important episode to McClelland, one of its prominent citizens:

> The burning of William and Mary College, which took part in the course of this fight, was not due to any fault of his [McClelland]. As his men were charging through the streets of Williamsburg they were fired upon by some of the inhabitants, from the doors and windows of houses. The soldiers were furious at this, and when they reached the upper end of the street where the college is located, driving the Confederates before them, McClelland ordered a halt. The lower part of the building had been used as a barracks for Rebel soldiers, and was filled with straw. Shortly after the halt Captain McClelland noticed smoke coming from the doors and windows, and ordered his men to put it out. He rode around the building several times, trying to find a way to save it, and did all he could to prevent its total destruction. There was no way of ascertaining how or what started the fire. Any Union soldier known to have done it would have been punished.[43]

The deposition of Maria T. Peyton was one of the two critical affidavits given to Williamsburg's magistrate, Dr. R.M. Garrett, in September 1862, following the Wren Building fire. Peyton deposed that she had gone to Lt. Colonel Smith, the commandant following Campbell's capture, to warn him she'd heard a rumor that Williamsburg would be set on fire, and was told, "No such orders had or would be given."[44] When the Wren fire started shortly thereafter, Peyton said that she had again gone to Smith. His reported response became part of the institutional saga regarding the Wren Building fire:

> Some time after, the affiant saw the College on fire, and immediately said to Colonel Smith, "See, sir, the destruction has begun." He replied, that it had, but that it would now be impossible to save the Building for want of buckets. He said further, that he had a set of drunken soldiers, and that it would take two sober men to control one drunken one. The affiant turned again to Colonel Smith and said, "Do, sir, try and save William and Mary College, for it will be a stigma on the page of history if you suffer it to be lost." He replied, "I have no means of putting out the fire, it cannot now be saved." The affiant distinctly understood from Colonel Smith, that no order had been given to burn

the College, but that it was done by drunken soldiers whom he could not control.[45]

As the armies of Generals McClellan and Johnston passed through, and in the progression of Union invasion and occupation between 1861 and 1865, Virginia's colonial capital remained a battle zone between Federal and Confederate troops on one level, and between the military and civilians on another. Ultimately, the protection and destruction of a historic past was at stake: residents tried to protect their own and others' property and belongings, but often failed or were forced to flee their homes. Along with periodic Confederate cavalry raids for supplies in Williamsburg, the Federals' hold was undermined by civilians supporting the Confederate military and communications across enemy lines.

By March 1863, Union authorities actively discussed how to deal with

Wise's Last Raid—
Skirmish at the College.
April 9th 1863.

This drawing (negative #57996), sketched by David E. Cronin, depicts the April 9, 1863, Confederate raid on Williamsburg, which resulted in heavy skirmishing on the William and Mary campus (collection of the New-York Historical Society).

such resistance, including drastic measures. Temporary Yorktown district commander Brig. Gen. Richard Busteed's plans vacillated between burning Williamsburg and protecting it, warning residents that they should cooperate to save their town, and ordering them to take oaths of allegiance to the U.S. government. His commanding officer, Maj. Gen. John A. Dix, disallowed burning Williamsburg, but decided that if residents' homes were known to harbor Confederate snipers, those houses would be razed to the ground.[46] Although Jefferson Davis declared martial law in Richmond and other Southern cities when either the possibility of invasion or lawlessness warranted, Federal forces encountered far more difficulties with hostility and resistance in captured areas like Williamsburg and Yorktown, in which the majority of the population was loyal to the Confederacy."[47] Resistance and retaliation continued throughout the war, adding to Williamsburg's physical vulnerability. In a February 10, 1863, Confederate military report from Brig. Gen. Henry Wise to Maj. Gen. Arnold Elzey about the thirty-five prisoners he sent him, Wise wrote, "These men are chiefly Germans, of the rascally 5th Pennsylvania Cavalry, who destroyed the records of Charles City County and who burned the buildings, library, &c. of the venerable William and Mary College. I trust they will be dealt with accordingly."[48]

Williamsburg's strategically located placement on the Virginia Peninsula made attacks and counterattacks between the Union and Confederate forces inescapable for the course of the war. Both enslaved and white townspeople found themselves caught in a power struggle between the sides. Periodically, Confederate infantry, at times under General Wise, would engage in skirmishes with Williamsburg's Union occupants, notably in 1863 and again in 1865, when a force under Col. John S. Mosby made a quick raid on the town. Interactions throughout the war were long remembered by civilians as well as soldiers and officers on each side. Mrs. Lee recalled Williamsburg girls detouring into the road to avoid walking under a large United States flag displayed outside a Union commissary building. In response, occupying troops "got a long flag pole [sic] and stretched it completely across the Main Street."[49] Another observer described the scene when Federal cavalrymen paraded down Williamsburg's Main Street in 1864, after an ineffectual raid on Richmond by troops under Union Maj. Gen. Judson Kilpatrick:

> Some of the gayer troopers wore conspicuous regalia, spoils taken not for their value but in the spirit of wanton mischief. One had adorned his horse with net armor, made out of a hoop skirt, another wore a lady's "skoopbonnet" with a huge bow. A large number wore stove pipe hats of antique models, piling them up one upon another. One boasted

of having a tower of eight telescoped in this style and waggishly asserted that the top one was "Jeff Davis's Sunday-go-to-meeting hat."⁵⁰

Fredericksburg endured similar treatment, according to eyewitness and author J. Clarence Stonebraker. He described vandalism, arson, robbery, and beyond that, the torture of women and children "horrible to relate," with churches and homes vandalized.⁵¹

For Provost Marshal David Cronin, Virginia's colonial history and Williamsburg's contribution to the nation's founding were enthralling, and he wrote about them with respect. Just as Williamsburg residents, particularly the ladies, tried valiantly to preserve the College's property as part of its heritage, they tried to protect their own property and belongings. However, such attempts often failed or were aborted when many were forced to flee their homes.

Appalled by the ransacking of homes in the town, Cronin himself put guards up to preserve what was left of private property. One case he described concerned the home of Robert Saunders Jr., a former professor and president of William and Mary. That residence is known today as the Robert Carter-Sauders House. Like many townspeople, the Saunders family left in haste as McClellan's army advanced, taking few possessions due to General Johnston's gathering all available conveyances for transportation. Families traveled on horseback to Richmond, using roads that were almost impassable due to heavy rains.⁵²

Cronin and the acting assistant adjutant general, Capt. E.V. Brown, found Saunders's home "in a state of complete wreck," littered with ruined documents, books, colonial newspapers, engravings, and evidence of the "heavy boots of cavalrymen who seemed to have played football with everything of value in the place." In the garret, they found minutes of secret sessions of Congress, letters from Thomas Jefferson to John Page, and others from prominent Revolutionary figures. These documents had been bequeathed to Saunders's wife by her father John Page, former governor of Virginia. Cronin and Brown took their "bundles of treasure" back to headquarters to protect them. Then, Cronin wrote:

> The following day the Captain sent to town an army wagon accompanied by infantrymen with shovels. The litter of garret and library was conveyed to the Fort where a number of ladies belonging to the families of officers assisted in carefully looking over the miscellaneous mass discovering many more relics of value nearly all of which, I was afterward informed, reached public historical collections as gifts.⁵³

According to Cronin, the documents sorted through at Fort Magruder went to the Rhode Island Historical Society, but there is little conclusive evidence of that.⁵⁴ An interesting counterpoint is that at least one account from a Massachusetts soldier written to his father in 1863 indicates that he "borrowed" books and letters to read from one ransacked historic home. This orderly, Sam Putnam, even sent letters written by Thomas Jefferson home so his father and sisters could read them. Further, although the house had been locked and military guards were watching the town, Putnam had found a way to reenter without being caught, to obtain more books.⁵⁵

As William and Mary president Lyon G. Tyler and others understood in reflecting on the past decades later, the protection and destruction of a way of life — and a seminal part of the nation's history — were ultimately at odds in the Civil War. In writing about Williamsburg's history, Tyler maintained that that "the most irreparable loss" during the war was the loss of the James City County record books, which ironically were sent to Richmond for safekeeping and perished there in an 1865 fire.⁵⁶ Although the College's heritage and resources had been protected, sometimes at great risk given wartime conditions, there were staggering losses in damage and vandalism. The Wren Building, so lovingly restored after the 1859 fire through Northern and Southern donors, was once again reduced to brick walls. William and Mary, like its faculty, students, and alumni, had gone to war; the resulting national conflict has never been resolved in some respects, including the wars of words represented in contradictory contemporary accounts.

Better-known Northern accounts such as David Cronin's demonstrate that Unionists' attitudes were not the same where the College and the area's historic significance were concerned. Despite the conditions of war, he and others resisted unauthorized practices of destruction and retaliation, and were willing to acknowledge blame. Lesser-known regimental histories, official war records, obituaries and recollections from Northern sources also reveal, through their contradictions, omissions and reinterpretations, the challenge of interpreting historical events and the ways in which an accepted narrative forms.

The accounts discussed in this chapter include some of the testimonies of townspeople and their recollections decades later. Edward McKinney and David Cronin wrote in distinctly different ways: McKinney as a veteran recalling the critical events of September 1862 — which included seeing his best friend Hannahs die — and Cronin, who penned a history of the military occupation of Williamsburg from his perspective as provost marshal. Add the testimonies of Williamsburg residents, stories of the war and occupation told to Colonial Williamsburg researchers in the 1920s, official reports, newspaper accounts, and College histories. The end result is a

3. A Bitter Demise 65

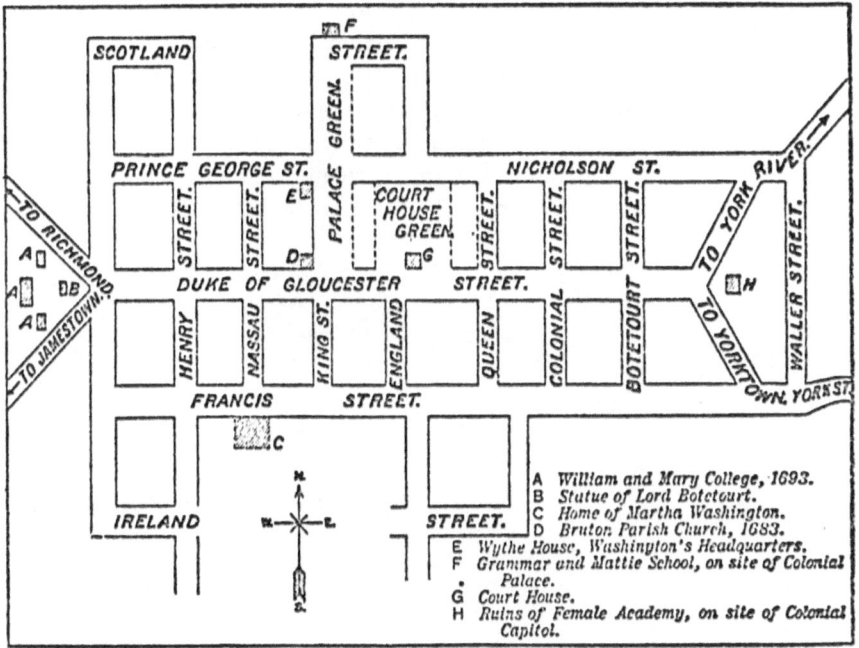

This 1886 map of Williamsburg is similar to what the town would have looked like during the Civil War era. From Herbert H. Adams, *The College of William and Mary: A Contribution to the History of Higher Education, with Suggestions for Its National Promotion* (Washington D.C.: U.S. Govt. Printing Office, 1887), 23.

densely woven narrative with multiple, often emotionally charged threads. This discord escalated to the halls of the U.S. Congress, when Benjamin Ewell and other College advocates (both Northern and Southern) persistently sought compensation for the Wren Building's destruction. Blame settled on unauthorized Union soldiers; that is the likely explanation when the September 9 fire is referenced in a sentence or a paragraph. Such a brief summary does not convey the realities of wartime occupation and contested ground.

In light of the College community's own contributions and sacrifices, the death of a promising young officer from New York might seem only distantly related to William and Mary's history. However, Hannahs' death demonstrates critical differences in Northern and Southern perceptions of the Civil War in relation to William and Mary, particularly the sequence of events during September 8–10, 1862. Piecing these accounts together shows that details about the Wren Building fire and who was responsible were contested, silenced, or used to reinforce shared realities, according to the tellers. As time would show, when President Ewell appealed for Federal compensation for damage from that fire beginning in 1867, the arguments for and against Union responsibility clashed in the public arena. However, while the William and Mary campus suffered immensely during the conflict, many of the College's students, faculty, and alumni had equally harrowing wartime experiences. Theirs is a story that must also be told.

CHAPTER 4

The College's Ambitious Sons

On April 9, 1865, Confederate Army Lt. Thomas H. "Tommy" Mercer and Privates Robert Armistead and John G. Williams laid down their arms at Appomattox Court House, Virginia, with the rest of their comrades, the remnants of Robert E. Lee's Army of Northern Virginia. There was little to distinguish these three young men from the rest of their comrades. They were all tired, hungry, and dirty from weeks of constant retreat from advancing Union armies. On this day of surrender, they were also undoubtedly amazed that they had survived all these years of ferocious fighting.

However, one undetectable factor bound this trio together. Just four years earlier, Mercer, Armistead, and Williams had been zealous William and Mary students who left their studies and their campus to go to war. They soon saw that day when their commitment to "the cause" was tested in battle, and many more like them. As these three men witnessed the historic surrender at Appomattox, one wonders whether they pondered the fates of their former classmates. History would later show that some died from wounds or sickness, while others surrendered with Confederate units in other parts of the country or sat it out in Union prisoner of war camps. A few of these former students even left the service altogether prior to 1865. Collectively, William and Mary students endured a wide variety of experiences during the war.[1]

At the beginning of the conflict in mid–1861, there was a great deal of excitement on the William and Mary campus. Although classes continued, the vast majority of the College's sixty-three students left for home to join the Confederate Army. Around April 25, 1861, William and Mary's last remaining Unionist student, William Reynolds, left for his native Baltimore to support the Union cause. Existing evidence suggests that he went on to serve as a private in the Union Army's 1st Maryland Infantry during the war's first year.[2] Thus, by May 10 with a virtually deserted campus and an imminent threat of war, the faculty decided to suspend classes. They hoped the College could resume operations later that year, but the proximity and intensity of the war did not make that possible. Although both armies later used the campus for military purposes, the College remained closed to students for the duration of the war.[3]

Meanwhile, other higher education institutions in Virginia attempted to stay open as the war raged around them. The Commonwealth's flagship civilian institution, the University of Virginia, struggled to survive with only a fraction of its student body. During the 1860 academic session, roughly 600 students were enrolled. However, only sixty-six were enrolled a year later, while over 515 left to join the Confederate Army.[4] That number dwarfs William and Mary's contingent of sixty-one students who pursued Confederate Army service, a sign of the College's diminished popularity during the 19th century. However, a higher percentage of William and Mary's student body served the Confederate cause. Around 97 percent of its student body joined the Confederate Army, while only 86 percent of University of Virginia students did the same.

With their academic days behind them, many William and Mary students began to make their own way in the growing Confederate Army. There were essentially two groups of students at this time: those hailing from various parts of Virginia and beyond, and those who were natives of Williamsburg or its surrounding area. The contingent of "locals" consisted of about nineteen individuals. The "out-of-towners" numbered about thirty-seven students, and they generally joined regiments in their home regions. Many of them hailed from central Virginia, the Norfolk area, or the rural sections of the state northeast of Richmond, known as the Northern Neck and Middle Peninsula. Most served in Virginia regiments and largely fought in the war's Eastern theater.[5]

However, five students (not including William Reynolds) were from other states: three from North Carolina, one from Maryland, and one from Mississippi. Halifax, North Carolina, native Sterling H. Gee served as a captain in the 1st North Carolina Infantry, and was later an assistant adjutant general on the staff of Maj. Gen. Robert Ransom.[6] Wounded initially in the thigh during the May 1863 Battle of Chancellorsville, Gee was later killed in action during the Battle of Five Forks on April 1, 1865.[7] William H. Day, a fellow Halifax County native, also served as a captain in the 1st North Carolina Infantry. He was captured at Spotsylvania Courthouse on May 12, 1864, and spent the rest of the war at various Federal prison camps, including Maryland's Point Lookout and Fort Delaware.[8] William and

Mary's other Tarheel student, Henry Ponton, served as a private in the 12th North Carolina Infantry, while Gresham Hough of Maryland served as a private in the Confederate Army's 1st Maryland Infantry and later the 1st Maryland Cavalry. The College's other out-of-state student, F.M. Wyman of Mississippi, went on to serve as a private in the 21st Mississippi Infantry, which was attached to the Army of Northern Virginia during part of the war.

Other notable examples of these "out-of-towners" who hailed from regions closer to Williamsburg were Richard A. Wise and Peyton N. Page. Born in Philadelphia, Pennsylvania, on September 2, 1843, Wise descended from a politically prominent family with deep Virginia roots. His father, Henry A. Wise, had been a member of the U.S. House of Representatives and U.S. ambassador to Brazil before serving as Virginia's governor from 1856 to 1860.[9] Richard was also a nephew by marriage of Union Maj. Gen. George G. Meade.[10] In early 1861, he was one of the several students who had joined the College's militia company. However, in the event of war, he had no plans to stay in the Williamsburg area.

In a January 9, 1861, letter to his father informing him of the College's militia company, Richard wrote, "I have joined, but do not intend to get a uniform, for if there is any fighting, I am going home and [will] go along with you."[11] True to his word, Richard went back to Richmond following the war's commencement to serve as a volunteer aide to his father, who was by then a brigadier general in the Confederate Army. In May 1862, Richard was appointed a second lieutenant with the 10th Virginia Cavalry, one of the regiments under Maj. Gen. J.E.B. Stuart's command. However, by that September he returned to his father's staff as an ordnance officer. For the rest of the war, Richard remained with his father as a captain and assistant inspector general.[12]

Peyton N. Page of Gloucester descended from one of Tidewater Virginia's most distinguished families. His great-grandfather, John

Brig. Gen. Henry A. Wise, CSA. From Henry A. Wise, *Seven Decades of the Union: A Memoir of John Tyler* (Richmond: J.W. Randolph & English, 1881), n.p.

Page, was a fellow William and Mary alumnus who served as a Virginia militia colonel during the American Revolution. He was also a close, lifelong friend of Thomas Jefferson, who, according to local tradition in Gloucester, wrote an early draft of the Declaration of Independence at Rosewell, the Page family estate.[13] His brother, Mann Page III, also attended the College and served in the Continental Congress during the American Revolution.[14] John Page went on to serve as Virginia's lieutenant governor in the 1770s, a U.S. congressman in the 1790s, and Virginia's governor between 1802 and 1805, succeeding James Monroe.[15] Along with John Page, Peyton was also directly descended from Robert "King" Carter, the influential colonial businessman and political leader who served as Virginia's governor in 1726 and 1727.[16]

Like his classmate Richard A. Wise, Peyton quickly joined the Confederate Army following the war's commencement in 1861. For the first half of the war, he served as a lieutenant and aide-de-camp to Brig. Gen. Gabriel J. Rains, who played a significant role in the early development of land mines. Later promoted to captain and then major, Peyton spent the second half of the war as an assistant adjutant general on the staff of fellow Gloucester native, then–Brig. Gen. William B. Taliaferro. Peyton was wounded in action in March 1865, captured, and later paroled by Union Army authorities on April 26, 1865.[17]

Apart from the "out-of-towners" like Richard A. Wise and Peyton N. Page, the Williamsburg natives made up the other large contingent of William and Mary students. These students were mostly members of prominent Williamsburg families who had resided in the area for generations and maintained close ties to the College. Although they dwelled in the dusty, old former capital, several of these families descended from friends and relatives of George Washington, Thomas Jefferson, and other Founding Fathers who made significant contributions to the American Revolution and the creation of the nation.[18] These families placed great value on their heritage as it gave them an aristocratic status within the region. It also kept Williamsburg immersed in the past, recalling the lost days of its 18th-century grandeur.

Student Thomas S. Beverly Tucker was one such member of this group. Thomas (or "Tom" as he was called) descended from a long line of prominent judges. His grandfather, St. George Tucker, studied law under George Wythe, served as a militia officer during the American Revolution, and later taught at William and Mary before becoming a judge.[19] Tom's sister, Cynthia Beverly Tucker Washington, was the widow of a former William and Mary professor and kinsman of George Washington.[20] Like classmate Richard A. Wise, Tom had been involved in the College's militia company during the secession crisis. After the war began, Tom spent the first year as a Confederate Army staff officer, serving as a second lieutenant and aide-de-camp to Maj. Gen. Lafayette McClaws.

During the December 1862 Battle of Fredericksburg, Tom was shot in the knee and permanently crippled. Over the next several months, he endured a slow and difficult recovery, despite regular assistance from family members. In an April 16, 1863, letter to his sister, he updated her on his condition:

> The day you left I dressed and moved my chair out into the porch where I enjoyed the fresh air for several hours. I can dress myself and get into and out of the chair without any assistance. I sat up yesterday for more than five hours — three longer than I have ever sat up before. I attempted to stand up with crutches but as soon as Mother let go of my arm I fell back into the chair. I expect to leave for Lynchburg in about a week.[21]

Thus, he eventually retired to the Invalid Corps on July 2, 1864. He later returned to service in July, working at the Conscript Bureau, and served in that capacity for the balance of the war.[22]

Thomas H. "Tommy" Mercer also belonged to this elite group of William and Mary students. His father, John Mercer, and grandfather, Robert Page Waller, were both prominent area doctors and landowners. Tommy also possessed a proud military heritage that fueled his ambition for battlefield glory. He was a great-grandson of Brig. Gen. Hugh Mercer, the esteemed Continental Army commander and close friend of George Washington who died from wounds sustained at the 1777 Battle of Princeton.[23] As such, he was also related distantly to Confederate Brig. Gen. Hugh W. Mercer of Georgia.

Although he enlisted initially in April 1861 as a private in the 32nd Virginia Infantry, Tommy showed great interest in military life and soon desired an officer's commission in the Confederate Army. He was appointed an officer cadet in October 1861 and spent the next several months as a drillmaster for the 1st Virginia Infantry.[24] An effective soldier, Mercer was cited by Lt. Gen. A.P. Hill for "coolness and daring" during the May 1862 Battle of Williamsburg, where he sustained a battlefield injury.[25] Following that battle, Tommy served as an ordnance officer on the staff of Maj. Gen. Lafayette McClaws. Later promoted to second lieutenant, he went on to serve the Army of Northern Virginia, first in Woolfolk's (Virginia) Artillery and then Madison's (Mississippi) Artillery Company during the war's later stages.[26] For students such as Tom Tucker and Tommy Mercer, who were members of these illustrious Williamsburg families, they had reasons to fight beyond simply achieving visions of battlefield glory. They were not just fighting to serve the Confederate cause, but also to preserve the honor of their distinguished family names.

While the College's non-local students scattered across a wide array of Confederate infantry, cavalry, and artillery regiments, the majority of Williamsburg natives joined the 32nd Virginia Infantry. This regiment was created around April 1861 and consisted of men from all over the Virginia Peninsula—Williamsburg, Yorktown, and what are now the cities of Hampton and Newport News. A reluctant Benjamin Ewell took command of this unit, commissioned initially as a major, and then a lieutenant colonel the following month. Although he despised disunion, Ewell could not bear arms against his native state and consequently aligned with the Confederacy.[27]

Residents of Williamsburg primarily served in Company C of the 32nd Virginia, better known as the Williamsburg Junior Guard. At least nine William and Mary students served in this unit, which was originally organized as the College's militia company in 1859.[28] The balance of its membership consisted of farmers, townspeople, and the sons of prominent community members. However, some students and several alumni were also present in other parts of the regiment. A small number of students also joined the 3rd Virginia Cavalry, which was formed in the same area.[29] Nevertheless, the largest concentration of William and Mary students in the Confederate Army was found in the 32nd Virginia Infantry.[30] Over the course of the war, this regiment served in various parts of Virginia and North Carolina. It participated in the Battles of Williamsburg and Fredericksburg in 1862, and later at Cold Harbor and Petersburg in 1864.[31] The 32nd was also present for the Appomattox campaign and surrender in 1865.[32] Throughout these campaigns, the regiment fought nobly, due in part to the work of students from the College.

Students from William and Mary made contributions to the war beyond solely the work of the 32nd Virginia. They served in a variety of capacities, ranging from privates to regimental and division staff officers. Out of the sixty-one students who served in the Confederate Army, at least thirty-eight enlisted as privates. This was likely due to their lack of military experience. However, at least a few of the college's students who enlisted had significant military training. For instance, John D. Myers had attended Washington College prior to enrolling at William and Mary and also trained at Virginia Military Institute. Although he enlisted initially as just a private in the 32nd Virginia Infantry, he was soon regarded as a highly accomplished drillmaster. Therefore, he spent time during the war's early stages training men of the 4th and 31st Virginia Infantry regiments. Myers later applied for appointment as an officer cadet, securing recommendation letters from Brig. Gen. William L. Jackson, Lt. Gen. Thomas J. "Stonewall" Jackson, Col. John F. Preston, and Col. Benjamin S. Ewell.[33]

Commissioned a second lieutenant in June 1861, Myers continued his service as a drillmaster and also served as an assistant aide-de-camp on Brig. Gen. Robert S. Garnett's staff. After completing additional service as a quartermaster and ordnance officer, John lost his commission in a regimental reorganization and went on to serve as a private in both the 4th and 1st Virginia Cavalry regiments. He was wounded slightly in the face during the August 9, 1862, Battle of Cedar Mountain, and later sustained a more significant shoulder wound at the Battle of Todd's Tavern on May 7, 1864. Possibly because of his injuries, he spent the war's final stages either on sick leave or tending to administrative matters for the regiment. John was paroled at Columbia, South Carolina, on May 3, 1865.[34]

Over the course of the war, some students advanced to noncommissioned officer ranks, such as corporal and sergeant. At least five students were promoted to the rank of corporal and about six advanced to the rank of sergeant or sergeant major. Still, roughly twenty-six students never advanced beyond the rank of private. Nevertheless, some still carried on tasks of great responsibility. For instance, Pvt. John G. Williams of Orange County, Virginia, served as a courier for Lt. Gen. Jubal Early for much of the conflict.[35]

Conversely, at least eighteen students served the Confederacy as officers. Six of them, including Tommy Mercer, enlisted first and worked towards earning a commission later in the war. Others, like Tom Tucker, used family connections with high-ranking Confederate officials to bypass enlisted status altogether. In Tucker's case, his sister Cynthia wrote to President Jefferson Davis, one of their late father's old admirers, to earn her brother a commission in May 1861. A week later, Tom was nominated for a second lieutenancy in the Confederate Army.[36] In a similar vein, Richard Wise probably benefited from his father's political and military standing in earning his commission. The remaining students in this group likely became officers through either election by their peers or promotion.[37] Regardless of his path to commissioning, no William and Mary student advanced beyond the rank of major over the course of the war.[38] That honor went to Peyton N. Page, who spent the war as a Confederate staff officer. Among the other students who served as officers, ten of them were first or second lieutenants and only six became captains. In addition, at least five joined Page serving as staff officers while the balance of the group held command positions.

Collectively, the College's students served in all branches of the Confederate Army.[39] At least thirty-one served in the infantry, making that the most common form of their military service. However, the artillery and cavalry were also well represented, as there were at least thirteen William and Mary cavalrymen and about seven artillerists. In most instances, the students remained in their original service branch for the duration of the war. However, at least five of them switched from one branch to another. In each case, they left the infantry to enroll in either cavalry or artillery units. There are several possible explanations for this occurrence. One was that injury or illness often necessitated service outside of the infantry, which was the most physically demanding of the three branches. For example, at least two students, Pvt. Henry S. Dix and Pvt. John N. Williams, were required to transfer from infantry to artillery units after suffering from ailments such as typhoid fever.

In addition, many people also viewed cavalry or artillery service as more dashing and sophisticated than menial duty as a "ground-pounder."[40] Therefore, after an initial period of infantry service, some soldiers possibly sought more exciting duty in another branch. Another possible explanation reflects a broader trend seen in both armies during the war. As some infantrymen had their fill of intense combat, they sometimes sought transfers to the cavalry or artillery, which were viewed as "safer" forms of military service. It is plausible that some of these students used this tactic, thinking it would get them through the war in one piece.

The wartime experiences of William and Mary students generally differed little from that of their colleagues. They faced periods of fear, boredom, and stress along with the rest of their Confederate peers. Supply shortages were also a common problem. In the following December 1862 letter to his sister, Lt. Tom Tucker asked for pajamas, an overcoat, socks, money, and other articles of clothing. Considering that Confederate officers were generally better equipped than enlisted men, this correspondence indicates the extent of material shortages in the Confederate Army:

> Headquarters Div. near Fredericksburg — Dec. 6, 1862
>
> I received your note and several since dearest sister and am truly glad to hear that you are well — also the Burg.[41] Everything is quiet just as it was when I last wrote you, so far as I know. It was thought a few days since that the enemy was leaving but it turned out to be a "false alarm."
> It snowed all day yesterday. It was one of the most disagreeable days I ever saw! We all had quite a "snowballing spree" last night begun by Major McClaws. I could not enjoy it as I have been quite lame for several days frost so much so as to hardly be able to draft this letter. Hope to be entirely well in the course of a day or two.
> I am much obliged to the Doctor for his offer of the shirts, but as I never wear undershirts will not deprive him of them unless you think it better for me to have them. Have you sent the clothes I wrote to you

for? I cannot make for sure from your note whether you have or not. I received the overcoat on Thursday just in time for the bad weather. Please get Davy two pair of socks if you can so he has some.

Any news from home? Do you think it possible for mother to send me some bed clothes? I lost all I had except for [illegible]. I am consequently very much in need of some.

I saw Uncle William Berkeley a day or two ago. He is looking as well as I ever saw him. Charley is if anything uglier than ever. Cousin Edward was wounded at the Battle of Sharpsburg and taken prisoner — has not been exchanged. Please get me three dollars worth of [illegible] in your next letter.

Love to all,
God bless you,
T.S.B.T.[8]

William and Mary students also experienced homesickness just like all other soldiers during the Civil War. For instance, Tom Tucker constantly asked for news from home, remarking in a November 24, 1862, letter to his sister that he was "very anxious to get news, any news from home."[43] He also indicated his intense displeasure when promised letters from his sister did not arrive on time. In an April 16, 1863, letter to his sister, he wrote, "We have been looking for your promised letter for several days past my dear sister, but have so far been disappointed in not securing it."[44] Although with modern forms of transportation Tom was only two or three hours from home, it felt like he was on the other side of the world in the 1860s.

Since the vast majority of William and Mary students fought in the war's Eastern theater, they largely served in regiments attached to the famed Army of Northern Virginia. Accordingly, most of them saw action in some of the war's most important battles. For instance, Lt. Alexander Tunstall of the 6th Virginia Infantry served in the Battles of First Bull Run, Fredericksburg, Gettysburg, and Cold Harbor, considered by many to be four of the war's most significant engagements.[45] Further, many of the students were present in the trenches outside of Petersburg during the war's later stages. Apart from the Army of Northern Virginia, a few students served in other Eastern commands. For instance, Capt. Richard A. Wise saw service in both the Shenandoah Valley and the North Carolina coast at Roanoke Island. Existing evidence also suggests he spent the war's final days, along with Maj. Peyton N. Page, with General Joseph E. Johnston's army in North Carolina.[46] Further, at least one student, Pvt. F.M. Wyman of the 21st Mississippi Infantry, may have served in the West, since that regiment fought in the 1863 Battle of Chickamauga.

As the war progressed, students from the College also experienced their fair share of combat and fatigue. Consequently, several experienced injury, capture, and even death. Union forces captured at least four students (including Capt. William H. Day of the 1st North Carolina Infantry) and either paroled them at a later time or sent them to Federal prisoner of war camps. For instance, Sgt. T.J. Barlow of the 32nd Virginia Infantry was captured during the Battle of Antietam in September 1862 and paroled a few weeks later at Shepherdstown, (West) Virginia. Sgt. George Fosque of the 39th Virginia Infantry was captured twice, once at Roanoke Island in 1862 and then again in 1865. He sat out the conclusion of the war at Point Lookout Prison in Maryland.[47] Sgt. Maj. Joseph V. Bidgood was captured in April 1865 during the Battle of Sailor's Creek, and also spent the war's final days as a prisoner at Point Lookout.[48]

There were several combat-related casualties among the students during the war. Lt. Tom Tucker sustained the devastating knee injury during the December 1862 Battle of Fredericksburg that nearly killed him. As outlined in his letter of April 16, 1863, the wound put him out of action for several months as he spent time recovering in Richmond and Lynchburg.[49] Lt. Tommy Mercer also sustained an injury during the May 1862 Battle of Williamsburg. Aside from injuries, there were also at least three combat fatalities among this student population, including Capt. Sterling H. Gee of the 1st North Carolina Infantry who was killed at Five Forks. Pvt. T.R. Argyle of the 4th Virginia Cavalry was killed in service near Goochland, Virginia, in September 1861, and Sgt. William Browne of the 12th Virginia Infantry was mortally wounded at Malvern Hill in July 1862 during the Seven Days' Battles, dying in Richmond the following month.[50]

As with other Confederate soldiers, disease proved to be as harmful to the students as exposure to combat. Consequently, at least four of them were either discharged from the Confederate Army for medical reasons or died in service from disease. For instance, Pvt. James H. Dix became the first casualty among the Williamsburg Junior Guards when he succumbed to typhoid fever in September 1861.[51] The Dix family's medical misfortune continued when his brother, Pvt. Henry S. Dix, was discharged from the 32nd Virginia for "disease of the spine" in October 1862. Although Henry reenlisted with the Mathews Light Artillery in 1863, he was detailed to assist an enrolling officer in Halifax County, Virginia, on account of his health.[52] John N. Williams, a private in the 6th Virginia Infantry, endured a similar ordeal as he was discharged from the Confederate Army after a tough bout with typhoid fever in April 1863. After a period of recovery, he later joined the Richmond Howitzers Artillery.[53]

Apart from physical injury, at least one student possibly suffered from the emotional strain of fighting and wanted a way to get out of the military.

Consequently, Pvt. E.W. Spratley of the 12th Virginia Infantry furnished a substitute, John L. Jeans, and was discharged from the Confederate Army on July 22, 1862.[54] Conversely, a fellow student, Norton C. Newton, served as a substitute for a John H. Williams. Newton joined the 6th Virginia Infantry as a private, with his desire for cash possibly outweighing his fear of the battlefield.[55] Although there were many casualties and some voluntary departures from service, most William and Mary students, including Newton, served for the duration of the war and lived to tell their tales.

Despite all of the pain and misery that they endured during the conflict, some William and Mary students experienced amusing moments on occasion. Portsmouth, Virginia, native Joseph V. Bidgood, a sergeant major in the 32nd Virginia Infantry who was born in 1841, was one such student.[56] In the years after the war, he wrote about his experiences during the Second Battle of Cold Harbor in 1864:

Wartime student Joseph V. Bidgood, ca. 1898 (*Atlanta Constitution*, July 23, 1898), 15.

> I had a first cousin, John Langhorne, a gallant fellow. No doubt many of the Richmond men remember him. He was just on the right of our line with two guns of his battery. The enemy had been worrying us a good deal with their artillery, and Lieutenant Langhorne made up his mind to give them some of their own medicine.
>
> He picked out a place just at the foot of a little rise in the ground, where, rigging his guns in mortar fashion, and getting the range, he commenced to drop shells in their lines and battery that made the enemy think they had started the worst kind of hornets. Langhorne had his fun, but overlooked the fact that it was a game two could play. After standing it as long as possible, they turned loose all their guns on our lines.
>
> We infantry boys did surely hug the ground. General Corse,[57] our brigadier, had been near us just before the fuss commenced. My colonel, Montague,[58] Major B.P. Lee[59] and myself had picked out the safest place we could find, when all of a sudden the colonel said to me, "Bid-

good, where is General Corse? Go out, find him and ask him to come with us." I looked at the colonel and said to myself, "Does he want to get rid of his sergeant-major this way?"

The shells were coming as thick as hail, bursting and kicking up such dust as no tornado could. However, when the colonel ordered it, and it was my duty to obey, I started to find the general, but as "Grand Old Dad," as we called him, was a wise man as well as a good general, he had doubtless selected a safe place. I dodged the shells and took a hasty look, but nothing was to be seen, not a man, nothing but the shells and dust. I finally made my way back to the colonel, and reported that the general could not be found. Colonel Montague looked me full in the face, smiling, and said, "Bidgood, this is the first time I ever saw you scared."[60]

After the Confederacy's fall in 1865, these veterans settled back into the civilian world to continue their lives. Some went on to distinguished careers in medicine, law, business, and public service, while others were content with a quiet and simple life in small-town America. Maj. Peyton N. Page returned to Gloucester and married Emily Daniel Kemp in 1875.[61] He also studied law during that period and became a prominent local attorney. For several years, he also served as the Gloucester County commonwealth's attorney. However, he succumbed to pneumonia at the age of fifty-one on January 7, 1891, and was buried at Abingdon Episcopal Church Cemetery in Gloucester.[62]

After his 1865 surrender to Union forces in Greensboro, North Carolina, Capt. Richard A. Wise decided to pursue a career in medicine. He earned a degree from the Medical College of Virginia in 1867, married Maria Daingerfield Peachy in 1870, and spent the rest of his career in Williamsburg. Richard was later a professor at William and Mary from 1869 to 1881, where he organized a militia company known as the "Wise Light Infantry."[63] He also served as superintendent of Eastern State Mental Hospital from 1882 to 1885.

However, as he grew older, Richard turned increasingly to his father's old profession of public service. He served in the Virginia House of Delegates from 1885 to 1887, and was also the circuit court clerk for Williamsburg and James City County between 1888 and 1894. With a growing interest in national politics, Richard served as a delegate to the 1892, 1896, and 1900 Republican National Conventions. His public service career culminated in the late 1890s with service in the U.S. House of Representatives. However, he was a longtime sufferer of Bright's disease, and Richard's health began to fail as the 1890s grew to a close. In his last days, a concerned Congressional colleague remarked to Richard, "You are a doctor and ought to know what will give relief." To that, he responded, "The doctors cannot cure a man with my disease."[64] Richard died in December 1900 at the age of fifty-seven and was buried at Hollywood Cemetery in Richmond, Virginia.[65] To honor Richard's life and work, an anonymous Williamsburg resident, who had been one of Richard's political opponents, wrote the following tribute:

> The feeling of deepest sorrow fills this entire community on account of the death of Dr. Richard A. Wise, which occurred about 10 o'clock yesterday morning, for they feel the loss of a good and skillful physician, who was ready at all times to respond to the calls of suffering humanity; and those who feel most heavily the loss of a kind friend and benefactor are the poorer class of people.
>
> This day have been heard on the streets and out in the country many heartfelt expressions of sorrow from the lips of white and colored: "What is to become of us, now that Dr. Wise is gone?" Many families can be mentioned — white families, not to speak of the colored people — upon whom Dr. Wise has been practicing for years without hope or expectation of remuneration.
>
> The devotion of the needy class to Dr. Wise was phenomenal. Day and night, it is known to the writer of this poor tribute, Dr. Wise would travel many miles to visit the sick, nurse them tenderly and carefully, when he well knew there was not the slightest prospect of any medical fees.
>
> The author of this notice differed in politics from Dr. Wise — one a lifelong Democrat, the other a Republican — yet we know that there are white Democrats in this part of the peninsula who never failed to vote for Dr. Wise whenever he was a candidate for office. But these men would never vote for any other Repub-

Wartime student Richard A. Wise, ca. 1895, A.M. — 1869. From *Memorial Addresses on the Life and Character of Richard Alsop Wise*, Fifty-Sixth U.S. Congress, 2nd session (Washington D.C.: U.S. Govt. Printing Office, 1901), 2.

lican. Their gratitude to the good physician and their generous friend always overcame their party loyalty.

Dr. Wise has proven a working and useful member of Congress, and it cannot be denied that he has secured at Washington large appropriations for this congressional district. Though regarded generally as a bitter partisan by the Democrats, it is well known that he has secured during his career in Congress many appointments for Democrats. One of his last public acts was to appoint as principal and alternate to the Naval Academy, at Annapolis, the sons of unwavering Democrats.

Dr. Wise had his peculiarities (and who has them not?), but he possessed a kind heart and generous disposition to those who knew him intimately and understood him well.

A lifelong Democrat, who has never voted any other than a Democratic ticket (save once, and that for Horace Greeley), who has known Dr. Wise for more than forty years — always differing with him politically — feels deeply distressed at his untimely death, and will place flowers upon his grave, with "peace to his ashes."[66]

Other students joined Wise in pursuing postwar careers in the public arena. Lt. W.H.E. Morecock returned to his native Williamsburg and served as circuit court clerk from 1870 to 1887, before passing away in 1896.[67] Pvt. William Reynolds became a well-known attorney in his native Baltimore, Maryland, upon concluding his service with the Union Army.[68] Following his surrender at Columbia, South Carolina, Lt. John D. Myers attended the University of Virginia from 1865 to 1866, training to become a physician. He later practiced medicine in Christiansburg as well as Lexington, Virginia, where he also served as a city councilman.[69] In later years, John's career prompted him to move to New York; Booneville, Missouri; and Caperton as well as Huntington, West Virginia. He died in Huntington on May 2, 1915, at the age of seventy-four, and was later buried in Lexington.[70] Lt. Alex Tunstall also went into medicine, studying at both Bellevue Hospital and the General Hospital in New York City. After earning his M.D., Alex returned to his native Norfolk, Virginia, where he joined his father's medical practice. Alex went on to become a highly respected medical leader, and "was ranked as one of the most skillful, courageous, and able physicians and surgeons in his city."[71] He died in 1905 at the age of sixty-two and was buried in Norfolk.

After his surrender at Appomattox, Pvt. John G. Williams went on to become a prominent lawyer and bank president in his native Orange County, Virginia, serving on three different occasions as a vice-president of the Virginia State Bar Association. Along with serving as circuit court clerk, he also served as commonwealth's attorney from 1883 to 1908, succeeding his father, who had served in the same office from 1832 to 1880.

John died at the age of sixty-eight on September 26, 1911, and was buried in Orange County.[72] Upon release from Union custody in 1865, Sgt. Maj. Joseph V. Bidgood went on to become a successful businessman, serving as vice-president of J.W. Randolph Publishers. He was also one of the few William and Mary students to continue a career in the military, serving for over twenty years as an officer in the Virginia militia, eventually reaching the rank of colonel.[73] Before his death in 1921, Bidgood lived to read newspaper accounts about another terrible conflict that utilized some of the technological innovations established during the Civil War: the First World War.

While some students lived long, productive lives after the Civil War, others were not so fortunate. Several suffered from the lingering physical effects of their lengthy service in the Confederate Army. After the Appomattox surrender, Lt. Tommy Mercer returned home to Williamsburg to resume his civilian life. Unfortunately, his postwar career was cut short when he succumbed to pneumonia at age twenty-two on September 7, 1865, a likely result of his weakened physical condition from months of heavy fighting. His grieving grandfather, Dr. Waller, noted, "Oh! His death is a sad blow, after his escape from all the great battles he participated in."[74] Lt. Tom Tucker suffered a similar fate. Although he was probably the only student to return to William and Mary in the postwar years to complete his education, his battle wounds continued to plague him. Upon his death in 1872 at age thirty-one, his sister Cynthia asserted that he was "as effectively killed by the ball on the battlefield of Fredericksburg as if he had fallen on the spot."[75]

It is difficult to determine whether the surviving students felt the same sense of devotion to "the cause" after four years of horrific fighting as they did in early 1861. Did they believe that their suffering and sacrifice had been in vain? One bit of evidence suggests that this was not so for some of them. At least four of the students were heavily involved in Confederate veterans' groups for many years after the war, in some cases well into the 20th century. Sgt. T.J. Barlow of the 32nd Virginia Infantry went on to become a member of the Portsmouth, Virginia, United Confederate Veterans (UCV) Camp in the years following the war. Pvt. John N. Williams went on to serve in the Norfolk, Virginia–based Pickett-Buchanan UCV Camp, while Lt. Henley T. Jones served as adjutant for the UCV's Williamsburg-based Magruder-Ewell Camp in the 1890s.[76] Along with serving as bureau chief for the Commonwealth of Virginia's Confederate service records in the 1890s, Sgt. Maj. Joseph V. Bidgood also served as adjutant general and chief-of-staff for the UCV in the late 1890s.[77] Even after all they endured, they seemed to want to preserve their memories of the epic struggle that had consumed so much of their youth.

However, not all of the College's Civil War–era students shared those pro–Confederate sentiments. In his later years, Capt. Richard A. Wise became an "uncompromising" Republican, serving as chairman of the James City County Republican committee for twenty years. He also spoke openly about his pride and relief in the Union's military triumph over the Confederacy. As a member of the Virginia House of Delegates, he created a sensation in the mid–1880s when, during a floor speech, he declared that "Appomattox was a great blessing to that section of the country, and that the people of the South should unite in paying the pensions of the men who saved the Union."[78] That statement created quite a stir, considering that Richard was the son of a former Confederate general, as well as a former Confederate Army officer who served under J.E.B. Stuart.

It is difficult to gauge the level of involvement that these former students had with their alma mater in the postwar era. Several likely never saw the William and Mary campus again after leaving it in spring 1861. However, other former students, particularly those who returned to live in the Williamsburg area, were actively involved in the College for many years following the war. Along with Capt. Richard A. Wise, Gloucester native Pvt. T.J. Stubbs of the 34th Virginia Infantry returned to the College to serve as a faculty member after he completed his education. Other former students kept abreast of the College's situation in the postwar era and did what they could to aid in its redevelopment. One such student was Lt. Henley T. Jones, who lived in postwar Williamsburg and worked as a farmer and pharmacist until his death in July 1902.[79] In this July 29, 1901, letter, he sought to assist William and Mary's president, Lyon G. Tyler, in determining the age of the College's walls:

> My Dear Sir,
>
> In reply to your inquiry in regard to the present walls of the College, I can only say that prior to the destruction of the building in February 1859, I had always heard and believed them to be those of the original structure. I was present at the burning of the College in the year above mentioned, and know the fact that the walls then resisted the ravages of the fire, they being two and a half or three feet thick. The College was rebuilt upon those walls during that year.
>
> I left Williamsburg with General Magruder's army in May 1862. When I returned in April 1865, nothing of this building remained save these same walls, the College having been again destroyed by fire applied by soldiers of the Federal army, as is well known. The present College building was, under the direction of Col. Benjamin S. Ewell, then President of William and Mary, erected upon the walls left by the fires of 1859 and 1862.

Please do not infer that I mean to convey the impression that no part of the walls were destroyed; such would not be true; where they were damaged the apertures were small, and the main walls were not materially effected. I hope what I have written may aid you in the object you have in view.

Yours truly, H.T. Jones[80]

The contributions of William and Mary students during the Civil War were extensive and varied. In a way, they were similar to those of their peers at other Southern schools. Collectively, their ages, outlooks, and motivations to serve primarily the Confederacy were very similar, paving the way for service as enlisted men or junior officers in the Confederate army. However, William and Mary's student body in this context was also unique. Despite their relatively small number, many of the College's students achieved significant levels of responsibility within the Confederate Army, serving as combat commanders or staff officers on the regimental and division levels. Further, several of the College's students served with or caught the attention of some of the Confederacy's most prominent military leaders, including Generals Jubal Early, A.P. Hill, Lafayette McClaws, and Thomas J. "Stonewall" Jackson. Conversely, other students were connected through family ties to well-known Civil War–era figures such as Virginia Governor Henry A. Wise and Union Maj. Gen. George G. Meade.

With their campus location in historic Williamsburg, the students also shared an interesting connection with America's Revolutionary War past that did not always exist to the same degree on other college campuses. This connection was further strengthened with the presence of descendants of friends and relatives of Washington and Jefferson in the student ranks. This potentially gave the students even more motivation to defend the honor and legacy of their families and native land. For many of the College's students, their dedication to honor also continued into the postwar era, as several went on to pursue public service in multiple capacities, ranging from holding local offices to service in the U.S. Congress. Despite the stress and trauma of war, these students upheld the College's time-honored tradition of service to the community, state, and nation. Consequently, their service constitutes a fascinating chapter of William and Mary history worth remembering.

CHAPTER 5

Warrior Scholars

Just as William and Mary students toiled through four long years of war, the College's faculty made significant contributions to the conflict. President Ewell and Professors Edward S. Joynes, Thomas P. McCandlish, Charles Morris, Robert J. Morrison, Thomas T.L. Snead, and Edwin Taliaferro were each devoting themselves to academic lives when the war broke out. However, as native Virginians they all rallied, though some reluctantly, to the Confederate cause. Although only Ewell could claim previous military training, these seven professors served in a variety of capacities throughout the war, ranging from government service to roles as army staff officers throughout the Confederacy. In this effort, they were joined by faculty members from other Virginia colleges, such as the University of Virginia and Virginia Military Institute, which provided Thomas J. "Stonewall" Jackson to the Confederate Army. While all of William and Mary's professors lived to see the end of the conflict, some passed away from illness shortly after the war, while others went on to enjoy long and productive postwar careers. Whatever course their postwar lives took, however, the Civil War left a lasting impact on them.[1]

As with their students, there were initially mixed emotions among the faculty in spring 1861 over the coming war. Ewell's opposition to the conflict was well known on the campus, and other professors shared his belief—at least initially—that secession was "unnecessary and inexpedient." Conversely, other faculty members, such as Edwin Taliaferro and Robert Morrison, were more excited about the looming war and were ready to fight for the Confederate cause. Taliaferro was among the first members of the College's community to join the Confederate Army in April 1861. Support for the South ran strong in his family, as his brother, William and Mary alumnus William Booth Taliaferro, ultimately became a Confederate general. However, for most faculty members, their allegiance to the Confederacy probably grew gradually, culminating after Virginia's secession from the Union. With the exception of Edward Joynes, every faculty member eventually served as a Confederate Army officer. Among the group, there were one colonel, two majors, and three captains. Joynes opted to take a civilian post in the Confederate War Department. Consequently, the war would keep some faculty members, such as Joynes, close to home, while taking others, like Ewell, to almost every theater of battle.² To gain a better understanding of their Civil War service, it is useful to examine the faculty members' individual wartime experiences.

Prof. Edward Joynes (Faculty-Alumni File Collection, Special Collections Research Center, Swem Library, College of William and Mary).

Edward Joynes began working at William and Mary in 1858 as a professor of modern languages. Born on March 2, 1834, in Accomac County, he was descended from some of the Virginia Eastern Shore's earliest settlers and possessed a distinguished family history. His grandfather, Maj. Levin Joynes, had served in the Continental Army during the American Revolution. His father, Thomas R. Joynes, was a prominent attorney and court official who had also served in the Virginia General Assembly. Edward Joynes received his early education at the Concord Academy and Delaware College, where he began to develop his lifelong interest in studying languages. Joynes later attended the University of Virginia and then spent 1856 to 1858 studying abroad at the Universities of Berlin and Paris, where he eventually became *l'uomo universale* (the universal man). Upon his return from Europe in 1858, he was appointed professor of Greek and German at William and Mary. Shortly thereafter, he married Williamsburg native Eliza Waller Vest and eventually had four children.³

Before the war, Joynes was an active faculty member at William and Mary, helping to reorganize the college's curriculum. The reasons he did not join the Confederate Army are unclear, but he made a significant contribution to the war effort as a civilian administrator. As chief clerk for the Confederate Bureau of War, Joynes reported directly to the secretary of war and interacted regularly with top military commanders, fielding requests for personnel and equipment.[4] It was also in this capacity that he first met Robert E. Lee, with whom he would eventually develop a cordial friendship. As chief clerk, Joynes appeared to play an influential role in Confederate governmental affairs and was at times solicited by job seekers for recommendation letters. During the war's later stages, Joynes also served as a private in the 3rd Virginia Regiment, which was a home guard unit consisting of government employees. However, it is highly unlikely that he ever saw any actual fighting. Joynes remained with the Confederate War Department until 1864, when he returned to teaching, serving at Hollins College prior to his return to William and Mary.[5]

Thomas P. McCandlish, a professor of ancient languages and mathematics in the College's preparatory department, began work only a year before the outbreak of war. As an 1857 graduate of the College, McCandlish was closer in age to his students than to some of his colleagues. A Williamsburg native, he enlisted in June 1861 as a private in the Peninsula Artillery, which was eventually incorporated into the 32nd Virginia Infantry. He was commissioned a captain later that month and served for most of the war as the 32nd Virginia's regimental quartermaster. In 1864, be became the quartermaster for his brigade, serving under Brig. Gen. Montgomery Dent Corse. McCandlish's father also served in the Confederate Army as a colonel.[6]

Charles Morris, a native of Hanover County, Virginia, came to William and Mary in 1859 to serve as a professor of law. Born in 1826, Morris was somewhat older than some of his faculty colleagues. After graduating from the University of Virginia in 1845, he spent several years practicing law and traveling abroad before choosing a career in education. He also served as commonwealth's attorney in Hanover County. In 1854, he married his cousin Mary Minor Morris, a granddaughter of James Plesants, a former U.S. senator (1819–1822) and Virginia governor (1822–1825) who had also attended William and Mary. Once the Civil War commenced, Morris returned home and joined the Hanover Troops, which was later attached to the 4th Virginia Infantry.[7]

After seeing his first action during the Peninsula Campaign, he was attached as an assistant quartermaster to Maj. Gen. Lafayette McClaws's division. He possibly served briefly in the same capacity on Maj. Gen. John B. Magruder's staff. After the Battle of Antietam, he was transferred to the staff of Brig. Gen. Alexander R. Lawton in Richmond, where he remained until the end of the war. In that position, he paid damage claims filed against the Confederate government. Morris held the rank of captain until March 9, 1865, when he was promoted to major. Maj. Gen. John Breckinridge, the Confederate secretary of war, personally signed his commission.[8]

Professor Robert J. Morrison also hailed from the Richmond, Virginia, area. Born in 1825 in Brunswick County, he attended the University of Virginia and was also known as an inventor. In 1854, Morrison married Catherine Heth Harrison, a member of Virginia's prominent Harrison family who was related distantly to Presidents William Henry Harrison and Benjamin Harrison.[9] He joined the William and Mary faculty in 1858 as a professor of history. Prior to that, he had taught at girls' schools in both Fredericksburg and Richmond and was a strong advocate for female education.[10] Existing evidence suggests that Morrison was a highly respected figure who was frequently solicited for recommendation letters and advice. For instance, he made a personal appeal in 1861 to President Jefferson Davis to help secure Lafayette McClaws a promotion to brigadier general. On another occasion that same year, Cynthia Tucker Washington Coleman had Morrison write a recommendation letter to the Confederate surgeon general to secure a commission for her then-fiancé.[11]

As for his own military service, Morrison joined the 32nd Virginia Infantry as a captain and was likely the regiment's first quartermaster. He also served as an ordnance officer with the regiment. His wife Catherine was also fully committed to the Confederate cause. During the war's early stages, she sacrificed her own wedding gown to create a blue and white silk regimental flag for the 15th Virginia Infantry, which was camped near the William and Mary campus. Meanwhile, her husband was busy tending to his military duties as well as the College's affairs. Even as the war raged, Professor Morrison played an instrumental role in attempting to reopen the College. On September 28, 1861, he participated in a faculty meeting that concluded, "The interests of the College require that it should be opened if possible" by January 1, 1862. Morrison was even placed on a committee charged with finding a way to complete that goal. However, his military and academic careers were cut short when he succumbed to typhoid fever on October 31, 1861. Reflecting on this tragedy, Cynthia Tucker Washington Coleman, the sister of former William and Mary student Lt. Tom Tucker, wrote, "No family could be left more destitute than his."[12] Around that time, one of his former students wrote this tribute, which summarizes the high regard in which many held him:

> Another of the great and good men of the Earth has fallen. Another of the numberless seeking sacrifices, laid on the altar of Freedom's God, has been rendered up, amid the anguish and tears of the heart-broken throng around. In the death of Prof. Morrison, William and Mary Col-

lege, Virginia, to repeat a commonplace phrase (but nevertheless a true one), has lost one of the best and bravest of her noble sons — one who was true and devoted to the great cause of Southern independence, and who, long before the events which have since reached their crisis between the two great sections of the country, assisted with his whole mental and physical resources Virginia and her sisters to maintain their independence of the North.

He, with his far-reaching eye, saw the impending storm which ere long burst upon our heads, and, with the assistance of his loved and able coadjutor, established the Southern Female Institute, and at this day the South would be far less able to cope with the North in educational ability had it not been for their united efforts in the cause of female education. And we do think every female in our fair Southern land should be sincerely grateful for the immense benefits derived from this valuable institution, but more especially should those bow their heads and hearts in humble tribute who were the recipients of his fostering care.[13]

Thomas T.L. Snead was another William and Mary alumnus who returned to teach at the College. Like Edward Joynes, Snead was a native of Virginia's Eastern Shore, hailing from the community of Onancock in Accomac County. Born on March 20, 1832, he graduated from William and Mary in 1856 and joined the faculty later that year as an adjunct professor of mathematics. In the war's early stages, he helped President Ewell survey the Williamsburg area to plan for a defensive line against Union forces. Desiring a commission in the Confederate Engineering Corps, Snead spent the summer of 1861 with Brig. Gen. Henry A. Wise surveying land in western Virginia.[14]

His hard work paid off on October 9, 1861, when he was commissioned a second lieutenant. During the summer of 1862, he served as an engineer under then–Maj. Gen. Thomas J. "Stonewall" Jackson, and was later on Maj. Gen. D.H. Hill's staff during the Battle of Chancellorsville. On account of disability, he was later stationed in Richmond as an adjutant to the Confederate Army's chief engineer, Maj. Gen. J.F. Gilmer, along with Col. W.H. Stevens. Professor Snead was promoted to captain in November 1863 and served for the duration of the war in that rank. Existing evidence suggests that he was not highly regarded by all Confederate Army personnel. The acclaimed Confederate mapmaker, Maj. Jedediah Hotchkiss, once called him "one of the worst rattle brains the world ever saw ... a red-haired mischief." Nevertheless, Professor Snead returned to teach mathematics at the College immediately following the war.[15]

On the issue of secession, Edwin Taliaferro was one of the most outspoken members of the faculty. Born in 1835, he was a member of a prominent Tidewater Virginia family of English-Italian origin. The Taliaferros had resided in Gloucester County for generations, and had over time married into several of the Commonwealth's most prominent families. Taliaferro was also a nephew of James Seddon, a two-time U.S. congressman from Richmond who would go on to serve as Confederate secretary of war. Following his graduation from the University of Virginia, Taliaferro won appointment to the College's faculty in 1858 and served as a professor of Latin and Romance languages. In 1861, he married Frances Bland Beverley Tucker, a sister of the former William and Mary student, Lt. Tom Tucker.[16]

During the secession crisis, Taliaferro was one of the most pro-secessionist faculty members on campus. He was also committed to revitalizing his native Virginia, which in his opinion had lost much of its Revolutionary War–era luster. During this period, Taliaferro wrote that, "Poor old Virginia [had lost] her influence and her caste.... It is a hard case for a State so long First in Councils of wisdom ... to be now in her old age [and] in the hands of ... temporizing, submissive politicians."[17] As war clouds loomed on the horizon, Taliaferro was active in organizing secessionist activity among his students, who shared increasingly in his belief that Virginians had a God-given right to rule over others.[18] During a November 15, 1860, speech to the Williamsburg Masonic Lodge, of which he was a member, Taliaferro outlined some of his thoughts concerning the chaotic political events unfolding around them. While he was on the surface discussing the impact of current events on the Masonic order, there are underlying themes in the following excerpt that reveal his thoughts about Virginia's status within the Union, as well as its future:

Maj. Edwin Taliaferro, CSA (Faculty-Alumni File Collection, Special Collections Research Center, Swem Library, College of William and Mary).

You bid me to speak to you of the benefits and glorious memories of our brotherhood. Forgive me if I couple with my eulogy the notes of elegy and warning. In a spirit of justice and love I deem it a duty incumbent upon me, as far as I may to awaken your energy and zeal, whilst I point out errors which would weaken your arm, shorten your step, and diminish the range of your influence.

In the days immediately following our political struggles, the powerful reaction, which ensued after a season of such high wrought excitement, seemed even to affect our own organization. The spirit which in the darkest days of our trials had bound our people in yet closer bonds, seemed to languish and die with the circumstances which called it forth. The zeal which had filled our lodges from North to South with ardent votaries became gradually more and more feeble. In many cases, the very name and site of our temples were forgotten; in others, their broken walls and neglected altars proclaimed eloquently the apostasy of their worshippers.

Even those who still proclaimed allegiance to the fraternity, seemed lukewarm in its behalf, until unable to maintain longer the pomp and state of early days, the successors of those who had reared on high, the sublimest monument of human architecture, were formed to assemble informally, as circumstances would permit, and renew their ancient ritual, or celebrate their solemn service in the garret or the cellar!

In many cases the record books were lost, and the memorials of our past history scattered to the winds, so that there remained not among us as Masons, memory, or name of those who, in the annals of our country, had left us the heritage of their fame and the influence of their virtues! But I rejoice to say, that for the last few years a new and brighter day has dawned upon us, and it is with anxious hope, that I look forward to that future, in whose mysterious folds lie involved the issues of our future destiny.

Virginia, as you know, despite all the dangers of lethargy and indifference, has kept pure and intact the traditions and mysteries of our association. It is to her that the states of our Union still look as the star whence emanates with purest ray the light of Masonic truth.[19]

Once the war began, Taliaferro followed most of his colleagues by joining the 32nd Virginia Infantry. Although he initially enlisted, Ewell saw great promise in him and helped Taliaferro secure a commission as a first lieutenant. From there, he served as an ordnance officer for the 32nd Virginia, and later played the same role in Maj. Gen. Lafayette McClaws's division as a captain. It was during this period that Taliaferro participated in some of the war's most important battles, including the Peninsula Campaign, the Seven Days' Battles, Antietam, and Fredericksburg.[20]

From early 1862 to late 1863, Taliaferro kept a diary chronicling his military experiences in poetic verse and song. In some instances, he also included illustrations of landscapes, people, and military equipment.

Taliaferro titled this work "Ballads of the Battlefield of McClaws's Division — Poems Written in Camp, Fredericksburg, Virginia." As a specialist in literature and languages, he possibly saw this as a way of relieving stress, maintaining his creativity, and avoiding boredom. In the diary's first passage, he wrote the following:

> Behold you live [among] warriors tall,
> All from the Southern Land,
> Whose names [in] his time of [need] shall call,
> In the roll of her patriot land.
> Who fought at Savage Station,
> At York and Malvern's Height,
> In the cause of our struggling nation,
> Bold champions of the right.[21]

As his diary progressed, he began to write poems about specific battles. The following selections illustrate his thoughts about the Battles of Antietam and Fredericksburg, respectively:

> Three days roll on, again is heard,
> The deep-mouthed cannons roar,
> As Federal hosts with vengeance stirred,
> Down the South Mountain pour.
> In rushing stream like winter's flood,
> They sweep yon narrow vale,
> Soon to be stained with crimson blood,
> And stream with corpses pale.
>
> And a nation's thanks to those who stood,
> Behind the wall of stone:
> Whose fame was writ in his blood,
> And spread in famous groan.
> Enduring monument of fame!
> To all who fought or fell,
> Long shall their now immortal name
> In grateful memory dwell.[22]

Promoted to major in 1864, Taliaferro spent the rest of the war commanding the Confederate arsenal at Macon, Georgia. After the war, he returned to teach Latin at the College.[23]

While the College's instructional faculty made noteworthy contributions to the Confederate war effort, William and Mary president Benjamin Ewell had the most extensive and far-reaching army service, which is ironic because he detested military life. Ewell was educated at West Point against his wishes solely for financial reasons, as his family was impoverished and the Academy was free. He dreaded his years there and stayed in the U.S. Army just long enough to satisfy his service obligation following his 1832 graduation. However, he kept in contact with some of his former classmates over the years and even worked with two of them, Gen. Joseph E. Johnston and Maj. Gen. John B. Magruder, during the Civil War. Despite Ewell's aversion to military life, his West Point education made him a valuable commodity to the Confederate Army, which was always in need of officers with prior military training. The war years saw Ewell serve in a variety of capacities: as a regimental commander, as chief-of-staff to a senior Confederate general, and as a mediator between feuding military and political leaders. While he was constantly frustrated and disillusioned by his assignments, the opportunity to work with close friends and relatives kept him motivated for much of the conflict.[24]

Although Ewell graduated from West Point, he quickly traded in his saber for an academic career. After a short career in engineering and teaching assignments at Virginia's Hampden-Sydney and Washington Colleges, he joined the faculty at William and Mary as interim president in 1848. After a brief return to teaching at the College, he assumed the presidency on a permanent basis in 1854. Born in 1810, he was by far the oldest of the Civil War–era faculty. His decision to align with the Confederacy was not an easy one. However, the desire to defend his native state overrode his Unionist sympathies, and he offered his services to Confederate authorities in late April 1861. Robert E. Lee, the commander of Virginia forces and a former West Point classmate of Ewell's, quickly commissioned him a major and ordered Ewell to organize a battalion of troops for defense of the Virginia Peninsula.[25] Within a few weeks, he was promoted to lieutenant colonel and assigned to lead the newly formed 32nd Virginia Infantry, effectively giving him temporary command of all area land forces. Ewell also continued his task of organizing and training recruits within the region. Although there was initially broad support for secession on the Peninsula, he often found it challenging to convince hesitant locals to join the war effort. The ominous presence of Federal forces at nearby Fort Monroe was also a cause for concern. Confederate military authorities, convinced that a Union attack on Richmond would come from that direction, urged all haste in organizing units of troops, making Ewell's job even more difficult.[26]

Therefore, Ewell must have been relieved in late May 1861 when he learned of John Bankhead Magruder's assignment as head of the Confederate Department of the Peninsula. As an old friend of Ewell's from West Point, Magruder was someone with whom he could work well. With Magruder at the helm, Ewell tended to his regiment when possible, but focused primarily on building a defensive line running through Williamsburg. Theoretically, this line was meant to stop a possible Union advance on Richmond. However, the project was plagued by constant infighting between Ewell and his superiors in Richmond, namely Robert E. Lee. Although Lee initially approved Ewell's fortification plans, he reversed his decision after one of his young engineering officers, Capt. Alfred Landon Rives, toured the terrain and criticized Ewell's approach.[27]

Although Ewell protested this action, Rives won out when Lee and Magruder ultimately approved his revised plans for entrenchments. This infuriated Ewell, who never forgot Lee's slight and presumed lack of confidence. However, he swallowed his pride for the good of the cause and assisted with implementing Rives's plan. Nevertheless, Ewell later maintained that the 1862 Union advance on Richmond would have been stopped in Williamsburg if his original plan for defensive lines had been adopted. He contended that Rives's plan was too complicated and took too long to construct.[28]

By March 1862, Ewell was still working frantically to complete those defensive lines, now in the face of a massive Federal army under Maj. Gen. George B. McClellan, which was arriving at nearby Fort Monroe. By this time, Confederate forces on the Peninsula were under the command of Ewell's good friend, Gen. Joseph E. Johnston, and Ewell's regiment was stationed at Fort Magruder in Williamsburg. Over the next couple of months, McClellan slowly moved his large army up the Peninsula, halting for a time at Yorktown to initiate a siege against local Rebel forces. Although McClellan's hesitant nature and skillful Confederate stall tactics slowed the Union advance, Johnston recognized that he was vastly outnumbered and decided to evacuate his forces west to Richmond in early May.[29]

A likeness of Col. Benjamin S. Ewell, CSA, in uniform (by Dr. Lisa L. Heuvel) based on his picture in Tyler's *The Making of the Union*. No actual photographs of Ewell in uniform are known to exist (collection of the authors).

Against his wishes, Ewell was ordered to evacuate his regiment from Williamsburg along with the rest of the Confederate forces. Ewell knew that a battle in the Williamsburg area was imminent and he wanted to stay and fight. However, Confederate military authorities only permitted a couple of brigades under then–Maj. Gen. James Longstreet to remain and engage Union forces in what became the Battle of Williamsburg on May 5, 1862. With no intention of holding Williamsburg, Confederate forces fought only until their colleagues were safely evacuated from the area and then pulled back that evening. The Confederates consequently left the town and College wide open to Federal forces, which then occupied the area for the remainder of the war. Ewell was highly disappointed to learn of this turn of events. Although he was upset that he missed the battle, his anger focused primarily on the Confederacy's willingness to abandon the defensive lines he built, as well as the community and College he loved. For years thereafter, he believed that the Confederate strategy was ill conceived, and that they should have made more of an effort to defend Williamsburg.[30]

Ewell's troubles continued in late May 1862 when he was not reelected colonel of the 32nd Virginia Infantry. For months the men had viewed him as an "absentee" commander because of his nonstop work supervising earthworks construction and his administrative obligations to General Magruder and other Confederate officials. Consequently, Ewell rarely commanded the entire regiment and had never led it in battle. The men opted instead to elect *in absentia* the popular Edgar B. Montague, a King and Queen County attorney and William and Mary alumnus with previous experience in the regiment. Before the election, Montague was a lieutenant colonel with the 53rd Virginia Infantry. Now, with Colonel Montague at the helm of the 32nd Virginia, Ewell's association with the regiment came to an end.[31]

Ultimately, this event was perhaps a blessing in disguise for Ewell, who was already pursuing his next wartime assignment. As early as May 1862, Confederate records indicated Gen. Joseph E. Johnston's desire to name Ewell his adjutant and chief-of-staff. With his administrative background and diplomatic nature, this appeared to be a perfect job for William and Mary's president. However, a dispute between Johnston and Jefferson Davis over Ewell's exact title and rank appeared to delay the appointment. Johnston, with John B. Magruder's support, originally wanted Ewell promoted to the rank of brigadier general to serve in this new position.[32]

However, Davis refused to authorize the promotion for two reasons. First, per Confederate military policy, Davis argued that staff officers could not hold a rank above colonel. Second, he contended that since Ewell was not re-elected colonel of the 32nd Virginia Infantry, he held no military rank, thus making him ineligible for promotion to brigadier general.

Despite these official reasons, the difficult relationship between Johnston and Davis may have also played a major role in this opposition. The pair had a history of problems that dated back to their days as West Point cadets. Further, Johnston and Davis were in the midst of their own bitter dispute concerning Johnston's degree of seniority within the Confederate Army. It therefore took several weeks to get these administrative matters sorted out. Consequently, it was not until November 1862 that Ewell assumed his new duties, at his original rank of colonel.[33]

While he was in between assignments in 1862, Ewell spent time with his family in Richmond and then served as a volunteer aide to his younger brother, Lt. Gen. Richard S. Ewell. Richard Ewell had commanded a division under Lt. Gen. Thomas J. "Stonewall" Jackson and later led a corps in Lee's Army of Northern Virginia. While campaigning with his brother, Ewell grew increasingly frustrated with the war, claiming that neither side had any coherent strategy. He also faulted Confederate commanders who, in his opinion, unnecessarily risked Richmond's capture and overall defeat by their actions during the Seven Days' Battles. Ewell always believed that the Confederates could have won the war in 1862 before Richmond. During this period, he also made several unsuccessful attempts to cross Federal lines to survey damage done to the College in Williamsburg. In mid–September, he had learned that the Wren Building was destroyed by fire following a September 6 skirmish between Union forces and Confederate cavalry commanded by Brig. Gen. Henry A. Wise. However, Federal authorities refused to allow him through the lines (under a flag of truce) to inspect the campus. It was very difficult for Ewell to be unable to tend to his campus during its time of need.[34]

However, his new job for General Johnston would take him away from Virginia to nearly all corners of the struggling Confederacy. In late November 1862, Johnston was assigned to command the Department of the West, which encompassed much of the middle and Deep South. Johnston and his staff, including Ewell, left immediately for Chattanooga, Tennessee, which served as the headquarters for the general's new command. Later in the war, Ewell would also serve with Johnston in Mississippi and Georgia.[35] As chief-of-staff, Ewell handled all of General Johnston's correspondence, dispatches, telegrams, orders, and personal letters. He also kept Johnston regularly updated on activities at headquarters while the general was in the field. These were not easy tasks since the general's command encompassed the majority of the Confederacy. Known as a "peacemaker," Ewell faced the additional responsibility of softening Johnston's blunt and unpredictable manner in dealings with subordinate officers. He proved to be an able assistant, enjoying Johnston's full confidence and trust. A fellow staff officer described Ewell as "the general's closest personal and official friend, consulting with him as no one else did." While his previous Confederate military experience was rocky, Ewell appeared to have found his niche serving with Johnston.[36]

Although this position was a good fit for Ewell, quarreling between Johnston and other high-ranking Confederate officials made it increasingly difficult. The general had never gotten along well with Jefferson Davis, and their relationship only worsened as the war progressed. It reached a boiling point in July 1863 when Davis blamed Johnston for the fall of Vicksburg. Upon learning of Davis's plans to call a court of inquiry to investigate Johnston's role in the defeat, the general threatened to resign. However, Johnston's supporters, including Ewell, talked him out of it, contending that Davis and his contradictory orders were to blame for the fiasco. After negotiating with Johnston, Davis, and John C. Pemberton, the former Confederate commander at Vicksburg, Ewell played a key role in smoothing over the dispute.[37]

Gen. Braxton Bragg, who was hated by all except Jefferson Davis, was also another consistent problem for Ewell. Despised by his subordinates, Bragg endured constant accusations of incompetence and votes of "no-confidence" after reports indicated that he ordered retreats against the will of his subordinate generals in late 1862. As he was assigned to the Department of the West, Johnston and Ewell constantly dealt with investigations and negotiations pertaining to General Bragg. The difficulties continued when Bragg, after a forced field resignation, became a senior advisor to Davis, and, in effect, served as Johnston's superior. By the end of 1863, these problems, along with bouts of ill health, proved to be more than Ewell could handle. In December, he resigned as chief-of-staff, claiming that the job should go to a younger and more able man. Although a replacement, Brig. Gen. William W. Mackall, was soon appointed, Ewell was talked into staying on as an assistant adjutant-general since he was one of the few people to whom General Johnston would listen.[38]

The year 1864 brought even more important work for Ewell on behalf of his friend, Joseph E. Johnston. Now commander of the Army of Tennessee, Johnston was frustrated over disagreements with Jefferson Davis concerning military strategy in northern Georgia. Davis was concerned that Atlanta and its vital railroad network would fall to Union forces and felt that Johnston was acting too cautiously. Conversely, Johnston believed that he did not have the resources to launch an offensive. He also speculated that there was a bias among top Confederate officials for Robert E. Lee and his Army of Northern Virginia. Overall, Davis wanted to attack, but Johnston urged patience until appropriate reinforcements could bolster his fledgling army. With no troops to spare, the debate turned into a stalemate.[39]

Gen. Joseph E. Johnston, CSA, Ll.D.— 1868 (Library of Congress).

Believing that telegrams and letters did not adequately articulate his position, Johnston decided to send Ewell to Richmond for service as his personal emissary. By virtue of Ewell's friendship with Davis's senior advisor, Gen. Braxton Bragg, Johnston felt the colonel could find success in explaining his position to the Confederate high command. Ewell spent a week in April meeting with Davis, Bragg, and Robert E. Lee. Although they were all cordial and engaged in negotiations, they ultimately offered no additional help to Johnston. Ewell returned to Atlanta empty-handed, and in July, Johnston was relieved of command. Ewell spent the rest of the summer defending Johnston's record to Confederate authorities.[40] He also criticized Johnston's successor, Lt. Gen. John Bell Hood, for reckless behavior and unacceptable casualty rates, writing:

> General Hood it was supposed had more dash and would force a battle at all hazards. He attempted it — lost a fifth of his army in making the attempt — gained no advantage, and has since quietly subsided in the course pursued by General Johnston. Had he persisted, doubtless ere this his army would be have been destroyed. A more triumphal vindication of General Johnston's policy could not be offered.[41]

Along with General Hood, Ewell viewed Jefferson Davis with a certain degree of contempt, pointing out that while General Johnston had been refused reinforcements, Hood had immediately received 4,000 men upon taking command. Nevertheless, Atlanta ultimately fell on September 2, 1864, which proved to be a total military disaster for the Confederacy. Disgusted by the leadership of his political and military superiors, Ewell wrote, "The ... executive that did this is responsible clearly and fully. We are now in imminent peril from the folly and incompetency of our rulers."[42]

Sick and exhausted after enduring endless political infighting, Ewell spent the last months of the war at home in Virginia. After a period of recuperation, he served about six months as an adjutant to his brother, Richard Ewell, who commanded the Confederate garrison at Richmond. However, in March 1865, persistent health issues, including chronic diarrhea and digestive problems, forced him to resign from military service altogether. A few weeks later, he watched helplessly as fires, set by retreating Confederate forces, consumed most of downtown Richmond, marking his end to the conflict.[43]

After the war, the six surviving faculty members settled back into their academic careers. Most of them taught at William and Mary for a few years before leaving later on to pursue other opportunities. Thomas T.L. Snead taught math at the College and worked on improving its postwar appearance by planting trees all over campus throughout the late 1860s.[44] However, declining health brought about by his wartime service resulted in his death on July 3, 1872, at age forty-one. Snead was later buried in the College graveyard near his beloved trees. Thomas P. McCandlish resumed his teaching of languages until he left around 1872. He later became an attorney and settled in Richmond, Virginia.[45] Edwin Taliaferro also resumed his position as a language professor and held the distinction of being the first to return to Williamsburg after the war. As such, he wrote a detailed letter to Benjamin Ewell in June 1865 describing the damage done to the campus. Unfortunately, his promising career was cut short when he succumbed to tuberculosis in 1867.[46]

Other faculty members spent less time at William and Mary and departed well before the 1870s. In the early postwar years, both Edward Joynes and Charles Morris left the College to teach at other Southern universities. In 1866, Joynes decided to work for his old friend Robert E. Lee, who was then president of Washington College in Lexington, Virginia, later becoming Washington and Lee University. At Washington College, Joynes quickly became one of the South's pioneers of modern language, and he later reflected on these years as "My Golden Age." He also considered it a privilege to work with his friend, General Lee, whom he held in high esteem.[47] During his stay at Washington College, Joynes was also the subject of an amusing story that Charles B. Flood outlined in his book, *Lee: The Last Years*:

> At the beginning of December [1866] an apparent murder attempt occurred in one of the college dormitories. Early one snowy morning, just after he had placed an additional stick of firewood in his potbellied stove, an explosive charge went off in the room of Edward S. Joynes, professor of modern languages. The stove blew into a hundred hot

metal fragments, every one of which miraculously missed Joynes, and set the college building afire.

The blaze was soon put out, but as a freshman said with a degree of understatement, "Of course it created something of a sensation." Professor Joynes had no doubt that an undergraduate had attempted to kill him by putting an explosive-filled log on the pile in his room, knowing that sooner or later he would slip it into his stove. Lee did not know what to think. At chapel service that morning he engaged in some understatement of his own: "He then said he would be glad to have any one who knew about the explosion call at his office during the forenoon."

At eleven A.M. two shaken freshmen appeared, and Lee told them to wait outside his office ... [and shortly thereafter] bade the two frightened boys to be seated. One of them, Jonathan Graham, explained that someone had been stealing wood from the room where he and three other students studied. In order to find the culprit, Graham had bored a hole into a stick of firewood, filled it with gunpowder, and sealed it with clay.

Then he replaced it on the pile of firewood, warning his study mates "under no circumstances to put that particular stick in our stove." Graham had thought that when the culprit, probably another student, put the loaded piece of firewood into his stove, wherever in the building it was, there would be a loud pop and a cloud of powder smoke — just enough to detect the offender, but not enough to do any damage.

What Graham had not known was that a janitor, charged with the responsibility for keeping sufficient wood in the professors' rooms, had been taking some that was already in the students' rooms rather than make a trip through the snow to a woodpile more than two hundred feet away. That was how the lethal log had come to Professor Joynes' room, and the rest was history.

When the unhappy student finished Lee laughed. "Well, Mister Graham, your plan to find out who was taking your wood was a good one, but your powder charge was too heavy. The next time use less powder." The matter was closed.[48]

Following Lee's death in 1870, Joynes's interest in Washington College waned, and he devoted the next several years to building schools and colleges across the South. Following his departure from Washington and Lee in 1875, he spent the next few years helping to organize Vanderbilt College in Nashville, Tennessee (which later became Vanderbilt University). In 1878, he then moved to East Tennessee University and helped transform it into the University of Knoxville. By this time, his reputation as a scholar and education advocate had spread to many parts of the South, and he was awarded honorary doctorates from both Delaware College (1875) and William and Mary (1878). In 1882, Joynes moved to South Carolina College, where he began to develop a strong interest in public education. For many years, he led annual summer teachers' institutes and became well connected with much of the state's political leadership. By the late 1880s, Joynes was at the forefront of the fight to develop a public education system for his adopted state. During this period, he was also a member of the first school board in Columbia, South Carolina, and was also instrumental in founding the city's public school system.[49]

While continuing his teaching at South Carolina College, Joynes went on to also help establish another higher education institution within the state. Frustrated as a school board member by the difficulty in finding trained teachers, Joynes helped co-found a teacher training school that later evolved into the modern-day Winthrop College, where he is now known affectionately as "the father of the University." Joynes continued his work with the annual teacher institutes, hoping to create a renaissance in Southern education. He received great acclaim for his work across the country, with the *New York Nation* once writing of him, "Probably few, if any American professors have taught so many students in foreign tongues, and certainly no other professor living has so widely influenced the study of modern language in America."[50]

In his later years, Joynes continued to teach Greek and German at South Carolina College, now known as the University of South Carolina, until his retirement in 1908 at the age of seventy-four. Two years later, he donated a valuable piece of property, along with a massive personal library, to Winthrop College, which later built Joynes Hall on its campus in his honor. Joynes died on June 18, 1917, and lay in state at the Imperial Hotel in Columbia before his burial in Elmwood Cemetery. For years thereafter, he was fondly remembered as one of the South's most prominent educators.[51]

Charles Morris enjoyed a similar record of distinguished service to Southern higher education. Highly popular with students, Morris "professed to be a typical 'old fogy' and clung to the manners and traditions of the *ante-bellum* days with a tenacity that never relaxed."[52] He continued teaching law at William and Mary until about 1869, when he abandoned the subject in favor of English and literature. Morris spent the rest of his career specializing in those subjects, teaching briefly at Randolph-Macon College. Except from 1872 to 1882, when Morris returned to teach at William and Mary, he spent his later years at the University of Georgia, where he taught until his death in April 1893, caused by the lingering effects of neuralgia and pneumonia. Like Joynes, Morris was highly regarded at the university, where many still addressed him as "Major Morris," a title of respect acknowledging his service to the Confederacy. His son, Professor Sylvanus Morris, went on to be a major force in the development of the University of Georgia's law school.[53]

While most of the Civil War–era faculty had either died or left William and Mary by the early 1870s, only Benjamin Ewell spent the rest of his long career at the College. This postwar tenure made his Confederate Army service look simple, as it was his job to save the decrepit and bankrupt institution from permanent closure. Over the next couple of decades, Ewell worked frantically to raise money and secure reparations from the Federal government for wartime damage done to the College. That difficult and important work is the subject of a later chapter.

William and Mary's faculty saw a wide range of service during the Civil War. As with most of the College's students, the entire faculty nobly served the Confederate cause, even if it was mainly to defend their native state. The two groups also shared the good fortune of surviving the conflict with only a few fatalities. However, there were some key differences between the experiences of the young students and their instructors. While every faculty member who joined the military served as an officer, only about a third of the students managed to obtain commissions. Furthermore, the faculty members often reached higher ranks than their student counterparts, with two majors and a colonel among the faculty and only one major among the students.

During the war, the College's professors also saw service in a much broader geographic area. Faculty members such as Benjamin Ewell and Edwin Taliaferro saw extended service in the war's western theater, while the College's students generally stayed within the confines of Virginia and North Carolina. Most of the faculty also maintained working relationships with some of the Confederacy's most important figures, including Jefferson Davis, Gen. Robert E. Lee, and Gen. Joseph E. Johnston. Conversely, only a few students saw direct service with senior Confederate officials, and none of them matched the prominence of Davis, Lee, or Johnston. Overall, greater age, maturity, and professional experience among the faculty are the most likely explanations for these differences. Therefore, although nine times as many William and Mary students fought in the Civil War, the faculty members made just as important a contribution to that long and brutal conflict.

What was the broader significance of the military service of William and Mary's faculty, beyond comparison to the College's student population? For one, despite their small numbers and the College's precarious standing in 19th century Virginia, William and Mary professors such as Benjamin Ewell reached high levels of responsibility within the Confederate Army. Several were also staff officers serving under some of the Confederacy's leading military figures, including Gen. Robert E. Lee, Gen. Joseph E. Johnston, and Lt. Gen. Thomas J. "Stonewall" Jackson. In some cases, such as with Benjamin Ewell and Edward Joynes, William and Mary faculty were close friends with some of these top Confederate leaders. In comparison, Virginia's leading higher education institution at the time, the University of Virginia, contributed among its faculty ranks to the Confederacy an assistant secretary of war (Albert T. Bledsoe), surgeons, scientists, and other junior officers and enlisted personnel. While that service was certainly significant, it is striking that the small faculty contingent from William and Mary, which was almost an afterthought in comparison to the larger and more prosperous University of Virginia, reached such important positions within the Confederate Army.[54]

Further, William and Mary's professors were unique in their Civil War service in that they all served the Confederate war effort in one form or another. One reason for this was that the College closed for the duration of the war, releasing its professors to pursue government or military service. Other schools, including Richmond College and Emory and Henry College, also closed their doors. In comparison, some other institutions within the Commonwealth, including the University of Virginia, Washington College, and Roanoke College, stayed open to varying degrees during the war.[55] Thus, at least some professors had to remain on those campuses to teach. Another reason for the uniform Confederate service of William and Mary's faculty was that they were all Virginians, and even if they did not agree with secession, they saw a need to defend their native state. This was unusual during the period, considering that some college professors working in Virginia hailed from the North. Pennsylvania-born George Junkin, who was president of Washington College just prior to the war, was one such example. With their Unionist sympathies, faculty members such as Junkin either refused to join the Confederate cause or simply left the state. While William and Mary certainly had northern-born professors on campus as late as 1859, all of the wartime faculty members were Virginia-born.[56]

Perhaps the most important role played by the College's faculty during this period was their contributions to higher education following the war. Three professors in particular, Benjamin Ewell, Charles Morris, and Edward Joynes, went on to devote their lives to revitalizing the devastated Southern higher education system during the late 19th century. While Ewell was busy rebuilding William and Mary, Morris was helping to develop the University of Georgia's academic reputation. Joynes arguably had the greatest impact on Southern higher education, taking direct roles in founding or developing Vanderbilt University, the University of Knoxville, the University of South Carolina, and Winthrop College. Along with his work in higher education, Joynes also played an instrumental role in developing public school systems in his adopted state of South Carolina. While the Civil War service of these faculty members was quite significant, their true legacy lies in the modern success and vitality of several colleges and universities across the South.

CHAPTER 6

The Old Guard at War

No examination of William and Mary's role in the Civil War could be complete without studying the wartime service of the College's alumni. Although they were not an everyday presence on campus, the alumni were still an important part of the College's community. Many of them were actively involved in their alma mater during their later careers, serving on the Board of Visitors, enrolling their own children as students, or helping to raise money for the College when they could. However, whether they maintained close ties to William and Mary or never gave it a second thought following graduation, the College was a significant part of their lives, helping to define who they were as individuals. Many of them benefited immensely from the classical education they had received during their time at William and Mary, and put it to good use in a variety of capacities during the war. Compared with the Civil War–era student and faculty ranks, the alumni also made the most significant wartime contributions.

In fact, some of the war's most prominent figures had close ties to William and Mary. Within the alumni ranks were three generals (including a commander-in-chief of the Union Army), two U.S. senators, at least ten members of the Confederate Congress, a top Confederate diplomat, and several other Confederate government officials. Further, two top Confederate military leaders, Gen. Joseph E. Johnston and Brig. Gen. Raleigh Colston, were awarded honorary doctorates following the war, permitting them to be counted among the College's alumni body. There were also within this group many regimental commanders, high-ranking staff officers, surgeons, and even a former president of the United States. Although William and Mary was a small, struggling institution compared with other mid–19th century Southern colleges, it still left through its alumni a significant mark on the nation's bloodiest conflict.[1]

Between 1825 and 1861, about 1,356 men attended William and Mary, and at least 360 graduates (attending the College between roughly 1804 and 1861) verifiably served in the Union or Confederate armies during the war (see Military Service Table), comprising nearly thirty percent of the entire alumni population.[2] However, the true number of Civil War veterans within the alumni ranks is likely higher. While significant, those numbers paled in comparison to the alumni service of the College's more prosperous competitors, the University of Virginia and Virginia Military Institute. Out of the University of Virginia's 8,000 living alumni in 1861, over 2,200 served in the Confederate Army, including twenty-six generals and ninety-eight colonels.[3] At Virginia Military Institute, approximately 1,788 of the institution's 1,902 living alumni joined the Confederate service during the war. Further, over a third of Virginia's sixty-four regiments of Confederate infantry, cavalry, and artillery were commanded by Virginia Military Institute graduates.[4] Nevertheless, despite its small size, William and Mary still contributed many alumni to the war effort, along with other colleges throughout Virginia and the rest of the South.

Despite the College's location in the South, there is enough compelling evidence to suggest that at least seven William and Mary alumni went on to don uniforms of Union blue, serving largely in the enlisted ranks or as junior officers. For instance, it appears that Illinois native Philip A. Johnson, who attended the College between 1849 and 1852, served as a first lieutenant in the 29th Illinois Infantry. Further, a couple of Maryland-born alumni, James Beatty and J.J.H. Newman, served as privates in Union regiments from that state. While this number is only a small fraction of the total alumni population, it challenges a traditional misconception that William and Mary's community supported the Confederate cause exclusively. While most of the possible Unionist alumni were fairly obscure, there were also some more prominent William and Mary alumni who aligned with the North, including a couple of high-level politicians. The three most distinguished examples were Lt. Gen. Winfield Scott, U.S. Sen. John J. Crittenden, and U.S. Sen. Lemuel J. Bowden.[5]

Born in 1786 on his father's farm near Petersburg, Virginia, Winfield Scott attended the College sometime between 1804 and 1806. However, Scott quickly discovered that his educational preparation was inadequate for William and Mary's demanding curriculum, and dropped out before graduating. Nevertheless, he was considered a natural leader even during his early days at the College. After studying law in Petersburg, Scott opted for military service and went on to a long and distinguished career. He was regarded as a hero for his service during the War of 1812, in which a brigade under his command bore the brunt of the fighting in the American victory at Lundy's Lane. Badly wounded during that engagement, Scott quickly became an international hero. After years of service in the peacetime army, he commanded all U.S. forces in the field during the Mexican War. He again received national acclaim for his masterful military campaign, resulting in the capture of Mexico City in April 1847. In 1852, Scott became the first officer since George Washington to hold the rank of lieutenant general. That same year, he sought to use this popularity in a run for the presidency on the Whig ticket, ultimately losing to Franklin Pierce of New Hampshire.[6]

By 1861, Scott's professional career was in its final stages, as he was already at the usual post-retirement age of seventy-five. Although he was a Virginian, he did not struggle over a decision to leave the Union, as his loyalty to the United States was absolute. When an old William and Mary classmate, Judge John Robertson, attempted to align him with the Confederacy, Scott replied:

> Friend Robertson, go no further! It is best that we part here, before you compel me to resent a mortal insult! I have served my country, under the flag of the Union, for more than fifty years, and so long as God permits me to live, I will defend that flag with my sword, even if my own native state assails it!

Branded as a traitor by his fellow Virginians, Scott spent the early stages of the war in his capacity as commander of the U.S. Army formulating Union military strategy. Too old, sick, and obese to mount a horse, he was unable to take a field command, leaving that task to younger subordinates. Surrounded by those who predicted a short and painless war, Scott was one of the first officials on either side to realize that the Civil War would be a long and

Lt. Gen. Winfield Scott, USA, attended the College between 1804 and 1806 (University Archives Photograph Collection, Special Collections Research Center, Swem Library, College of William and Mary).

bloody process. His greatest contribution to the conflict was his advocacy for the "Anaconda Plan," which called for a complete blockade of the South and control of the Mississippi as essential Union strategy for winning the war. Although Federal military authorities initially ridiculed him, much of Scott's plan became official Union policy during the war's later stages, helping to starve the Confederates of supplies and munitions.[7]

Although Scott's military instincts were as sharp as ever, many believed that the ailing general was no longer up to running a war. During the July 1861 Battle of Bull Run, President Lincoln had to awaken Scott from a nap in order to get an update on the battle's progress. Upon Lincoln's departure, he immediately composed himself for another nap. Following the battle, Scott was blamed for the errors of his subordinate commander, Maj. Gen. Robert Patterson, which allowed Confederate forces under Gen. Joseph E. Johnston to affect a junction with Gen. Pierre G.T. Beauregard, resulting in the Union rout at Bull Run. Scott was also burdened with a poor working relationship with Maj. Gen. George B. McClellan, commander of the Army of the Potomac. McClellan resented Scott for not supporting his appointment, and the pair consequently never got along. Thus, Scott requested retirement on October 31, 1861, and Lincoln approved it, ending the general's fifty-year military career. Fortunately for Scott, he lived to see his beloved Union survive its greatest crisis, passing away in 1866.[8]

John J. Crittenden was another Southern alumnus who refused to side with the Confederacy. A native of Versailles, Kentucky, Crittenden was born in 1786 and attended prep schools in that state as well as Virginia before enrolling at William and Mary in 1804. The College had a profound effect on Crittenden and helped to shape his future in public service. At the time, William and Mary was described as "an exciting place with young ideas of joyful revolt against the past [and] of spirited dreams for the future. Jefferson's influence was at its height [and] he was almost deified by the students."[9] Influenced heavily by this spirit of Republicanism, Crittenden studied works by John Locke, William Godwin, Rousseau, and Voltaire (to name a few). Although Crittenden was a diligent student, he also spent many lively evenings playing cards and talking to young Williamsburg ladies at Raleigh Tavern. However, the death of Crittenden's father forced him to accelerate his studies, leading to his early graduation in 1806.[10]

Following his studies at the College, Crittenden returned to Kentucky and studied law before embarking on an extraordinary political career. Over the first half of the 19th century, he served as an attorney general of the Illinois Territory, a Kentucky state legislator, a U.S. congressman, a U.S. senator, and governor of Kentucky. Crittenden also served as U.S.

attorney general in the administrations of Presidents William Henry Harrison and Millard Fillmore before returning to the U.S. Senate in the late 1850s.[11] Further, "no other American was nominated for the Supreme Court by presidents as far separated in time as [John] Quincy Adams and [Abraham] Lincoln."[12] Crittenden's prominence and influence during the antebellum era was best summarized by historian Albert D. Kirwan:

> Crittenden's service in the United States Senate began on the day of Monroe's inaugural, before Calhoun, Webster, or Benton had yet entered that chamber; and he died, still a member of the Congress, more than a dozen years after they had passed from the scene. His path also crossed those of Adams, Jackson, Van Buren, Harrison, Tyler, Polk, Taylor, Fillmore, Pierce, Buchanan, Lincoln, Seward, Douglas, and Jefferson Davis. With all of them he was intimately associated, and there is hardly a major political event in the three decades prior to the Civil War in which he did not figure.[13]

As clouds of war loomed over the country in late 1860, Crittenden worked feverishly to prevent a conflict. His most noteworthy achievement in this period was the Crittenden Compromise, presented to the Senate in December 1860. His bill proposed extending the Missouri Compromise line to the Pacific, thus offering the expansion of slavery as an enticement to keep Southern states from seceding. However, both sides rejected this last-ditch peacekeeping measure, which was ultimately unsuccessful in preventing war. Crittenden's anguish increased when his two sons took up arms on opposite sides, serving as generals in the Union and Confederate Armies. While Crittenden himself had Southern persuasions, his antisecessionist beliefs kept him from leaving the Union. During the first years of the war, he served in the U.S. House and supported the Lincoln Administration. More importantly, Crittenden worked tirelessly to keep Kentucky from seceding. Despite his death around the war's midpoint in July 1863, his efforts were instrumental in keeping his native Kentucky, a key border state, from joining the Confederacy.[14]

The Unionist alumnus with the most trying Civil War experience was undoubtedly Lemuel J. "Lem" Bowden. A James City County native born in 1815, Bowden studied law under Judge James Semple and graduated from the College in 1832. Intensely ambitious, Bowden quickly embarked upon a political career, serving in the Virginia House of Delegates from 1841 to 1846. He was also a delegate to both the 1849 and 1851 state Constitutional conventions. While moving up the political ladder, Bowden also became Williamsburg's leading attorney in the 1840s and 1850s. This success brought him great wealth and prestige, along with the jealousy of some of his Williamsburg neighbors. As he was hot-tempered and fiercely independent, the relations between Bowden and many of the town's leading families gradually soured in the late antebellum era. His passionate opposition to slavery also eventually severed Bowden's ties with the Democratic Party on the eve of the Civil War.[15]

When Virginia seceded from the Union in 1861, Bowden and his brother Henry were among the only Williamsburg residents who refused to accept secession. Instead, they proclaimed publicly their support for the Union cause — a move that won them few friends in this secessionist town. It was said that even Bowden's mother, an ardent secessionist, refused to live under his roof following this pronouncement. Meanwhile, Brig. Gen. Henry A. Wise issued a warrant for Bowden's arrest, prompting him to flee to Union-held Norfolk to evade capture by Confederate authorities. His son, William and Mary student Thomas R. Bowden, joined him in this exile. However, when Federal forces took control of Williamsburg in May 1862, they promptly installed Bowden as mayor, prompting him to be hated by town residents more than ever. One resident, Harriette Cary, noted in her diary around that time, "Bowden the traitor is mayor of our town." She later added, "The band serenaded Mayor Bowden tonight — loud cheering heard in conclusion, 'down with the traitor!' If we ever recover our power..."[16]

U.S. Attorney General John J. Crittenden graduated from the College in 1806 (Library of Congress).

Bowden's tenure as mayor was short-lived, however, as he chose to seek asylum in Norfolk once again following Maj. Gen. George B. McClellan's departure from the Peninsula after the Seven Days' Battles. In late 1862, he declined an appointment by President Lincoln to a Federal judgeship, electing to remain in Norfolk. A few months later, he was elected to the U.S. Senate (representing Virginia) by the Unionist Wheeling Convention, which considered itself Virginia's legitimate state government.

However, Bowden's tenure as a Republican U.S. senator was cut short when he died from smallpox at age forty-eight after only ten months of service. He was buried in January 1864 in Washington, D.C.'s, Congressional Cemetery.[17] A colleague, U.S. Sen. Henry Wilson,[18] delivered a eulogy that summarized effectively the sacrifices that Bowden made to support the Union:

> Lemuel J. Bowden owned a 2,000 acre estate on the Peninsula that was overrun by both armies, and crops, buildings, barns, and fences were swept away.... He also owned a large number of slaves and sustained a large loss in their emancipation, but he never complained. He held this and all other political questions subordinate to the preservation of the Union.[19]

Like Lem Bowden, fellow alumnus Alexander Hugh Holmes Stuart endured the difficult process of balancing Unionist sympathies with a desire to continue residing in his native South during the war. However, while Bowden associated himself mostly with Federal authorities, Stuart had the added emotional burden of maintaining deep family ties to the Confederate cause. Several of his kinsmen, including Maj. Gen J.E.B. Stuart, were top military and political leaders within the Confederacy. His oldest son, Alexander H.H. Stuart Jr., was also a member of the famed Virginia Military Institute Corps of Cadets which fought at the Battle of New Market in 1864. Thus, instead of following alumni such as Scott, Crittenden, and Bowden into active wartime service for the Union, Stuart attempted to remain neutral despite entreaties from both sides to join their respective cause. This approach culminated in one of the more unusual stories of alumni engagement during the Civil War.[20]

A Staunton County, Virginia, native who was born in 1807, Stuart was a third-generation American of distinguished Scots-Irish and English ancestry. He studied at the College from 1824 to 1825 and later graduated from the University of Virginia. After gaining admittance to the bar in 1828, Stuart embarked upon a career in law and public service. From 1836 to 1839, he served in the Virginia House of Delegate, and was later a U.S. congressman from 1841 to 1843. The pinnacle of Stuart's public service career was when he served as U.S. Secretary of the Interior in the early 1850s under President Millard Fillmore. However, as the politically charged 1850s progressed, he shifted his focus back to Virginia, serving as a state senator from 1857 to 1861. Although he was a member of the 1861 Virginia Secession Convention, Stuart was an avowed Unionist. In speeches before that body, he argued against secession, maintaining that Virginia was neither prepared for war nor likely to benefit from joining the Confederacy. As the nation moved toward civil war, Stuart tried to do everything in his power to prevent it. On April 12, 1861, he was part of a delegation that met with President Lincoln in a last-ditch effort to achieve compromise. When that meeting failed to achieve any results, Stuart went back to Virginia in an attempt to sit out the war.[21]

Torn between his Unionist beliefs and sentimental attachments to Confederate-aligned Virginia, Stuart had a difficult time maintaining his neutrality during the Civil War. While he disagreed with Virginia's allegiance to the Confederacy, he could not help but engage in the ebbs and flows of his native state's fortunes. Stuart celebrated when Virginia military forces won great victories and mourned when they suffered bitter defeats. As the war progressed, Stuart found it increasingly difficult to remain on the sidelines, particularly when Confederate authorities tried to obtain his professional services. In January 1864, Stuart was asked privately by President Jefferson Davis to serve as the Confederacy's operations chief in Canada. In this capacity, Stuart would have directed Confederate espionage operations and controlled large sums of money. However, in meetings with Davis and Confederate Secretary of State Judah P. Benjamin, Stuart declined the appointment, explaining that with multiple relatives under his charge, he was not in a position to leave the country. Privately, his Unionist sentiments likely played a large role in his refusing the post. Stuart therefore sat out the rest of the war outside the realm of public life.[22]

However, Stuart's troubles continued even after the war, despite his efforts to return his native state back into the Union fold. Although he was elected to the U.S. House of Representatives in 1865, he was not permitted to take the oath of office nor serve in that body. The problem centered on his inability to take a loyalty oath that was passed by Congress in 1862:

> I do solemnly swear that I have never voluntarily borne arms against the United States since I have been a citizen thereof; and that I have voluntarily given no aid, countenance, counsel, or encouragement to persons engaged in armed hostility thereto; ... that I have never yielded a voluntary support to any pretended Government, Authority, Power, or Constitution within the United States, hostile or inimical thereto.

While Stuart never openly supported the Confederate cause, he had rendered material aid to Confederate forces and interacted with Confederate government officials over the course of the conflict. Thus, as far as Federal authorities were concerned, Stuart was ineligible to serve in the U.S. Congress. However, Stuart challenged this verdict, arguing that very few, if any, newly elected Southern congressmen could truthfully take that oath. Further, he noted that Confederate conscription laws required many of his relatives, including a son, five nephews, and three brothers-in-law, to join the Confederate Army. Thus, despite his Unionist sympathies, Stuart was compelled to render material aid to Confederate forces in order to assist his own family members. Consequently, Stuart felt that considering his challenging circumstances, U.S. government officials were holding him to a standard of loyalty that would have been impossible for him to achieve.[23]

Stuart's arguments fell on deaf ears, and he was never permitted to resume his Congressional career. Ironically, the strict loyalty regulations were later loosened, allowing several ex–Confederate officials, who were much more engaged in the Confederate cause than Stuart, to serve openly in the U.S. Congress. Nevertheless, Stuart continued his career in public service, serving in the Virginia House of Delegates from 1874 to 1877. Along with serving as president of the Virginia Historical Society, he was also rector of the University of Virginia from 1874 until 1882. Stuart was for some time the last surviving member of the Fillmore Cabinet until his own death at age eighty-three in 1891. In the end, his life and wartime experiences served as a powerful reminder of the difficult choices that many had to make between supporting their nation or native states. For Stuart himself, the war still took a powerful toll on him despite his best efforts to stay out of it.[24]

Although a few William and Mary alumni, such as Scott, Crittenden, and Bowden, worked to preserve the Union, while others like Stuart remained neutral, they were certainly the exception. The vast majority of the College's pre–Civil War graduates aligned with the Confederacy and served it through military, political, or diplomatic assignments. Several alumni made important contributions in the latter two categories. A few graduates, including former U.S. Rep. Jeremiah Morton and Samuel Garland (a grandnephew of Patrick Henry), served as delegates to state secession conventions. Further, at least ten alumni served in the Confederate Congress as members of the House of Representatives. One alumnus, Jackson Morton (attended 1814–1815), represented Florida in that legislative body. A native of Fredericksburg, Virginia, Morton moved to Pensacola in 1820 and later represented Florida in the U.S. Senate from 1849 to 1855. However, most of these alumni helped comprise the Virginia delegation to the Confederate Congress. They included Waller R. Staples, William H. Macfarland, James Lyons and John R. Chambliss Sr. (L.B.—1830), who was the father of Brig. Gen. John R. Chambliss Jr. One notable example, William Cabell Rives (attended 1809–1810), served in sessions of both the provisional and regular Confederate Congress. This service marked the end to a long career in Virginia politics, including terms as a state legislator, congressman, and U.S. senator in the 1830s and 1840s. Along with serving in the Confederate Congress, Judge John W. Brockenbrough (attended 1824–1825) served as rector of Washington College following the war. He was also the individual who first approached Robert E. Lee to lead that venerable institution, known today as Washington and Lee University.[25]

Alumnus Austin M. Trible also had ties to the Confederate Congress.[26] A native of Essex County, Virginia, Trible became a prominent attorney following his 1839 graduation from William and Mary. Becoming active in local politics, he went on to serve in the Virginia Senate during the late antebellum period. After he moved to Lynchburg to reside in his second wife's hometown, health issues prevented Trible from active involvement in the Civil War. Nevertheless, he was elected to the Confederate Congress in 1864, but ill health prevented him from taking the seat before the body dissolved in spring 1865. Despite his inability to take his seat, he still had strong family ties to the Confederate cause. His daughter Julia married Col. Frank Huger, who was an artillery commander in the Army of Northern Virginia. He was also the son of Maj. Gen. Benjamin Huger, who commanded Confederate forces in both the Eastern and Western theaters.[27]

Along with alumni who became Confederate congressmen, there was a host of others who served in various government posts at the state or national level during the war. President John Tyler's son Robert (L.B.—1837) served as registrar for the Confederate Treasury. Meanwhile, his brother John Tyler Jr. (A.B.—1837) served as an assistant secretary of war. On the state level, Col. George W. Munford (L.B.—1824) served as Virginia's wartime secretary of the Commonwealth, reporting directly to Gov. John Letcher. Some of his responsibilities included furnishing the state's flag to Virginia military units within the Confederate Army and affixing the state seal to government documents. One of his sons was Col. Thomas T. Munford, a cavalry commander in the Army of Northern Virginia who served under Generals Jubal Early and Thomas J. "Stonewall" Jackson.[28]

The alumnus who engaged in arguably the most unusual form of Confederate government service was Robert Ould. Born on January 31, 1820, in Washington, D.C., Ould studied law at the College and graduated in 1842. Prior to the war, Ould was a militia general and prominent Washington, D.C., district attorney. In one famous 1859 case, he prosecuted the infamous U.S. Congressman Daniel Sickles for the murder of his wife's lover, Philip Barton Key II. Despite being weighed down by a plethora of personal scandals, Sickles was acquitted and went on to become a Union general during the Civil War. Meanwhile, Ould went on to support the Confederate cause, and served briefly as an assistant secretary of war in early 1862. However, the Civil War service for which he was best known came about during the war's later stages. Based on his considerable experience as a prosecuting attorney, Ould was appointed Confederate agent for the exchange of prisoners with the rank of colonel in July 1862. In that capacity, Ould was in charge of negotiating and making arrangements for the exchange of all Confederate prisoners in the war's eastern theater. Along with serving as a judge advocate general in Richmond, Ould remained busy in his work, securing the release of Confederate prisoners through the end of the war.[29]

Among all of the College's alumni, two graduates stood out as contributing the most political or diplomatic service to the Confederacy: James Murray Mason and John Tyler. Born in 1798 in what is now the District of Columbia, James Mason graduated from the University of Pennsylvania in 1818 before earning a degree in law from William and Mary in 1820. A grandson of George Mason, he spent his early career serving in the Virginia House of Delegates and the U.S. House of Representatives. However, the bulk of his prewar political service was spent in the U.S. Senate, where he served from 1847 until 1861, when he resigned to join the Confederacy. After serving briefly in the provisional Confederate Congress, Mason earned an appointment as commissioner for the Confederacy to Great Britain and France. It was in this capacity that he contributed his most important Civil War service, lobbying the two great European powers to recognize the fledgling Confederacy. However, Mason will be forever remembered for his instrumental role in the infamous 1861 *Trent* Affair.[30]

After earning his appointment as Confederate commissioner, Mason and his colleague, John Slidell of Louisiana, left immediately for Europe. However, their October 1861 departure from Charleston, South Carolina, on a blockade-runner was an open secret. Consequently, after they transferred to the British mail steamer *Trent* in Havana, Cuba, for passage to Europe, Union authorities from a nearby Federal naval vessel boarded the ship without authorization and took the pair into custody. Although Northerners viewed the Federal officials as heroes, the British condemned this action as an act of war and immediately dispatched over 11,000 troops to Canada. Eager to avoid a second war, the Lincoln Administration eventually reached a settlement with Great Britain, releasing the Confederate commissioners to continue their journey on January 1, 1862. For the balance of the war, Mason worked diligently in an unsuccessful effort to secure European support for the Confederate government. After the war ended, he resided in Canada as a political exile before returning to the United States in 1868. Although his efforts to secure European recognition of the Confederacy failed, Mason will be long remembered for his role at the center of an international incident that almost caused a war between the United States and Great Britain.[31]

While John Tyler's Confederate service was not nearly as dramatic as that of James Mason's, his wartime activities made a noteworthy impact. As a former president of the United States, Tyler could be considered William and Mary's most distinguished 19th-century alumnus.[32] Born in 1790 at his family's plantation in Charles City County, Virginia, Tyler was the son of a Virginia governor and friend of Thomas Jefferson. A class of 1807 alumnus, he arguably maintained the closest ties to William and Mary of any prominent graduate in the 19th century, with decades of service as a Board of Visitors member, benefactor, and chancellor from 1859 until his death in 1862. Upon learning of his appointment as chancellor, Tyler described it as "an honor of which I am quite as proud as of any other ever conferred upon me by my fellow man."[33]

Although Tyler was devoted to William and Mary, he spent most of his career engaged in public service. Through the early and mid–19th century, he served as a state legislator, U.S. congressman, Virginia governor, U.S. senator, and ultimately vice-president under William Henry Harrison. Upon Harrison's unexpected death after only a month in office, Tyler was propelled into the presidency. After a tumultuous term in office from 1841 through 1845, he declined to seek a second term. Though he enjoyed retirement, Tyler remained active and kept current on public affairs. As the nation drifted towards war in early 1861, he was instrumental in organizing and leading a peace convention consisting of representatives of twenty-one Northern and Southern states. Although he was a proud Southerner, Tyler wanted to do everything possible to avoid a bloody conflict. However,

Former U.S. President and Confederate Congressman John Tyler, A.B.—1807, Ll.D.—1854 (Library of Congress).

when Abraham Lincoln respectfully declined to adopt the convention's resolutions, designed largely to protect slavery, Tyler threw up his hands and aligned himself with the Confederacy.[34]

Early in the conflict, Tyler was a driving force in urging Virginia to secede from the Union. Once the war commenced, he served in the provisional Confederate Congress and ultimately won election to the regular Confederate Congress in late 1861. However, he died before he could take his seat early the next year, marking a unique end to the life of an American president. John Tyler is still the only president in American history to affiliate formally with and support an enemy of the United States, a fact that was not lost on angry Northerners, who branded him as a traitor. Consequently, as an act of retribution, Union troops vandalized the Tyler home in the war's later stages, and it was not until 1915 that the U.S. Congress authorized a memorial at his gravesite.[35]

Although several William and Mary graduates contributed political and diplomatic service to the Confederacy, most alumni supported it through joining the military. College records identify 188 graduates who served in the Confederate Army in regiments scattered all over the Southern states. However, there are many more who bore arms for the Confederate cause, and the true total number is likely in the 400s. The vast majority of graduates served in Virginia, as most of them resided in the state's Tidewater, northern, or central regions. As with the students and faculty, there was a concentration of alumni in the 32nd Virginia Infantry, where at least nine graduates served as privates on up to regimental commanders. However, there were at least ten alumni who served outside of the Commonwealth, hailing from such states as North Carolina, Maryland, Alabama, Texas, and Mississippi. At least forty-one served in infantry regiments, with a further sixteen in the cavalry, about four in the artillery, and one in the engineering corps. However, since research has only yielded information regarding specific military service for roughly 60 percent of this group, those numbers are undoubtedly low.[36]

Along with the College's faculty, most alumni served as commissioned officers in the Confederate Army. Out of the roughly 360 graduates, at least 178 were officers, including three generals, twenty-eight colonels, twenty-two majors, seventy-nine captains, and forty-six lieutenants. Four additional alumni were listed in College records as officers of unknown rank. Included within this group were at least thirty-two alumni who served as surgeons in the Confederate Army, including Tazewell Tyler, a son of John Tyler, who attended the College around 1850. Conversely, only about a third of William and Mary's students earned commissions as Confederate officers during the war. Though several junior alumni served as officers, almost all of the older alumni, graduates from about 1830 to 1850, were officers or surgeons, a likely reflection of their mature age and professional experience. There also appeared to be a rich blend of command and staff officers among the graduate ranks, including individuals who led regiments as well as those who worked for senior officers.[37]

The enlisted contingent of William and Mary graduates generally consisted of younger alumni, who attended the College in the middle 1850s and beyond. Some of them had only recently graduated when the war commenced. At least 150 alumni had identifiable enlisted experience, but there are probably many more. This group consisted of twenty-six sergeants or sergeants major, twelve corporals, and 112 privates. Although most of these individuals remained in the enlisted ranks, at least three earned commissions in the war's later stages.[38]

The College's alumni who served in the Confederate Army consisted of several individuals from many of Virginia's most distinguished and well-known families, underscoring William and Mary's reputation as a producer of statesmen. George D. Wise and Obadiah J. Wise, respectively a nephew and a son of former Virginia Governor Henry A. Wise, joined student Richard A. Wise in serving the Confederate cause. As graduates from the middle 1850s, they each served as army captains. An 1855 graduate, B. Hill Carter Jr., descended from the wealthy and influential Carter family of Shirley Plantation, served as a second lieutenant in the 3rd Virginia Cavalry. His ancestor, Robert "King" Carter, was one of Virginia's most powerful figures in the 18th century. Additional sons of a former Virginia governor also served the Confederacy. Capt. P. Bell Smith and Col. Thomas P. Smith were 1856 graduates and sons of Governor William "Extra Billy" Smith, who went on to become a Confederate major general. Further, Capt. William Marshall of Fauquier County, Virginia, was a grandson of the first Chief Justice of the United States, John Marshall.[39]

Through family ties, several William and Mary alumni were also connected with some of the Civil War's best-known figures. Brig. Gen. Edwin Gray Lee, who attended the College between 1851 and 1852, was a second cousin of Gen. Robert E. Lee and interacted with him frequently during the war. Maj. Abram H. McClaws, who attended the College between 1842 and 1845, was a brother of Maj. Gen. Lafayette McClaws. A lawyer by trade, Abram spent the war's early stages as a quartermaster on his brother's staff. However, a double hernia led to his July 1863 resignation from active duty, and he spent the rest of the war behind a desk. Col. Henry M. Ashby, who commanded the 2nd Tennessee Cavalry in the war's western theater, was a first cousin of Brig. Gen. Turner Ashby. Henry would go on to hold brigade and even division commands in the war's later stages. Following service in the enlisted ranks, Capt. James B. Pannill served as a staff officer in the 26th Virginia Infantry. A class of 1856 graduate, Pannill was a first cousin of Maj. Gen. J.E.B. Stuart, though it is unlikely that they ever served together during the war.[40] In addition, Col. Julien Harrison, a wealthy Goochland County farmer and 1847 graduate, was a brother-in-law of Maj. Gen. Henry Heth.[41]

Among all of the alumni with family connections to prominent Civil War figures, Lt. Samuel H. "Sam" Early likely spent the most time during the war with his better-known relative. A Franklin County, Virginia, native who graduated from the College in 1832, Sam was the older brother of Lt. Gen. Jubal Early. For most of the war, Sam served as his brother's aide-de-camp, and participated in major battles such as Antietam and Gettysburg.[42] He acted primarily as a courier and liaison for his younger brother, relaying and explaining orders to other Confederate commanders. However, Sam's influence on General Early predated the Civil War, going all the way back to his days as a cadet at West Point in the early 1830s. While Sam was embarking upon a career in law, his brother was struggling to find his way at the Academy, questioning whether all of his effort was worth it. Sam played an instrumental role in keeping his younger brother enrolled, asserting in letters that the unique training West Point provided would be highly useful in future career pursuits. Sam also informed his brother of the limited prospects he would face by dropping out, noting, "For any [job] you could obtain in this country — money is scarce — people are hard run and prospects are gloomy in every respect, it seems to me." In the end, Jubal Early stayed at the Academy and stayed on his military career track. Ironically, his brother, the William and Mary graduate, unwittingly helped cement the future of one of the Confederacy's top military commanders.[43]

The battle experiences of the alumni compared in some ways to those of the College's students. For instance, most alumni served in regiments affiliated with the Army of Northern Virginia, participating in battles largely within the war's eastern theatre.[44] However, because of the dynamics of each group, there were also some key differences. Since there were more alumni serving in non–Virginia regiments, a larger number served in other areas, including the North Carolina coast and the western theater. The graduate contingent was also much larger than the student body, resulting in more alumni casualties. At least seven alumni were killed in battle, including Capt. George Wise, Capt. Obadiah Wise, and Lt. Hill Carter. George Wise was killed before the Battle of Petersburg, Obadiah died earlier in the war at Roanoke Island in North Carolina, and Carter died during the Battle of Chancellorsville in May 1863. Furthermore,

Union forces captured Lt. Col. George Blow (B.L.—1831) of the 14th Virginia Infantry during the fall of Norfolk in 1862. Capt. Octavius Coke (attended 1857–1858) of the 32nd Virginia escaped death but suffered serious injuries at the Battles of Antietam and Five Forks, including a gunshot wound in the left hip. As future research is conducted on alumni casualties, the numbers will likely increase substantially.[45]

Over the course of the war, several alumni made noteworthy military contributions to the Confederate cause. Many graduates, including Col. Edgar Montague, served as regimental commanders for much of the conflict. Montague, an 1856 alumnus, replaced Benjamin Ewell as commander of the 32nd Virginia Infantry in 1862 and remained in that post for the duration of the war. Described as a "splendid man and officer" by his wartime brigade commander, Montague went on to become a prominent Virginia judge following the war. A pair of alumni who were brothers followed Montague's lead into wartime service as regimental commanders. Born on February 6, 1827, the aforementioned Julien Harrison came from a wealthy Goochland County family and graduated from the College in 1847. Prior to the war, he served as a militia officer and married Lavinia Heth, a sister of Confederate Maj. Gen. Henry Heth. Originally commissioned a lieutenant colonel in the 6th Virginia Cavalry, Harrison spent the war's early stages commanding that regiment as a full colonel. Following an injury sustained during the October 1863 Battle of Brandy Station, Harrison was deemed unfit for field service and spent the remainder of the war as a military judge. Meanwhile, his brother Randolph Harrison pursued wartime service in Confederate infantry forces. Prior to the war, he attended the College in the early 1850s and became a respected physician. However, Harrison went on to serve as colonel of the 46th Virginia Infantry during the war until he was wounded and taken prisoner during the siege of Petersburg in 1864. He went on to become a distinguished physician in Williamsburg after the war.[46]

Col. William Lamb, CSA, B.P.—1854, L.B.—1855. From *Battles and Leaders of the Civil War*, Vol. 4 (New York: Century Co., 1888), 646.

Unlike his fellow alumni who served as regimental commanders, Col. William Lamb made his military contributions to the Confederacy by serving as a garrison commander. A Norfolk native, Lamb was a member of a wealthy family who first enrolled at the College in 1852. He originally had no intention of studying a profession, but Lamb's attitude changed quickly once he was immersed in Williamsburg's historic atmosphere. Specifically, "the speeches he heard at the [1853] commencement from Ex-President John Tyler, Henry A. Wise, James Lyons, and others kindled an ambition for professional and public life." After earning degrees from William and Mary in 1854 and 1855, Lamb served as a newspaper editor and militia officer during the late-antebellum era.[47]

Following the outbreak of war, Lamb was appointed a captain in the 6th Virginia Infantry. However, he was promoted to major later in 1861 and served on the staff of Brig. Gen. Joseph R. Anderson at Wilmington, North Carolina. It was in this capacity that he began his wartime career as a garrison commander. Following a short tenure commanding Fort St. Philip on the Cape Fear River, Lamb was appointed commander of Fort Fisher, which was also located along the North Carolina coast, on July 4, 1862. President Jefferson Davis also promoted him to full colonel shortly thereafter. An avid student of military history and defensive fortifications, Lamb oversaw extensive modifications to the installation's defensive works, and by December 1864, it was regarded as the largest and most powerful earthen fort in the Confederacy. However, Union forces overran Fort Fisher in January 1865, during a large battle in which Lamb was wounded and taken prisoner. Nevertheless, even after the fortress fell to Federal forces, Fisher's design and physical features drew praise from Union authorities. Lamb would go on to serve as mayor of Norfolk in the postwar era.[48]

Two alumni, Edwin Gray Lee and William Booth Taliaferro, reached the rank of general in the Confederate Army. While they are not normally listed among the ranks of the most famous Confederate commanders, Lee and Taliaferro both achieved levels of high authority and interacted with some of the Confederacy's top military and political leaders. Born on May 27, 1836, in northern Virginia, Edwin Gray "Ned" Lee received his early education from Hallowell's School in Alexandria before enrolling at William and Mary in 1851. At the College, he formed several close friendships that continued into his later life. One of his best friends was William Lamb, with whom he would interact again, a fellow Confederate officer during the Civil War. Although he was a key player in forming a debating society on campus, Lee's behavior at the College left much to be desired, and he was frequently reprimanded for mischievous behavior. He was finally suspended in December 1852 after ringing the Wren Building's bell in the middle of the night. Although he was later invited to return to

William and Mary, it was determined that an Alexandria boarding school was a better fit to complete his education. Lee later studied law at Washington College and pursued a career as an attorney and militia officer in Shepherdstown, (West) Virginia.[49]

Lee began to establish a reputation as a competent military officer even prior to the Civil War. During John Brown's 1859 raid on Harpers Ferry, Lee was among the Virginia Militia forces on hand to diffuse that situation. In that capacity, he also ran into his second cousin, Robert E. Lee, who later wrote of him, "I first made [Edwin's] military acquaintance at Harpers Ferry ... where though a youth he displayed great bravery and firmness." J.E.B. Stuart, who was also present at Harpers Ferry, displayed similar positive sentiments about Lee, writing, "my acquaintance with him began simultaneously with Gen. R.E. Lee at Harpers Ferry ... and the favorable opinion formed then has been steadily enhanced ever since." Upon his return to Shepherdstown, Lee married Susan Pendleton, the daughter of future Confederate Brig. Gen. William N. Pendleton, on November 17, 1859.[50]

Upon the outbreak of war, Lee entered the Confederate Army as a second lieutenant and earned rapid promotions to major and lieutenant colonel. As a full colonel, Lee later led the 33rd Virginia Infantry and was a temporary commander of the famed "Stonewall" Brigade. During the first half of the war, he served as an aide to Stonewall Jackson and also saw service in the Shenandoah Valley as well as with the Army of Northern Virginia. Further, he participated in the Seven Days' Battles, Second Manassas, Antietam, and Fredericksburg. Lee was even captured briefly by Federal forces in September 1862 during a quick trip home to visit his parents. One of his captors during the short period of custody was none other than George Armstrong Custer,

Brig. Gen. Edwin G. Lee, CSA, attended the College in the early 1850s (National Archives).

who was then a Union cavalry captain. While Lee had been an active battlefield commander during the war's early years, his frail health prevented him from sustaining that vigorous pace. Health problems stemming from tuberculosis forced Lee to take leaves of absence on multiple occasions through 1863 and 1864. Nevertheless, he was promoted to brigadier general on September 23, 1864, and held various administrative posts when his health permitted.[51]

Despite Lee's failing health, he grew restless as the war raged on without him and was eager to obtain a more substantial assignment. This led to one of the more intriguing stories of Confederate military service provided by a William and Mary alumnus. In fall 1864, Confederate Secretary of State Judah P. Benjamin appointed Lee to head up espionage operations in Canada, which was by then the center of intrigue for the Confederacy. The assignment would also give Lee the opportunity to revitalize his health, as doctors had suggested that a colder climate would help alleviate his tuberculosis. In December 1864, Lee and his wife started their arduous journey to Canada, which required running the Union naval blockade. Along the way, they stopped at Fort Fisher to see Lee's old William and Mary classmate, Col. William Lamb, who was by then commandant of that installation.[52]

Following a visit with relatives, Lee reached Canada in April 1865 and set up his headquarters at a Montreal hotel, going on to direct a variety of planned Confederate initiatives. With the war in its final days following Robert E. Lee's surrender at Appomattox, Confederate authorities were desperate to try anything to reverse their fortunes. One project Lee worked on was a plan to free between 15,000 and 25,000 Confederate POWs from Elmira Prison in New York. With the Confederate Army near total collapse, government officials felt that this infusion of soldiers could possibly keep the war going. For this mission, Lee ordered Confederate agent John Surratt (an associate of John Wilkes Booth) to travel to Elmira to survey the prison and its security apparatus. However, the plan was interrupted when President Lincoln was assassinated and Federal agents began looking for Surratt. He was forced to flee to Italy before being captured later. Meanwhile, Lee was at the center of suspicion regarding the possible involvement of Confederate agents in Canada with Lincoln's assassination. In a Montreal newspaper, he rebutted Federal claims that Lincoln's murder had been organized in Canada by writing, "No official of the Confederate States authorized, or was cognizant of, that assassination." Lee further indicated that he had no knowledge of any assassination scheme ever being hatched by Confederates in Canada. Following Lee's return to the United States, he and his wife traveled in vain to find a place that could treat his failing health. Lee died from tuberculosis on August 25, 1870, and was buried in Lexington, Virginia.⁵³

Along with Brig. Gen. Edwin Gray Lee, fellow alumnus Maj. Gen. William Booth Taliaferro provided active battlefield and administrative leadership to the Confederate Army. During the war he commanded Confederate troops and departments in multiple theaters and worked with such prominent figures as Lt. Gen. Thomas J. "Stonewall" Jackson and Gen. Pierre G.T. Beauregard. Born into Tidewater Virginia aristocracy in 1822, he grew up in Gloucester County, studied at Harvard, and graduated from William and Mary in 1841. Although he actively participated in Virginia politics, serving in the House of Delegates from 1850 to 1853, his primary interest was military affairs. Taliaferro served as a major in the 9th U.S. Infantry during the Mexican War and was later major general of the Virginia Militia. In that capacity, he commanded Virginia militia forces at Harpers Ferry in the aftermath of John Brown's raid.⁵⁴

Once the Civil War commenced, Taliaferro spent the first months of the conflict as a colonel, commanding troops in Tidewater and then western Virginia, where he drew praise for his gallantry at the October 1861 Battle of Greenbrier River leading the 23rd Virginia Infantry. Promoted to brigadier general in March 1862, he spent much of that year serving with Stonewall Jackson in and around the Shenandoah Valley. Over the next several months, the pair maintained a poor working relationship, stemming from Taliaferro's supporting an official complaint against Jackson in January 1862. At the time, Taliaferro and some of his fellow officers believed that Jackson was subjecting their men to brutal conditions and freezing winter marches for minimal strategic gain. For his part, Jackson believed that Taliaferro was too slow in moving his troops and was "demoralizing" as a commander. The dispute cul-

Maj. Gen. William B. Taliaferro, CSA, A.B.–1841 (University Archives Photograph Collection, Special Collections Research Center, Swem Library, College of William and Mary).

minated when Jackson threatened to resign, only to be talked back into resuming active service by high-ranking Confederate government officials. Despite this difficult relationship, Taliaferro and Jackson achieved much success in repelling Federal forces from the Shenandoah Valley.[55]

As a brigade commander and under Jackson, Taliaferro fought in several engagements, including the Battles of McDowell, Cross Keys, and Port Republic. On at least two occasions during this period, he also assumed temporary division command when his commanding officers were wounded in battle. For instance, Taliaferro took command of Stonewall Jackson's old division when its commander, Brig. Gen. Charles S. Winder, was "frightfully mangled" by a shell during the August 9, 1862, Battle of Cedar Mountain. Winder died a few hours later, leaving Taliaferro in command until a permanent replacement could be found. Later that month, an injury sustained while leading the Stonewall Brigade during the Battle of Second Manassas kept Taliaferro out of action for several weeks. However, he recovered in time to command his troops during the Battle of Fredericksburg in December 1862.[56]

During the war's second half, Taliaferro left Virginia and held a series of commands along the southern Atlantic coast, working closely with Gen. Pierre G.T. Beauregard. In March 1863, he took command of the district of Savannah, where he was responsible for defending the South Carolina and Georgia coastline against Federal attack. He was therefore the top Confederate official in the field during the famous July 1863 attack on Fort Wagner, and was in the thick of heavy fighting during the 54th Massachusetts Infantry's famous charge. During the battle, heavy Union shelling actually caused Taliaferro to be buried in a sand slide. However, he was quickly dug out to resume his command of Confederate forces. For his service at Fort Wagner, Taliaferro later received a commendation, having brilliantly repelled a numerically superior force. By early 1864, he was temporarily reassigned to the District of East Florida, in time to oversee Confederate troops during the Battle of Olustee, before returning to the South Carolina coast later that year. In the war's final months, he was military commander for all of South Carolina, reportedly earning a promotion to major general in January 1865.[57] In that capacity, he spent most of his time evacuating Confederate forces from the path of Maj. Gen. William T. Sherman's Union forces. Taliaferro finished his wartime service with Gen. Joseph E. Johnston's army, participating in the surrender of that force in April 1865. Although he hit occasional rough patches, Taliaferro was regarded by most of his peers as a competent commander who provided active service throughout the Confederacy's Atlantic seaboard.[58]

While Edwin Gray Lee and William Booth Taliaferro are acknowledged universally as Confederate generals, at least two other alumni are listed as such in only selected historical records. Conversely, other wartime records identify them as colonels. While this inconsistency over rank appears odd at first glance, it was actually a quite common occurrence for several reasons. For one, in the chaos of the war's closing days, promotions made in the field were not always approved (or even made known) to government officials in Richmond. On the other hand, commissions issued during the war's final days did not often reach the appropriate officers and were often lost or destroyed, leaving no evidence of the promotion. On occasion, promotions were also held in limbo because of political controversy or other disputes. In other cases, field grade officers who held administrative posts such as "inspector general" or "adjutant general" were sometimes referred to as "generals" in military records or postwar publications. Thus, while the legitimacy of two alumni, Henry M. Ashby and John W. Grigsby, as Confederate brigadier generals is highly disputed, the stories of their wartime service are no less compelling.[59]

Henry M. Ashby, the aforementioned cousin of Brig. Gen. Turner Ashby, was born in Virginia's Fauquier County in 1836. He attended the College from 1853 to 1854 but did not graduate, choosing instead to pursue work as a merchant in Chattanooga, Tennessee. Following the outbreak of war, Ashby quickly organized a cavalry company and was appointed its captain, going on to serve in the Army of the Tennessee. On May 24, 1862, he was elected colonel of the 2nd Tennessee Cavalry, and engaged in guarding east Tennessee from Union Army advances. Serving under Brig. Gen. John Pegram, Ashby also mounted raids into Union-occupied Kentucky and saw action at the Battles of Stones River and Chickamauga. During the 1864 Atlanta Campaign, he saw heavy fighting as a brigade commander serving in Brig. Gen. William Y.C. Humes's division. Regarded as a "born leader" by many of his colleagues, Ashby was a favorite of his corps commander, Maj. Gen. Joseph "Joe" Wheeler. He finished the war during the 1865 Carolinas campaign as a division commander, following the wounding of General Humes. Ashby finally surrendered with Gen. Joseph E. Johnston's forces in April 1865.[60]

Although Ashby spent most of the war as a colonel, he was identified as a brigadier general in an April 1865 report written by General Wheeler. Apparently, Confederate War Department officials had informed Wheeler unofficially that three of his colonels (including Ashby) had received generals' commissions. However, the commissions were never delivered because of uncertainty over where to send them in the chaotic final days of the war. Thus, Ashby signed his May 3, 1865, parole as "Colonel, commanding Division." Whatever his rank, he proved to be a quite effective cavalry commander who made a respected name for himself in the war's western theater.[61]

Like Henry M. Ashby, John W. Grigsby spent most of his Civil War career in the states of Kentucky and Tennessee. Born on September 11, 1818, in Rockbridge County, Virginia, he graduated from William and Mary in 1838 with a bachelor's degree in law. From 1841 to 1849, Grigsby spent several years abroad and served as a U.S. diplomat in Bordeaux, France. He later returned to the United States and opened a small legal practice in New Orleans before moving to Lincoln County, Kentucky. While establishing himself as a farmer, Grigsby married Susan Shelby, a granddaughter of Kentucky's legendary governor, Isaac Shelby. With the outbreak of war in 1861, he did not follow Henry M. Ashby's prompt lead into Confederate Army service. Like other Southern-leaning Kentucky residents, Grigsby abided by that state's attempted neutrality in the war's early months. However, following the fall 1862 Confederate invasion of Kentucky and subsequent presence of a friendly military force, he joined the Rebel cause. Grigsby assisted in organizing cavalry units and was later elected colonel of the 6th Kentucky Cavalry in September 1862.[62]

Serving in a cavalry brigade in the Army of Tennessee, Grigsby quickly became good friends with Maj. Gen. Joe Wheeler, who was the top cavalry commander. After sustaining a wound during an engagement near Milton, Tennessee, on March 20, 1863, Grigsby was later attached to Brig. Gen. John Hunt Morgan's cavalry brigade and helped lead several raids into Union-occupied territory. He narrowly escaped Federal capture during Morgan's ill-fated 1863 Ohio raid by swimming across the Ohio River back into Kentucky. Meanwhile, Morgan and much of his force were taken into Union custody. During the 1864 Atlanta Campaign, Grigsby led a cavalry brigade under Maj. Gen. Joe Wheeler and saw heavy fighting against advancing Union forces.[63]

Although he was a highly regarded combat commander, he was later moved into more administrative roles. In summer 1864, he was appointed inspector general of all cavalry forces in the Army of Tennessee. Grigsby then concluded his Confederate Army service by serving as Maj. Gen. Joe Wheeler's chief-of-staff during the war's closing months. A fellow officer described him as "brave, determined, fearless, and enterprising." Although some sources like the *Southern Historical Society Papers* and *Confederate Veteran* later referred to Grigsby as a brigadier general, he was paroled as a colonel in May 1865. His service as an inspector general likely prompted reference to him as "general."[64]

Overall, the wartime political and military service of the College's alumni was quite extensive considering William and Mary's small size and troubled state during the antebellum era. Despite the College's many challenges, it produced several alumni who went on to play highly significant roles during the Civil War. However, while the wartime service of the College's alumni was broad and varied, their service in the postwar era was just as noteworthy. Several alumni played key roles in rebuilding the war-torn South, particularly within the realms of politics and education. Other alumni went to work in a valiant attempt to revitalize William and Mary during the postwar era, assisting in fundraising efforts or serving in leadership positions on the Board of Visitors.

Like all other Civil War veterans, William and Mary alumni settled back into civilian life upon the war's conclusion in spring 1865. Although most graduates probably enjoyed the tranquility of everyday life, several pursued careers in the public eye. In some cases, a few alumni achieved high political office in states outside of Virginia. For instance, Capt. Octavius Coke of the 32nd Virginia Infantry left his native Williamsburg in 1867 to pursue a career in North Carolina politics. He served as a state senator, state Democratic Party chief, and secretary of state before his death in 1895. Alumnus Richard Coke reached even higher political office in the postwar era. Although he originally hailed from Williamsburg, Coke moved to Waco, Texas, after graduating in 1848 and later served the Confederacy as a captain in the 15th Texas Infantry. After the war, he involved himself in Texas politics and eventually served as the state's governor from 1874 to 1877. His administration was known for its efforts to balance the state budget and revise the Texas Constitution. As governor, Coke was also influential in creating the Agricultural and Mechanical College of Texas, which later evolved into Texas A&M University. Coke was elected to the U.S. Senate in 1877 and served there until his retirement in 1895.[65] Coke County, Texas, created in 1889, is named in his honor.

During the same period, alumnus William D. Bloxham achieved great success in Florida politics. Born in 1835 on his family's plantation in Leon County, Florida, Bloxham graduated from the College in 1855 and later served the Confederacy as a captain in the 5th Florida Infantry. Following the war, he served in the Florida House of Representatives and was also a two-term governor, serving from 1881 to 1885 and 1897 to 1901. As governor, Bloxham devoted himself to restricting monopolies and eliminating government fraud and waste. Further, his planned opening of Florida to railroad construction was later heralded as a key turning point in the political and financial development of that state.[66]

While a few William and Mary alumni such as Richard Coke and William Bloxham enjoyed successful political careers in other states, most who pursued public service following the war did so within Virginia.

Moreover, certain alumni played key roles in rebuilding the war-ravaged Commonwealth and easing it back into the Union fold. In the late 1860s, alumni Alexander Hugh Holmes Stuart and Wyndham Robertson negotiated Virginia's readmittance into the Union as leading members of the "Committee of Nine." Chaired by Stuart, this committee consisted of leading moderate conservative politicians who negotiated the wording of Virginia's new constitution with Federal authorities in order to reach a compromise. This agreement allowed for the Commonwealth to be readmitted to the Union in January 1870. A Chesterfield County native who graduated from the College in 1821, Robertson was also instrumental in securing the agreement. Prior to his service on the committee, Roberson had been a longtime member of the House of Delegates and also served as Virginia's acting governor from 1836 to 1837. Like Stuart, Robertson had been a staunch Unionist who did everything in his power to prevent Virginia's secession as well as a civil war. These efforts included his passage of the "Anti-Coercion" Resolution in January 1861, which was part of an ultimately unsuccessful strategy to reject secession. However, while Stuart and Robertson failed to prevent Virginia from seceding, their combined efforts following the war were crucial in securing the Commonwealth's readmission to the Union.[67]

Within Virginia, other alumni chose to serve in elected office during the postwar era. King William County native Beverly B. Douglas (B.L.—1843) served in the U.S. House of Representatives from 1875 through his death in 1878. This capped off a long career in political life, which included service in the Virginia Senate from 1852 to 1865 and wartime duty as a major in the Confederate Army's 5th Virginia Cavalry. Meanwhile, former Confederate General William Booth Taliaferro was again elected to the Virginia House of Delegates, where he served from 1874 to 1879. A fellow alumnus, Edmund Bagwell (attended 1858–1859), also served in the House of Delegates in the postwar era. A native of Virginia's Eastern Shore, he attended the College in the late 1850s and served as a second lieutenant in the 46th Virginia Infantry during the war. Taliaferro and Bagwell were joined by several other alumni who served as postwar state legislators, including Oswold B. Finney (attended 1840–1841), Abner W.C. Nowlin (B.P.—1855), and John W. Lawson (attended 1856–1857), who all served in the Virginia Senate. During the war, Finney and Lawson served the Confederate Army as surgeons, while Nowlin served as a captain in the 24th Virginia Infantry.[68]

While some alumni distinguished themselves during the postwar period as elected officials, others focused their efforts on other tracks to help rebuild war-torn Virginia. The most notable example was John Baytop

Cary, who devoted himself to building Virginia's educational system following the war. Born on October 18, 1819, in Elizabeth City County,[69] Cary earned an A.B. from the College in 1839 and was later awarded an honorary M.A. in 1854. Prior to the war, he operated the Hampton Male and Female Academy, better known as the Hampton Military Institute. Along with serving as principal, he also taught ancient languages and mathematics. An ardent defender of the South, Cary promptly joined the Confederate cause and was commissioned a major of artillery at the beginning of the war. He was at the center of a famous historical incident in May 1861 when he contacted Union Maj. Gen. Benjamin Butler at Fort Monroe to request the return of three escaped slaves who had sought refuge at the Federal installation. Butler promptly refused, setting a precedent for Union confiscation of slave property and eventual military emancipation of slaves.[70]

Following later Civil War service as colonel of the 32nd Virginia Infantry and as a staff officer under Maj. Gen. John B. Magruder, Cary devoted his postwar career to rebuilding Virginia's devastated educational system. After moving to Richmond to set up a lucrative insurance business, he served on the city school board from 1884 to 1886. From 1886 to 1889, Cary served as superintendent of Richmond public schools, the largest public school system in the state with 8,300 students and nearly 200 teachers. As superintendent, he focused on raising teacher salaries and increasing expenditures for the education of African American students. In supporting African American education, Cary desired "to educate every child, so that he can read his Bible and the Constitution of his country ... and thus fit him for the privileges, the duties, and the responsibility of citizenship." From 1890 to 1894, Cary served on the Richmond City Council, where he continued his advocacy for public education. Along with chairing the city council's school committee, he was instrumental in developing what would later become the Museum of the Confederacy. Through Cary's efforts, a variety of Richmond educational institutions were given the necessary resources to grow and prosper during the difficult postwar era.[71]

Like other alumni during the postwar period, Cary was also committed to supporting Virginia's higher education system. Specifically, he was active with his alma mater, serving on the William and Mary Board of Visitors from 1892 until 1897. Two other alumni who were active College supporters during this period were William Booth Taliaferro and William Lamb. While serving as a judge in his native Gloucester County, Taliaferro served on the Board of Visitors for William and Mary as well as Virginia Military Institute before his death in 1898. He was also actively engaged in fundraising efforts for the College during that difficult time. Along with serving as mayor of Norfolk from 1880 to 1886, William Lamb also served on William and Mary's Board of Visitors, taking a lead role in supporting the College's reconstruction. In later years, he also served as the College's rector as well as a University of Virginia Board of Visitors member. Along with their work in redeveloping other sectors of Virginia's governmental infrastructure, the active engagement of alumni such as Cary, Taliaferro, and Lamb in Virginia's higher education system helped set the foundation for those institutions to prosper in the 20th century.[72]

Overall the College's alumni provided the widest-ranging scope of political and military service during the Civil War era when compared to the student and faculty ranks. Scores of alumni became active participants on both sides of the conflict, ranging from entry-level privates to high-ranking generals and political officials. Though the numbers are small when compared with Virginia's other leading institutions of the day, the College's alumni contributed admirably to the war effort, with more than 30 percent of the entire alumni body donning military uniforms. Although the vast majority of alumni fought for the Confederate cause, a small but noteworthy number chose instead to fight for the Union cause. However, apart from Winfield Scott, few of the College's alumni who provided military service are well known to history. Even graduates who achieved high military rank, such as Generals William Booth Taliaferro and Edwin Gray Lee, are little known beyond the ranks of Civil War historians. Nevertheless, Taliaferro, Lee, and scores of other alumni veterans provided important military service on all of the war's key fields of battle. Thus, the story of their service deserves to be known and better acknowledged as an important part of William and Mary's history.

While many of the College's alumni performed valuable military service during the Civil War, the areas in which William and Mary alumni arguably left the most important mark were in the political and diplomatic realms. Perhaps owing to William and Mary's tradition of producing public servants, several alumni were in high-profile political positions prior to the war's commencement in 1861. Thus, while some took lead roles in creating and advancing the Confederacy, other alumni were just as active in their efforts to preserve the Union. Within the Confederate ranks, alumni such as James Murray Mason, John Tyler, Jackson Morton, and William Cabell Rives played instrumental roles in forming the Confederate government and attempting to secure recognition for it within the international community. Even one of the South's most prominent and ardent secessionists, Edmund Ruffin, was a William and Mary alumnus.[73] Conversely, other alumni including John J. Crittenden, Alexander Hugh Holmes Stuart, Wyndham Robertson, and Lemuel J. Bowden did everything in their power to either prevent the war from occurring or advance the Union cause. John J. Crittenden alone played a crucial role in keeping his native Kentucky within the Union, a highly important strategic action that contributed enormously to the Union's eventual victory. Meanwhile, alumni such as Stuart and Robertson within Virginia did their best to prevent secession and the war that would follow. Even after the brutal conflict came to a close, they played key roles in gaining Virginia's readmission to the Union and also laid the groundwork for the Commonwealth's political, social, and economic revitalization. It is therefore in these political and diplomatic arenas that William and Mary's alumni body made its most lasting and indelible contribution to the Civil War effort.

CHAPTER 7

One Faithful Heart

As noted in previous chapters, members of the William and Mary community made significant contributions to Virginia, the South, and the nation in their military service and postwar lives. Many found ways to support William and Mary in the wake of four devastating years, as faculty members and alumni. An important sector of the College community resumed responsibility for its future: members of William and Mary's Board of Visitors, who gathered in July 1865 for their first postwar meeting.

America's higher education landscape was dotted with schools facing differing degrees of potential and loss, having adapted to a variety of circumstances during the Civil War. In Virginia, Richmond College (now the University of Richmond) closed in 1861 after its students and faculty left to enlist. Like William and Mary, its main building served for some time as a Confederate hospital, and Federal troops later were quartered on the campus.[1] Other schools such as the University of Virginia and Hampden-Sydney formed wartime cadet corps, staying open as Confederate military training schools.[2] Virginia Military Institute and Washington College in Lexington also remained open, with V.M.I. contributing its cadets to the Battle of New Market, as well as producing one of Lee's most valued generals, Prof. Thomas J. Jackson. Both Lexington schools faced the onslaughts of Union Brig. Gen. David Hunter and his troops in 1864 on their march through the Shenandoah Valley. Neither institution escaped damage: Virginia Military Institute's buildings were set ablaze, and although Washington College's buildings were spared, books, records, and scientific apparatus were destroyed at both schools.[3] At Richmond College, library books, equipment, and other property were taken and never returned.[4] The University of Virginia fared better in 1865: when Maj. Gen. Philip H. Sheridan and his Federal troops occupied Charlottesville, city and university officials persuaded then–Brig. Gen. George A. Custer to protect the university from harm.[5] In the South, the University of Virginia and the University of North Carolina were the only state schools to remain open throughout the Civil War.[6]

Virginia Military Institute made significant contributions to the Confederate war effort, and its buildings were targeted by Union soldiers as part of a general attack on Lexington.[7] For Washington College, the connection to its namesake George Washington (who provided a gift of stocks to support the school in 1796) was a saving grace, as was its civilian status when compared to neighboring V.M.I.[8] Ultimately, William and Mary was not the only Virginia college that suffered destruction at Union hands, nor was it the only one to eventually seek compensation from the United States government.

Interaction with Southern schools suffering wartime damage was one connection between the federal government and higher education; educational reform was another. There were landmark changes to these institutions as they made the transition to Reconstruction and beyond. In the South, the modern university model would evolve, as it already had in Northern schools. On the national level, major changes in curricula, admissions policies, organization and governance were underway, mirroring the growing influence of local, state, and national governments on education in general.

Leadership was another crucial component in higher education's changes. Fortunately for William and Mary, by 1864 Benjamin Ewell was already dealing with the grim realities of starting over. He was one of a cadre of former Confederate officers who would head Southern institutions of higher learning after the Civil War, using their military leadership skills in the education arena. William and Mary's Visitors, faculty, and Benjamin Ewell had shepherded the College through one major rebuilding and other prewar crises, but without the formidable hurdles of Reconstruction sentiments and a postwar economic depression. As a Confederate officer, Ewell asked three times unsuccessfully in the fall of 1862 to cross Federal lines under a flag of truce and secure the College. Its fate remained on his mind. He wrote in 1864, "If I could contribute to ... [the rebuilding of William and Mary] I should think I had lived to some purpose."[9] In June 1865, when Ewell made the first of several visits, the President's House and other College buildings were in Federal possession and remained so until September 20 that year. His first report to the Visitors picked up from their last 1861 meeting, accessing how the College fared structurally and financially during the war. Ewell had not yet returned to campus officially. However, his report signaled a readiness to come back, to pick up the pieces, and to begin again. Friends of the College had preserved what they could of its history and resources: books, most of the philosophical apparatus, portraits, the Seal and Charter, and some records were safe, most of these at the Eastern Lunatic Asylum.

The rest of the July 5, 1865, report he made was less promising. As the College's acting bursar, or academic "keeper of the purse," Ewell could report that of its $153,000 endowment, $32,000 had been invested in now-worthless Confederate bonds. He had already tallied the total campus losses at $70,000, with $57,000 of the damage to the Wren Building, but realized that his estimate was about $30,000 too low.[10] Ewell had also turned his attentions to the College securities, which were transferred for safekeeping to one of the Visitors, Hugh Blair Grigsby. The financial bottom line Ewell gave the Visitors was that the College could depend on a total of $74,500 in various stocks and municipal bonds.[11] Prior to the war, William and Mary had revenue from sources that dried up afterwards, including income from renting lands and slaves; however, control over loans and other investments had not been rigorous, according to surviving records.[12]

William and Mary Chancellor Hugh Blair Grigsby, Ll.D.—1855. From Henrietta H. McCormick, *Genealogies and Reminiscences* (Chicago: Geo. K. Hazlitt, 1894), 7.

In the Reconstruction South, Republican governments faced a litany of fiscal crises: rising expenditures draining state resources, escalating taxes on property that was worth less and less, and the decreasing value of state bonds.[13] A major cause of College's downward spiral in the 1860s and 1870s came from unproductive private bonds secured by lands declining in value. In the postwar period, President Ewell and the Visitors authorized the College bursar to collect on several bonds totaling almost half of the endowment. Through a complex series of legal actions and transactions between 1865 and 1878, the College attempted to regain liquid capital to boost the endowment. Unfortunately, nothing was collected; calling in the bonds incurred additional losses from legal fees, back taxes, and sales expenses. Smaller debts collected went to satisfy other College creditors.[14]

The serious financial situation was worsened for President Ewell and College bursar John Sargent Wise because they had authorized acceptance of a private bond from William C. Mayo in 1876 as a safe investment. The Visitors had trusted Ewell to make investments, Wise also having endorsed this one, and the situation was further complicated when the bond in question became security for a College debt. Wise tried to rectify his bad judgment by applying his bursar's salary and commissions to cover interest on the debt, which totaled $13,431 in 1888 when Ewell retired.[15] President Ewell blamed himself for this consequence. He also blamed himself for mishandling a debt of longer standing connected to one of William and Mary's most illustrious alumni.

In 1823, Thomas Jefferson borrowed $24,707 from the College to cover the principal and interest of a loan for which he assumed liability as first endorser when the borrower, Wilson Cary Nicholas, defaulted. According to his grandson Jefferson Randolph (who inherited the debt), the College's loan enabled his grandfather to live his last three years in comfort. The College loan seems ironic, given Thomas Jefferson's earlier turning away to found the University of Virginia. Even so, pursuing repayment was difficult due to the former president's involvement. By 1878, $17,000 was due, and Ewell felt responsible for a bad decision. He could have insisted on the Randolph home as security rather than Shadwell, which Jefferson Randolph had inherited from his grandfather. Although it was Thomas Jefferson's birthplace, the disappointing sale of Shadwell in 1878 brought more financial loss for William and Mary.[16] In 1869, Ewell then loaned $2,000 to the College to help reopen it. He supplied the remaining $5,000 of the $28,000 building debt due in 1872 from borrowed funds plus the last of his inheritance from Richard Ewell's estate.[17]

In addition to funding issues, President Ewell once again had to argue against moving William and Mary. This time, Richmond was proposed as a healthier, more accessible location with greater potential for enrollment. Although Ewell felt it was improper to advise the Visitors, he presented historical and practical reasons for not doing so. Most of his points echoed those of earlier decades and people again joined both sides of the debate. Typically, urban board members favored removal while those from rural tidewater Virginia disagreed. Ewell emphasized that should removal be attempted, "a strong opposition would be made by the people of the Tidewater Counties, and the friends of the University."[18] He added:

> Legislative action would be necessary. If this commences there is no telling where it will stop. It is believed that money could be collected in the North by individual subscription to rebuild the College in Williamsburg but not elsewhere; and it is thought the attempt should

be made. If removed, to use the language of one of your own Body, "It would no longer be William and Mary."[19]

President Ewell feared relocation on a temporary basis, as several Visitors suggested that it might become permanent. Therefore, he focused on the positive in his communications. On August 2, Ewell reported that as long as the United States military authorities remained in place, nothing could be done to initiate repairs. However, he emphasized that the Brafferton, the College Hotel, and the President's House were or could be in habitable condition once repairs were made and that the Wren Building walls were sound. He also reported that the U.S. military commander was prepared to turn over the buildings and grounds to the faculty "in the event the College is reopened."[20]

Meanwhile, across the state, a presidential search was underway. Washington College was in dire straits, its trustees and remaining faculty struggling to reopen the stripped and damaged school. They turned to Robert E. Lee for leadership. On August 24, 1865, Lee accepted the presidency of Washington College on two conditions: First, that he could focus his energies solely on leading the institution and not take on extra duties as an instructor; and second, that his acceptance not "draw upon the College a feeling of hostility."[21] The rector announced after the board's August 31 meeting that Lee would be the next president, marking "this most auspicious event."[22]

Washington College's fortunes did begin to change for the better. Early in December 1865, President Lee appeared before the General Assembly of Virginia with a board member and successfully requested financial assistance.[23] Legislators responded, and thousands of dollars also came from private citizens like inventor Cyrus McCormick during that period.[24] New research on Washington College enrollment records suggests that the school also benefited substantially in its in-state and out-of-state enrollment during Lee's presidency.[25] On January 21, 1867, General Lee wrote this letter in response to an appeal for support from Mrs. Cynthia Tucker Coleman, who was seeking funds to restore the Wren Building:

> Your beautiful appeal in behalf of William & Mary College was not needed to excite in me an interest in its welfare; for that I have felt all my life, & have mourned not less than yourself over its destruction. I have watched with anxiety the prospect of its recuscitation [sic], & hope that the completion of the Richmond & Newport News R. R. will make it so accessible, that the beauty & salubrity of the situation with its other advantages, will cause the youth of the Country to flock to its Halls. It must necessarily suffer under the depression incident to the calamities which oppress the State, but they will pass away, & William

& Mary will again receive her place in the first rank of the Colleges of the Country.

Time which brings a cure to all things, will I trust remove the difficulties in the way of her progress, & her friends must patiently labour in hope & Confidence for her restoration. Although without the influence you subscribe to me, it will give me pleasure to do all in my power for her advancement & prosperity....[26]

Like Benjamin Ewell, Lee committed personal funds to support his institution. Both leaders also advocated conciliation at a time when Southern feelings ran high about accepting the outcomes of war. Reconstruction was viewed much differently in the North, as were administrative policies and public opinion regarding the defeated South. The postwar history of its colleges and universities reflects growth in some areas, such as African American opportunities for advanced education, and stagnation in others.[27] Southern institutions of higher learning had to find a new place within the social order. As these schools struggled to regain their footing in academe and American society, their methods of adapting alternately changed or reinforced aspects of their identities. For example, the call for William and Mary's removal to a different site was only one of the challenges to its public persona. Although some Visitors, notably Virginia historian Hugh Blair Grigsby and former Gov. Henry A. Wise, were Ewell's allies in preserving the College and its heritage intact, others saw too much risk in rebuilding in Williamsburg with endowment funds. Ultimately, those dissenters yielded with some caveats from the Visitors as a group. By establishing an elementary preparatory school, reducing the faculty size, and essentially making do with the Brafferton as class space and the President's House as laboratory space, William and Mary reopened in October 1865.

As Virginia's collegiate institutions began to regroup from their losses of physical resources, faculty, and funds, they turned to the men most likely to help them: former Confederate officers who could apply leadership experience to these schools' often daunting postwar circumstances. With Benjamin Ewell, William and Mary had an experienced academic who combined leadership and organizational skills with a great capacity for mentoring students. In spring 1866, the trustees of Hampden-Sydney College attempted to lure Ewell by offering the Jackson Professorship of Mathematics for life, with the benefits of a home, $500 in moving expenses, a salary of $1,500, and the promise of a salary increase as soon as possible. He declined, unwilling to desert the struggling College unless its authorities felt his services were unnecessary.[28]

One bright spot in September 1866 was that the English Court of Chancery appointed the William and Mary faculty as trustees of a colonial fund dating to 1741, intended to teach the neediest children in Williamsburg.[29] Ewell also managed to attract a few Northern benefactors from his correspondence and personal visits, as this chapter discusses later. With the limited reopening of the College underway and immediate threats of relocation silenced, Ewell's campaign to publicize its history to potential donors surged to the forefront. He readied *A Historical Sketch of the College of William and Mary in Virginia* and wrote persuasive articles about the importance of the College, in the hope that people in the North would contribute to its restoration. As Professor Robert Morrison had done for William and Mary after the 1859 fire and President Lee had done on behalf of Washington College, President Ewell headed to Northern cities in 1867 to seek support. He also had asked for a letter of recommendation from Ulysses S. Grant, and received this reply:

> Washington, D.C.
> Apl. 30th 1867.
>
> Dear Sir:
>
> Your letter of the 27th of Ap. asking for a recommendation from me in favor of aid for the re-establishment of Wm & Mary College, Va. is just received. The advantages secured to a government by educational privileges being extended to all the youths of the country is are appreciated by everyone. That the south, as a result of the rebellion, is unable to rebuild at once, from her own resources, college buildings destroyed, and to provide the necessary means for securing instruction to the masses, is also well understood. I hope therefore you may be successful in procuring the means to re-establish Wm & Mary College, over which you preside, on as good a basis as it has ever had, and that it will continue to teach loyalty to the general government as I understand it has done under [your] able supervision.
>
> The North, and more prosperous sections of our country, has been very liberal

Lt. Gen. Ulysses S. Grant, USA (Library of Congress).

in providing for the pressing needs of the South. Education is a material want to a nation if it is not to each individual, and I hope, in making contributions, this want will receive a due proportion of the bounty bestowed.

> With great respect,
> Your obt. Svt.
> U.S. Grant
> Gen.1 U.S.A.[30]

Ewell's "begging tour," as he called it, achieved little. Despite Grant's endorsement and despite the case Benjamin Ewell made for preserving part of the nation's history through the College, individuals and foundations were unenthusiastic about contributing. In 1866 and 1867, he appealed to the U.S. Congress — in what he could not foresee as the start of a decades-long effort — for reparations stemming from the major 1862 Wren Building fire. His 1867 petition with the House Committee on Southern Claims was rejected, although he submitted supporting affidavits from Williamsburg residents.

Adding to Ewell's load, he faced another round of calls to remove William and Mary. Governor Francis Harrison Pierpont recommended the move, with Norfolk the potential destination. Therefore, Ewell offered a new defense: By virtue of the 1693 College charter, if the College was moved, it would no longer exist.[31]

President Ewell gained the Visitors' commitment to keeping the College in Williamsburg. William and Mary essentially limped along, opening in October 1867 with plans for construction completed in 1868. Keeping only the grammar school open, it closed for the 1868–69 academic session by faculty vote to speed the rebuilding process, with the Wren Building ready for classes in October 1869. Ewell's presidential efforts continued to be spread between supervising the school's rebuilding, serving as its chief administrator, seeking financial support in myriad ways, and planning how to secure indemnification for Civil War damage. Prior to 1866, he had tried to collect on outstanding loans to individuals totaling $57,377, plus another $13,752 in arrears of interest, and had pursued the collection of dividends from College-owned stocks and bonds, but with limited results.[32] Looking back later in life, this staunch advocate would observe:

> Since 1865, the restoration of the College has been the object of my thoughts by day, and of my dreams by night.... At various times since 1865 the College has, seemingly, been on the eve of receiving the aid it so much needs. But in each case, some obstacle would appear against which the cup filled up with pleasing hopes and anticipations would be

dashed to pieces, bringing often to my mind the well known line, "Man never is, but always to be, blest."[33]

Notwithstanding Ewell's loyal efforts and financial limitations, other factors may have intervened in the College's postwar status. The president's expressed beliefs were a mixture of old traditions and new realities in the Reconstruction South. An advocate of positions that could be considered progressive in the North, such as securing Negro education and suffrage, he retained some views that strongly shaped William and Mary's public persona in the North and South as tied to the past. To Ewell, restoring the College meant restoring traditions that marked its unique heritage. After the 1859 conflagration, when the Wren Building was rebuilt in Italianate style, the March 29, 1860, *Weekly Gazette* reported, "The bell which heretofore was suspended in the College lawn, was adjusted in one of the towers of William and Mary, on Monday last." The newspaper reported that the bell's tone was "admirable," and could be heard "at the distance to nine or ten miles."[34] By July 1870, Ewell renewed that tradition by having the College bell recast and rehung in the Wren Building. Commencement was held for the first time since before the war; but no undergraduates were candidates for degrees that year.

The tradition of honorary degrees was also renewed, with the Bishop of Japan awarded a doctor of divinity degree in 1866. Two honorary degrees were awarded in 1867, five in 1868, thirteen in 1869, and thirteen in 1870.[35] Many recipients were Episcopalian clergymen, including the bishops of Virginia, Michigan, and other states, which suggests President Ewell's attempt to strengthen or renew relations to the Episcopal Church in the face of declining enrollment of Episcopalian students.[36] Others were editors, educators, poets, philologists, lawyers, soldiers, and legislators, including Joseph E. Johnston, the former Confederate general, lawyer, and U.S. congressman, who was awarded an Ll.D. in 1868.[37] From 1870 forward, honorary degrees went to individuals in these and other career categories; in retrospect, some stand out for other reasons. Legrand W. Perce and George F. Hoar, two members of the U.S. Congress who strongly supported the College's cause in the House of Representatives and the Senate, received Ll.D. degrees in 1872 and 1873, respectively.[38]

There were honorary degree recipients of note within the history of higher education, such as Charles Landon Carter Minor, who received an honorary doctor of laws degree in 1875 during his tenure as the first president of Virginia Polytechnic Institute and State University (1872–1879).[39] Henry A. Strode, awarded an honorary A.M. degree in 1870, established a preparatory school for the University of Virginia in 1872, became the head of the mathematics department at the University of Mississippi in 1889, and then served as the first president of Clemson Agricultural College (now Clemson University) from 1890 to 1893.[40] Frances Henney Smith, a United States Military Academy graduate and Confederate Army colonel, received an honorary doctor of laws degree in 1878. Smith was the first superintendent of Virginia Military Institute, first appointed in 1840. Although his presidential tenure was interrupted by the Civil War, Smith returned to rebuild V.M.I. following the conflict and served until 1889.[41]

The spirit to rebuild and the determination to see it through were shared by Smith, Lee, Ewell, and other educational leaders in the shattered South. Ewell dedicated himself to keeping William and Mary afloat, and as the 1870s began, he offered to resign his position as president to teach there instead. Ewell's life in Williamsburg before and after the war had been filled with challenges, including marital discord. In 1862, as he reminisced about his life, Silas Totten wrote epitaphs about his former colleagues at the College, including Ewell. Having been cut off from communicating with them during wartime, Totten wrote, "I will write their epitaphs even as though they were dead," and later noted his error about Benjamin Ewell's demise.[42] Totten was writing about the man chosen president of William and Mary in his stead. This may account for his less-than-charitable approach, despite his having received an honorary doctor of laws degree in 1860 when he was president of the University of Iowa. Totten critiqued Ewell's education, teaching methods, and character, typically damning him with faint praise and implying that his former colleague's church attendance, wine and beer consumption, and marriage were not good examples to set for students.[43] Letters and other surviving sources other than Totten's do indicate that Julia and Benjamin Ewell's relationship became unraveled at some point, and that something was perceived as amiss regarding Julia McIlwaine Ewell. It is conjecture to say how much their marriage in 1839 was undermined by the age difference of ten years between this young woman from York, Pennsylvania, and her husband, by their personality differences, or by deeper psychological issues.

Ultimately, the Ewells' family life with their daughter Elizabeth ("Lizzy") was split apart before Benjamin Ewell first joined the College faculty. Julia McIlwaine Ewell went to live with her parents until attempting a September 1850 reunion with her husband and child in Williamsburg. After months of conflict, she returned to Pennsylvania in the fall of 1851. Students, friends, and neighbors referred to her mental and emotional instabilities, and Julia Ewell's letters to friends raise the possibility of some form of depression or schizophrenia.[44] In letters to his brother, Richard

Ewell regularly sent greetings to his sister-in-law "Mrs. Ewell"; however, that appears to have ended sometime between 1852 and 1854. When asking female family members to care for Lizzy, Benjamin Ewell referred to Julia's violent nature, which had manifested to the point that he "did not know how to keep her indiscretions of speech & temper secret any longer."[45] Totten's alternative account portrays Julia McIlwaine Ewell as a mentally ill woman who was "irritated to madness" by a controlling husband who even stipulated that she dress below her station. Although Totten claimed that the couple had reconciled somewhat before arriving in Williamsburg, he said "the two years she remained there were filled up with brawls and battles in which neighbors and friends became involved and all who knew the parties were glad when a final separation took place."[46] Totten then repeated a rumor that Ewell kept a mulatto woman as his mistress:

> This woman was his slave and his housekeeper and confidential servant and dressed much above her condition. I do not think he had religious principle enough to restrain him from such conduct and what was worse the students generally believed the rumor true.[47]

In sum, Silas Totten's negativity was so intense that bias has to be considered as a factor in his account.

Whatever the degree of accuracy about Ewell's personal habits and relations, the College's Board of Visitors in 1854 supported Ewell as William and Mary's fifteenth president over Totten, who considered himself the frontrunner for the position despite his own Northern roots. Praise for Ewell and sympathy for his personal life were consistent with many individuals through the years, unlike Totten's views. George M. Dabney, one of Benjamin Ewell's peers at Washington College, expressed this opinion in 1854:

> I can only testify to his eminent success as an instructor at Washington College, and to the remarkable degree in which he won the affection of his students by his plain yet kindly manners, and to the singular exemption from duplicity, humbug, and ostentation which marked his character.[48]

As noted in Chapter 1, Ewell's family had supported him in raising Lizzy, who first lived in the President's House, taking an active prewar part in the life of the campus, and then at Ewell Hall, his farm in James City County. She relocated to Richmond during the war to work at the Confederate Officers' Hospital, and after her marriage, she lived for a year in Prince Edward County with her husband's family. However, that arrangement ended in 1868 when Lizzy's husband Beverly Scott agreed to run his father-in-law's farm.[49] It brought her back at a significant time: Benjamin

Ewell's sister "Becca" had died in 1867, and like his mother, was buried in the little College cemetery.

Both as a professor and as president, Ewell's strong educational mission and his abiding love for William and Mary were well known. Family members' requests that he take on less demanding work were unsuccessful, but President Ewell was not obsessed to the point of territoriality. The College may have truly been the love of his life, and he was willing to step down if it would secure the school's future. After the war he made an initial unsuccessful attempt to attract his brother, former Confederate Lt. Gen. Richard Ewell, to the presidency, or at least his name and financial support. Later recommending Gen. Joseph E. Johnston as the next president, Ewell reasoned that his West Point friend and former commander's stature could be as beneficial as Robert E. Lee's had become at Washington College. The Visitors refused to accept Ewell's resignation. Yet, solely from the standpoint of effective fundraising, there was reason to consider it. Using today's criteria for college and university presidents, Benjamin Ewell had exceptional plusses: his devotion to the College; his bonds with students, the community, and a wide circle of friends and colleagues; and perhaps most intriguing, innovative communications and fundraising efforts that foreshadowed modern media and development techniques in higher education.[50]

During the Civil War, Ewell's leadership abilities and communications skills made him an effective chief-of-staff to General Johnston. Unfortunately, despite his extensive public relations efforts in the North and South with letters, brochures, and tours, he could not match Robert E. Lee's success at attracting donors. He did not have Lee's immense fame nor did he carry the name recognition in the North of generals like his brother Richard or Joseph E. Johnston. The significance of renown, or in Lee's case, reverence, was demonstrated after Lee's death in 1870. To retain Washington College's ties to the South's most famous figure of the Civil War, its trustees changed the school's name to Washington and Lee University and successfully offered Lee's eldest son Custis the presidency, in which position he served from 1871 until 1897.[51] George Washington Custis Lee, a major general and aide-de-camp to Jefferson Davis, had become a professor of military science and engineering at V.M.I. following the war. The trustees also secured endorsements for the university from thirteen former Confederate generals.[52]

Benjamin Ewell's survival strategies for his institution, like those of the Washington College trustees, dealt with harsh realities. Neither fully church nor state in its affiliations, William and Mary had only a remnant of its former colonial support from England in the trust fund mentioned earlier.⁵³ In addition, Ewell's deep regard for the College's history and traditions was not universally shared and did not help generate financial support. In fact, William and Mary's history as an arguably elite Southern school worked against it in Northern circles after the war. To make matters worse, although most Southerners probably respected the College and its constituents supported it, few if any were in positions to donate substantial funds, even the Visitors.⁵⁴

Having accepted the Board's decision, Ewell soldiered on as president in spite of family difficulties, his own economic condition, and the realities of Reconstruction. His tour of the North in 1868–1869 seeking contributions for the Wren reconstruction was largely unsuccessful except for book contributions from publishing companies. Ewell's letter to the editor of the *Richmond Whig*, published on September 16, 1868, stressed the losses to the College during the war ("greater than those of any Southern institution") and the successful rebuilding efforts underway. Ewell also acknowledged the "liberality of W.W. Corcoran, Esq., and other distinguished gentlemen of New York City" in allowing that rebuilding to proceed.⁵⁵

Having traveled from Baltimore on a fundraising trip, Benjamin Ewell wrote to his daughter Lizzy on January 4, 1869, from the Union Palace Hotel in New York City, where rain, overcrowded street cars, and a cold made his efforts difficult: "I am entirely in doubt how long I shall remain here. So far I have abundance of good wishes but nothing like currency. I shall make a fair trial though if I don't break down."⁵⁶ A day later, he wrote a letter to the editor of the *New York Times* to "set forth the present condition and necessities of the institution."⁵⁷ In his letter, Ewell again paid tribute to philanthropist William Wilson Corcoran (who contributed to many universities, including the College, George Washington University, and Washington and Lee), New York entrepreneur Alexander Tunney Stewart (who previously had contributed funds to restore William and Mary after the 1859 fire), industrialist W.E. Dodge (founding member of the Young Men's Christian Association and New York congressman), August Belmont (businessman and chairman of the Democratic National Committee), Robert Bonner (founder of the *New York Ledger* weekly newspaper, which had a readership of 377,000 by 1870), "and others in New York and elsewhere, [who] enabled the college authorities to begin last year the work of reconstruction."⁵⁸

Thomas Dunn English, a New Jersey politician and journalist with medical and law degrees, also a friend of Edgar Allan Poe, wrote to Benjamin Ewell on March 2, 1869, having heard that "the library of William & Mary College was destroyed by vandals during the late Civil War." Although he had no means to replace the library's losses on a large scale,

Dunn offered to send a package of books via steamer to Norfolk and on to a landing on the James River at no expense to the College, also offering to contact others who might help and suggesting names including the publishers, Appleton & Co. He added, "In any way that I can render service to the institution, command me."[59] The same year on December 13, President Frederick Barnard of Columbia College wrote on Ewell's behalf to Rev. B.L. Haight, noting the College's contributions in the cause of church education and Ewell's visiting New York "for the purpose of laying before the friends of education among us the condition of the college under his charge, and to endeavor to obtain assistance in restoring the college buildings, wantonly destroyed in 1862, by Union troops."[60] Ewell's sister Rebecca, who died of bilious dysentery on August 9, 1867, was a strong supporter of the College. Her bereaved brother wrote to Hugh Blair Grigsby on August 21:

> She is a greater loss to me than any of my family. She was an active & earnest friend to the College. She, by her representations & exertions, induced Mr. C__ran [Corcoran] to subscribe. Without the subscription he made I doubt if measures to rebuild would have been so soon undertaken. In other directions too she did a great deal.[61]

With William and Mary's financial hardships and limited resources, there was little hope of making postwar academic progress in league with better-supported institutions. One can argue, though, that its reopening and subsequent fight for survival signaled the will to do so. The war and its effects constrained further Southern reforms while higher education was making massive strides in the North, West, and Midwest, as evidenced by President Charles Eliot of Harvard and other educators moving their institutions toward university status in the post–Civil War era.[62]

William and Mary's curricular status was less problematic in the 1870s than its limited enrollment and mounting debts from structural repairs and new construction. Its declining fortunes were consistent with the depressed economic state of tidewater Virginia. William and Mary's isolated location meant significant distance and travel time from the rest of the state, and the lack of funds available to its traditional tidewater constituency hampered enrollment. With no hope of those conditions improving soon, Benjamin Ewell continued to seek state aid with the help of allies.

One unrealized source of Federal funding was the Morrill Land-Grant College Act of 1862, which became available once Virginia rejoined the Union. Members of the Virginia General Assembly struggled from 1870 into 1872 to decide which educational institutions should benefit. The

University of Virginia, Washington College (now Washington and Lee University) and Virginia Military Institute all lobbied for funds, with V.M.I. offering to move to Richmond as an enticement.[63] Ewell's appearances before the Virginia General Assembly failed to secure major funding that instead went to the establishment of Virginia Agricultural and Mechanical Institute (now Virginia Polytechnic Institute and State University) and to Hampton Institute in 1872. Compounding the College's problems were political, social, and educational changes in the state, Virginia's postwar debt, and a national financial crisis beginning in 1873. Enrollment would fall from forty-two in 1870–71 to twenty in 1877–78, with decreased tuition fees contributing to an average annual income of less than $4,000 to the College.[64] By 1876, the endowment dropped $18,000 from $85,000, and debts increased $10,000 to $20,000.[65] For Benjamin Ewell, there were unending challenges: funding, faculty retention, encouraging enrollment, attempting to stop further decline to the endowment, and preparing strategic appeals to Congress for compensation from war damages. If there was moderately good news, it was the 1875 reorganization of the Alumni Society with active supporters and the 1874–1876 involvement of the Southern Orphans Educational Association and the Southern Association for the Benefit of Widows and Orphans, which funded the education of approximately eighteen young men at the College whose fathers had been Confederate military casualties.[66]

In 1877, the Virginia General Assembly demonstrated where its higher education priorities lay, increasing support to the University of Virginia, the new Virginia Agricultural and Mechanical Institute, and Hampton Institute—but not William and Mary.[67] Public and legislative sentiment lay with educational institutions seen as having growth potential and political capital, not the College. Federal aid was even less likely. Ewell's efforts to obtain indemnities from Congress from 1870 to 1878 aroused deep-seated animosities related to the Civil War, degrees of indifference to William and Mary's history, and conflicting views of how the Wren Building's destruction had come about.

David E. Cronin, the Union officer and journalist previously mentioned in Chapter 2 as the provost marshal of Williamsburg in 1864, wrote this in his history, published four decades later:

> I shall not dwell further upon such repellant features of petty partisan war and have alluded to them so particularly in order to indicate the conditions under which we were scouting and the vengeful feelings toward the enemy that animated us. As a matter of fact, I am inclined now to believe, viewing the history of the war as a whole, including all sections where the contest raged, that in the matter of reprisals and

departure from so called strict rules of war fare, neither Unionists nor Confederates could boast of much in the way of clemency, in actual combat when vindictive passions were uppermost. It should be remembered that official records give us no true history of the war. The true history, of course, never can be written.[68]

Cronin's statement was not written directly in response to Ewell's Congressional appeals, as others were. His balanced assessment placed blame on both sides for wartime damage and aggression. Perhaps from his reportorial background, Cronin's reasoning appears far more balanced than discourse on the Wren Building fire, even decades after the event. These sensitivities created a tightrope for Benjamin Ewell to walk as a petitioner. On one hand, he had to detail the circumstances surrounding William and Mary's wartime damage; on the other hand, to accuse Federal soldiers of wanton, drunken destruction could inflame Northern feelings and destroy the chance of compensation.

Ewell's 1870 appeal described the Wren Building's destruction as a reality of war. Six Union generals wrote letters of support at his request: Ambrose E. Burnside, Ulysses S. Grant, George B. McClellan, George G. Meade, John M. Schofield, and William T. Sherman. In 1869, General Burnside sent encouraging words to Ewell from Providence, Rhode Island, writing:

> Professor Benj. S. Ewell
>
> My dear Sir
>
> I am glad to recommend you to the kind attention of the people of the north. It has given me great pleasure to read the strong testimonials of Genls. Grant, Schofield, Meade, and others in behalf of the good work you have in hand. I hope you will meet with abundant success in securing the means to rebuild, and reestablish William and Mary College upon a firm basis. When you feel disposed to visit New England I will take pleasure in presenting you, and your work more particularly to our people.
>
> Yours truly,
> A.S. Burnside.[69]

General Meade, an ex–West Pointer like Grant and Ewell, wrote:

> I am satisfied, on examination of the facts of the case, that the destruction of the buildings of William and Mary College by our troops was not only unnecessary and unauthorized, but was one of those deplorable acts of useless destruction, which occur in all wars.
>
> In this view, and believing that its reconstruction, under the direction and superintendence of Professor Benjamin S. Ewell, will tend to cement and strengthen the bonds of Union principles, I take great

pleasure in recommending the appeal of Professor Ewell to all those who have the means and the disposition to assist him in the good work in which he is engaged.[70]

College alumni met in the Wren Chapel on July 6, 1870, to discuss ways and means of restoring the College and increasing its endowment. Once again, Virginia Gov. Henry A. Wise stepped forward as a top William and Mary advocate, volunteering to garner support for those goals and to seek a Congressional appropriation for war damage.[71] Additional support came from Federal Judge Robert W. Hughes, a Virginia Republican whose son was a student at the College.[72] William and Mary had Northern supporters within the U.S. Congress, including Rep. Benjamin Butler of Massachusetts, who had been a Union major general during the war and assigned to the command of Fort Monroe and the Department of Eastern Virginia. In February 1870, Butler sponsored the House bill on the College's behalf, asking for $69,000. President Ewell personally made his case in front of members of the House Committee on Education and Labor. His carefully crafted arguments steered clear of inflammatory rhetoric, although he did not take Rep. Butler's advice to omit references to the war, requesting support for William and Mary solely as an institution of higher learning. Ewell stressed the College's venerable history and contributions to the nation, emphasizing its future value in providing teacher education in the state.[73]

Although his first appeal failed overall in Congress, President Ewell had gained the backing of the House committee and its chair Rep. Legrand Perce of Mississippi, as well as Rep. George Frisbee Hoar of Massachusetts. Ewell strengthened his second appeal on January 24, 1872, by adding affidavits from Williamsburg residents on how the conflagration occurred. These testimonies specified Union soldiers for the retal-

U.S. Senator George F. Hoar (R–Massachusetts), Ll.D.—1873, one of the top supporters of the College in the postwar U.S. Congress (Library of Congress).

iatory but unauthorized arson at the Wren Building, and they became a contested element of the College's Civil War narrative. The affidavits were not automatically accepted—nor were the arguments that William and Mary's heritage was sufficient reason to support its reconstruction. The 1872 *Congressional Globe* details speeches and debate about conflicting issues between members of the House of Representatives during the 42nd Congress.

On February 24, 1872, Rep. Milo Goodrich of New York gave a lengthy speech paying tribute to the College's renowned alumni and its history, but contesting war damage compensation and rebutting the arguments made in the College's favor by Rep. George F. Hoar of Massachusetts. Goodrich cautioned that even if unauthorized soldiers had caused the destruction, a "shoreless ocean of liability" from the war would result from such reimbursement.[74] He also called attention to how the College dismissed its students to join the Confederate ranks and yielded its buildings to use as barracks in the "grand conspiracy for the overthrow of the Union."[75] Likewise, Rep. Charles W. Buckley of Alabama and Rep. H.R. Hawley of Illinois pointed out that other higher education institutions in the South were destroyed, with Hawley stressing:

> Just before I took the floor one of the members from the State of Mississippi called my attention to the fact that in his State four colleges had been destroyed root and branch, "from turret to foundation-stone," during the war, and if we are to pay for the damage to this college, if we are to pay for its destruction we ought to pay for the public edifices destroyed in the Carolinas, for the schoolhouses and all the public buildings throughout the South.[76]

Hawley expressed his astonishment that such a bill "could find a standing place upon the floor of this House" since so many claimants had what he considered to be just claims. With "loyal people" such as Union soldiers' widows and children unpaid for their losses, Union soldiers unpaid for service to their country, and many members of Congress concerned that adjusting claims would drain the U.S. Treasury, Hawley questioned how such a generous donation to The College of William and Mary could be made.[77]

The House first dismissed the College's request on December 13, 1872. A second bill passed on February 17, 1873, but never reached the Senate floor because its members had adjourned.[78] Ewell then threw his support behind Ulysses S. Grant's reelection campaign, in part because of Grant's supporting the College's funding appeals. Undaunted, Ewell continued to press for Federal compensation, making another personal appeal on April 1, 1874. He reminded Congressional listeners that the French government, not the American government, had contributed monies for repairs following damage to William and Mary during the American Revolution, even though Princeton University and Rhode Island College had received such Federal compensation. Strong resistance overcame positive support once again and this third appeal did not even reach a vote in the House.

During a fourth try with Rep. George Hoar speaking on March 3, 1876, another bill for College compensation passed the House but failed in the Senate. In the next session of Congress, the House rejected William and Mary's latest claim by a vote of 127 to eighty-seven. The College's friends in the House from Virginia and Massachusetts could not overcome the political sentiments against assisting a private institution, which, no matter how ancient, had supported the Confederate cause. Although some could look past that so-called treason, other legislators and citizens felt that supporting William and Mary would open up a Pandora's box of Southern collegiate war claims.

Throughout the 1870s, Benjamin Ewell and his allies in the North publicly campaigned for the College through the media, attempting to raise funds and support. In November 1875, *Scribner's Monthly* published John Esten Cooke's lengthy article, "William and Mary College," extolling the history of the venerable College and Williamsburg. Cooke attributed the cause of the 1862 College fire to "a disorganized force of Federal cavalry," who "fired and destroyed the principal buildings with the furniture and apparatus, subsequently, injuring the property to the extent, in all, of about $80,000." [79] Cooke's sympathetic portrayal identified friends of education supporting the College from Virginia, other states and other countries, listing the Archbishop of Canterbury, the Earl of Derby, and a host of prominent supporters in New York, Philadelphia, Baltimore, and Georgetown, "the list being far too long to present in this place."[80] He also wrote enthusiastically that even if excelled in wealth and enrollment by other universities, William and Mary was "unsurpassed for the excellence of its moral and intellectual training" and by its refined and historic surroundings in Williamsburg.[81]

If Ewell possibly was behind the scenes as a booster for this article, that is less likely with an 1877 article that appeared in *The Chronicle: A Weekly Insurance Journal*, examining the history of American college and university fires. Although it focused on fires between 1874 and 1877 in Wisconsin, South Carolina, and Indiana, the front-page article took note of colonial colleges including William and Mary:

> The president's house of the college of William and Mary, in Virginia, was burned while occupied by the French at the siege of Yorktown, but was afterwards rebuilt by Louis XVI, and the main college building was

destroyed by accidental fire in 1859, and was rebuilt only to be again destroyed in 1862 by the incendiary act of some stragglers from the Fifth Pennsylvania cavalry, who were quartered in the neighborhood.[82]

Although consensus grew over decades that Federal troops had been involved in the Wren Building fire, there were significant omissions in published Northern histories and records of the 5th Pennsylvania about the September 1862 events in Williamsburg, including both the Wren Building fire and the death of Union officer Diodate C. Hannahs. One notable exception to this appeared in the memoirs of E.P. McKinney, friend to Capt. Diodate Hannahs. His account, *Life in Tent and Field, 1861–1865*, was published in 1922 in Boston. McKinney devoted a chapter to the assassination of his friend, Captain Hannahs. In the next chapter, "The Destruction of William and Mary College — Not Done by Union Soldiers," McKinney charged that the accusation of Northern vandalism had had "a potent influence in keeping alive a feeling of animosity toward the North in Virginia" over the intervening half century.[83] He also examined the "curious affidavits" of Williamsburg residents Mrs. Maria T. Peyton and Miss Mary T. Southall and concluded that they did not stand as sufficient evidence in comparison to the facts he presented, adding, "It was generally believed that the fire was the result of carelessness on the part of the Southern troops."[84] That McKinney was adamant in this defense sixty years later suggests that he was contesting a widespread perception of Federal troop involvement that became stronger over time. This was thanks in no small part to Benjamin Ewell's tireless lobbying on behalf of the College, but the outcome was not yet clear.

In the summer of 1877, Ewell felt his efforts to shore up the school through any means possible had been reduced to a final solution. In a report to the Board of Visitors, he recommended operating at minimum level rather than closing William and Mary completely.[85] Facing no appropriations from the Virginia General Assembly, faculty protests over workloads and salaries in arrears, and dissent with the Board of Visitors, President Ewell fended off the College's closing until April 1879, when the Visitors met in Richmond to consider a new proposal for removal. This time, the threat came from the University of the South as a form of rescue. The offer was to absorb the College as the "College of William and Mary in Virginia at the University of the South," in Sewanee, Tennessee, and renew its Episcopalian ties. Once again Ewell argued that William and Mary must remain — and close if necessary — where it was royally chartered. His strong arguments succeeded and the Visitors voted in mid-July to reject the proposal. Still not ready to give up, Benjamin Ewell then unsuccessfully sought funding related to the Yorktown Centennial of 1881. The College faced closing for lack of funds.

The following January, a new future beckoned, if William and Mary would join the Readjuster-Republican effort to bring public teacher training and education reform to Virginia. Gov. William E. Cameron advised President Ewell that the College could receive state funds in the form of an annual $12,000 appropriation. Another $8,000 for teacher training in the South was available through a Northern philanthropic organization, the Peabody Education Fund.[86] President Ewell had asked Boston philanthropist George Peabody for support in 1866 and applied to the Peabody Fund in 1867, and was denied because the foundation then focused its support on elementary education.[87]

In order to meet the funding criteria, Ewell supported transforming William and Mary into a state normal school for white male teachers. This time, it was the Visitors who resisted, not the state legislature: Conservative members on the board opposed such a major change in William and Mary's stature, thus shutting the door on the College's best chance for survival at the time. Virginia Normal and Collegiate Institute (now Virginia State University) was founded in 1882 as Virginia's first normal school for teacher training and African American education. The effort to save William and Mary seems Herculean in retrospect.

Much later, when Ewell had laid his burden of office down, Virginia lawyer, poet, and alumnus Charles Washington Coleman recited the poem "Alma Mater" at the 200th anniversary of the College of William and Mary in 1893.[88] His verses read in part:

> For loud have echoed against her walls
> The tramping of armies, the booming of guns;
> Thrice at the thrilling of trumpet calls
> To do and to die she hath sent her sons.
>
> Thrice hath the fire-fiend's lurid glow
> Leapt at the laurels about her head;
> The vandal smote her and struck her low
> And we turned from our mother and called her dead.
>
> We turned, did I say? Ay, one was true!
> When nights were bitter and days were drear,
> One faithful heart to her misery drew,
> And kept him a lonely vigil here.
>
> He held the hands of the high struck low,
> This prostrate, pitiful mother of ours;
> He shared in her poverty, bore her woe,
> A seneschal true in her shattered towers.

> To William of Orange, to Mary of York,
> We would render thanks for their royal names;
> To good James Blair whom no trial might balk,
> For the noble fulfillment of noble aims.
>
> And another name would we link with theirs,
> The man who kept faith with a fallen trust;
> 'Tis the glorious crown of his fourscore years —
> He was true when our mother lay prone in the dust.[89]

Eleven years before Coleman's William and Mary audience listened to his poem, the College had a total enrollment in June 1882 of three students and two professors, including Ewell. Its dwindling endowment and mounting debts were beyond stopgap measures, with no public or private support in sight. In a last gesture of tradition, defiance, or both, the Visitors did not officially close the College. Just as they refused to remove William and Mary from Williamsburg, they would not invalidate its charter.[90] This stance followed two decades in which Benjamin Ewell spoke, wrote, and lived his conviction that William and Mary was a national historic treasure. More than any other argument that Ewell skillfully wielded, his consistent drumbeat of heritage called people of prominence to lobby on William and Mary's behalf. Through their support of the College's 18th- and 19th-century history, they kept it visible to the public. Beyond that, they contributed to the heroic saga of its survival, as time would tell.

Wartime damage and severe postwar conditions hindered the recovery of Southern institutions of higher learning. However, William and Mary suffered also from the general perception that time and educational progress had passed it by. Benjamin Ewell's heavy emphasis on the College's historical significance was a double-edged sword: heralding William and Mary's ties to the colonial past brought it attention, but also branded it as a relic in the public consciousness. Also, higher education institutions with scientific and technical courses of study stood out as progressive representatives of the New South, not the struggling College with its primary adherence to the fading classical tradition. William and Mary's antebellum advances in curriculum development and scientific education, which were ahead of their time for Virginia institutions, were cut off by the Civil War and its aftershocks.

It is possible that one of the periodically recommended geographic removals to urban locations would have moved the College in a more progressivist direction. Embracing the overture for merger from the University of the South conceivably could have done so, or added to conflicts between that university's faculty members. Some, like Ewell, were West Point–trained supporters of scientific instruction; others were classicists who argued for retention of a more conservative curriculum.[91] Rejecting the potential for growth (or survival) posed by all these proposals, William and Mary's traditionalists chose to preserve the College's unique institutional identity at all costs and in some cases, to resist the societal change around them.

During the 1870s and 1880s, Ewell's peers advanced curricular reforms in the Southern collegiate system, modernizing science offerings, adding agronomy, and instituting professional and commercial courses.[92] They were hindered to some extent by the financial challenges that halted William and Mary's academic operations.[93] Benjamin Ewell's 1882 recommendation to initiate teacher training was prescient, for that new direction would finally reenergize the school in 1888 and enable it to evolve toward university status. In 1884, William and Mary was proposed as a location for the first normal school for training female teachers, but this effort also failed. Unfortunately, it would take six years for the idea of William and Mary as a professional teacher training institution to take root, years in which the aging Benjamin Ewell watched with continued care over the College and its remaining holdings. His stewardship during this period is embedded in the William and Mary narrative; as George Coleman's poem demonstrates, Ewell's dedication to the College already had been romanticized in just over a decade as part of its institutional saga. Ewell himself discussed this development in a January 19, 1887, letter to Herbert Baxter Adams, chairman of Johns Hopkins University's History Department. Concerning the popular assumption that he daily rang the College bell to maintain the royal charter during the school's closure, Ewell wrote, "It has given me a wide reputation as a 'bell-ringer,' equal to or superior to that of the celebrated 'Swiss bell-ringers.' So I laugh at the story without murmuring or contradicting." It had actually been Ewell with Malachi Gardiner, an African American tenant farmer at Ewell's farm outside Williamsburg. Ewell took a buggy ride to the College from Ewell Hall each day with Gardiner as his driver. Staying on campus five to six hours, the two men would first check all the buildings. Afterwards Ewell went to the President's House to correspond, to greet visitors, and take care of other College matters.

The president known affectionately as "Old Buck" kept William and Mary in the public eye as much as possible through his correspondence, interactions, and research regarding the College's history, poised for what he envisioned as its next stage of renewal. Ewell already had been made an honorary fellow of the Royal Historical Society of Great Britain in 1880. His seemingly tireless efforts attracted appeals and publications on behalf of William and Mary during the 1880s, such as the historical account written by Herbert Baxter Adams, chairman of Johns Hopkins University's Department of History and Political Science. In his eighty-nine-page publication *The College of William and Mary: a contribution to the history of higher education, with suggestions for its national promotion* (1887), Adams chronicled the College's history and contributions to America in scholarly detail, having learned "many interesting facts connected with the political and social development of Virginia" from President Ewell.[94] Adams also reiterated many points Ewell had made justifying William and Mary's war damage claims in the U.S. Congress. Herbert wrote:

> The hallowed associations which surround this college prevent this case from being a precedent for any other. If you had injured it, you surely would have restored Mount Vernon; you had better honor Washington by restoring the living fountain of learning where service was the pleasure of his last years, than by any useless and empty act of worship or respect toward his sepulcher.
>
> No other college in the country can occupy the same position. By the fortune of war that sacred institution, which has conferred on the country a hundredfold more benefit than any other institution or college in the South, has become a sufferer. I desire to hold out the olive branch to the people of Virginia, to the people of the South, to show them that we will join them in rebuilding the sacred place laid waste by the fortunes of war.[95]

However, during William and Mary's drastically reduced circumstances, there were more frustrations Ewell had to endure. Herbert Adams's study proposed that it would be a "grand possibility of life for the old College of William and Mary" to move it to Richmond. In a counterargument to Benjamin Ewell's contention that any removal would risk revoking the conditions of the College charter, Adams stated that the legislature could modify the geographical provision of the royal charter just as the Board of Visitors changed the chancellorship of the College from the Bishop of London to Washington after the Revolution.[96] Herbert's recommendation for the College's removal and his critique of persistent refusals to do so in the past forced Benjamin Ewell to debate that point once again.

In an earlier twist of fate, a deceased Bostonian's bequest of $400,000 to the College in 1885 could not be honored since the College was closed at the time. Instead, the University of Virginia received the legacy under the terms of the will's codicil. Ewell was a realist; he wrote that year:

> With respects to the future of the College, there are it seems to me but two lines of action. The one is to turn it over to the State, and the other is to continue it in its present condition, paying off its debts and taking all possible care of the College Property. It is my conviction that its restoration will in time be effected.[97]

Supporting Ewell and the College were friends like Maj. Gen. William B. Taliaferro and Judge Warner T. Jones, who previously had lobbied on its behalf in Richmond. Both were influential alumni and Board of Visitors members seeking funds despite opposition to new appropriations in the face of existing state debt. In 1887, the two men led the campaign for Virginia General Assembly funding in the form of a $10,000 appropriation in return for the establishment of teacher training at the College, helped by lawyer William W. Crump of Richmond, former Virginia legislator James N. Stubbs of Gloucester, and Dr. Richard A. Wise of Williamsburg, a former College student, faculty member, and superintendent of the Eastern Lunatic Asylum.[98] They took strategic parts in the lobbying effort along with Delegates A.W. Harris and Lyon G. Tyler, the latter a former faculty member.[99]

Together, they contended that William and Mary would fill a void in Virginia as a professional teacher-training institution, particularly for male teachers taking roles as principals and secondary school instructors. Again, the road through committees was not easy, and although the measure was reported favorably by two House committees, it was voted down by the House Committee on Schools and Colleges on February 1, 1888. On February 14, Senate Bill No. 53 was passed by a vote of forty-four to five, and returned to the House. Like its Senate champion James N. Stubbs, Lyon G. Tyler supported the College bill during an intensive House debate on February 23. The bill passed by forty-two to thirty-seven, but a majority vote of fifty-one was required in finance-related measures. By March 1, when the next vote was taken in the House, the William and Mary lobbyists had negotiated what was needed: a total of fifty-seven to twenty-seven votes.[100]

Northern leaders in the higher education community showed their support as well. H.N.R. Dawson, commissioner of the Bureau of Education in the U.S. Department of the Interior, corresponded with Benjamin Ewell and agreed with him that "the time will yet come when your old institution will rise from its ashes and renew, in the prosperity which seems to be awakening throughout the country, its usefulness in the future."[101] D.C. Gilman, president of Johns Hopkins University, wrote to Ewell the same month following a previous visit to see him at William and Mary, recalling the experience of seeing Williamsburg and the College with him:

> The familiar history has been made real by our visit. I esteem it a very great privilege that we could see what we saw under your guidance. You seem to me the very embodiment of the "genius loci"— the watchful and faithful guardian of a grand idea. As long as you live we may be sure that the spark of fire will not disappear from the sacred altar.[102]

On June 10, 1887, the secretary of the Phi Beta Kappa chapter at Dartmouth College wrote to Benjamin Ewell, asking that he attend the one-hundredth anniversary of that chapter's founding "and participate in the exercises of the day, when The College of William and Mary will be mentioned with the esteem which is its due." Should he not be able to attend, he was asked to send written words of greeting: "In any case, it will express its earnest hope that The College of William and Mary, under its ancient name and charter, may yet renew its youth."[103]

In his lengthy response of June 22, 1887, Ewell expressed his pleasure at the invitation and his regret that he would have to decline due to his age and health. Reflecting that William and Mary would celebrate its two-hundredth anniversary in less than seven years, Ewell also confirmed the belief of College governmental authorities that friends and patrons would never consent to the College's extinction when it was so intertwined with the nation's history. Further, Ewell emphasized — and perhaps referred to himself most of all in this statement — that "the existing authorities of William and Mary, though at times their position may be painful and mortifying, deem it a privilege and an honor to share in the work of preserving and perpetuating its 'historical continuity.'"

Thirty-five years of Benjamin Ewell's life had been devoted to the College by the time he made his last report to the Board of Visitors on May 10, 1888. This made him equal to Bishop James Madison in tenure and second to James Blair in length of presidential service to William and Mary. In an 1868 letter to his longtime friend, Hugh Blair Grigsby wrote these words with unerring prescience:

> And when more days of prosperity, which we think and hope will ere-long dawn upon us, shall arise, and the tread of numerous pupils shall resound through her walls, the friends of the College will hail you as its greatest friend in its hour of peril, and applaud you as its Deliverer. You will have the just credit of having aided more effectually than any other man in opening anew the fountains of knowledge and wisdom in the most venerable institution, with a single exception, in our whole country.[104]

Epilogue

The Old College Moves Forward

After all of William and Mary's tribulations, its absorption into the state's teacher training program promised stability, growth potential, and relief from a long funding drought on the state and national levels. The Virginia General Assembly enacted a bill in March 1888 authorizing funds for William and Mary's reorganization, approving a $10,000 annual state budget appropriation for training white male public school teachers.[1] The legislature enlarged the Board of Visitors by eleven: ten to be appointed by the governor, with Dr. John Lee Buchanan, Virginia's superintendent of public instruction, as an ex officio member.[2]

The College's Board of Visitors met in Richmond on April 10, 1888, and formally accepted the school's change in institutional identity on April 11.[3] On May 10, as the Visitors met again in Williamsburg to prepare for William and Mary's reopening, they faced another monumental transition: after four decades of service, the nearly 78-year-old Benjamin Stoddert Ewell was resigning. He agreed to supervise College renovations until a new president was in place. When Dr. Buchanan declined the Visitors' invitation to become Ewell's successor that July, they considered other applications but ultimately elected 31-year-old Lyon G. Tyler, who accepted the presidency.[4] As Richmond's freshman delegate to the General Assembly, Lyon G. Tyler demonstrated that he was cut from the same cloth as his father, John Tyler, the former president of the United States and William and Mary chancellor. The younger Tyler had strongly pressed the College's case in the Virginia House of Delegates from his multiple perspectives as a state legislator, educator, and former William and Mary faculty member (1877–78).

After President Tyler took the helm at William and Mary, a new era began. Over the next three years, faculty members whom students would call "the Seven Wise Men" came together: John Lesslie Hall (professor of language, literature, and history), Thomas Jefferson Stubbs (professor of mathematics), Lyman B. Wharton (professor of languages), Van Franklin Garrett (professor of natural science), Hugh Stockdell Bird (professor of pedagogics,), Charles E. Bishop (professor of Greek, French, and German), and Tyler himself (professor of moral philosophy, political economy, and civil government).[5] A succession of achievements followed at a steady pace: William and Mary alumni reestablished the Alumni Society (1888); the College's first literary magazine was published (1890); and the first number of the *William and Mary College Quarterly Historical Papers* was published (1892).[6]

Assured that William and Mary was in safe hands, Benjamin Ewell enjoyed a slower pace of life with family, friends, and visitors at his nearby farm, Ewell Hall. As president *emeritus*, he continued to chronicle history by recording wartime events and his own role at the College. Ewell would help to revive the College's Phi Beta Kappa chapter (Alpha of Virginia) in December 1893; it had been founded originally by William and Mary students in December 1776 and met there until 1781. Ewell had participated in the first reestablishment of the honor society on campus in the early 1850s, but it was halted by the start of the Civil War.

The College was not out of the woods yet in terms of obtaining secure funding for growth. A faction of state legislators and some private philanthropists were slow to fund its new mission in training public school teachers.[7] William and Mary's leaders kept appealing for support. They stressed its service to the Commonwealth's schools training educators, and emphasized the opportunity now available to young men who might not otherwise afford a college education.[8] However, the College's historical precedents were still the foremost argument, just as they had been under President Ewell.[9]

By March 1893, two hundred years after William and Mary's founding, the U.S. Congress partially indemnified the College in the amount of $64,000 for its Civil War losses.[10] There were also accolades for the man considered its greatest champion in the post–Civil War era. Like poet George Washington Coleman, J. Allen Watts was on William and Mary's 200th anniversary program to pay tribute to the College and to Benjamin Ewell. Watts, a lawyer and state senator, remarked in his June 21 address:

> The resolute purpose and intense determination of the man was shown in this protracted, unequal fight for the rights of this College, which he loved so well. Of his relation to his students I need not speak. His kindness, his consideration, his interest in their welfare, was known and appreciated by all, and all received benefits from their association with

him. I wish, Mr. Chairman, that I had the skill to depict the life and worth of this Virginia gentleman in true and accurate words as an example and model for those who had not the privilege of association with him, and to leave a proper memorial of this steadfast friend of William and Mary. I trust that now that the dearest wish of his heart has been gratified, he will enjoy the rest he so richly deserved.[11]

Before Benjamin Ewell's death in 1894, he had the satisfaction of seeing the College set on a new course: the joining of its aristocratic past to a progressive future, one in which young men could rise professionally as teachers through their education at William and Mary. Although it retained aspects of its classical curriculum, the College, like the Commonwealth, was adjusting to the realities of the New South. Responding to politics, social change, and the fortunes of war had been an almost insurmountable challenge. Whereas the College's English roots and unique royal lineage had been variously deemed antiquated or romantic, this heritage intersected with an important societal trend in the last part of the 19th century: increased interest in the Anglo-Saxon culture's heritage in America.

Higher education mirrored the blend of progress and heritage that characterized much of the South after the Civil War. Academics there saw scientific education and industrialization as the key to the region's future and many believed that the lack of these strengths led to the South's defeat.[12] Some higher education leaders like Benjamin Ewell saw postbellum reconciliation with the North as essential, attempting political and media connections as well as academic ones. Northern and Southern educators began to find common ground in crediting America's Anglo-Saxon roots for the nation's technological progress.[13] For Southern scholars, technical education was a stepping stone to invigorating the New South. However, their promotion of Southern history within a framework of scientific study did more than align their work within the discipline's modern perimeters. The *William and Mary College Quarterly Historical Papers* edited by President Tyler (now the notable history journal, *The William and Mary Quarterly*) and other scholarly works had the capacity to contest Northern historians' views of the war and Southern history in general.

As president, professor, and recognized scholar, Lyon Gardiner Tyler shared Ewell's deep appreciation for the history of the College. The Tyler family's bond to William and Mary spanned generations. His grandfather John Tyler studied at the College and served as Governor of Virginia (1808–1811), later becoming a member of his alma mater's Board of Visitors.[14] Former President John Tyler followed in his father's footsteps as a William and Mary student (1802–1807) and as governor of Virginia

(1825–1827). Awarded an honorary degree from the College in 1854, he became its chancellor in 1859, serving until 1862.[15]

Although Lyon G. Tyler attended the University of Virginia for his undergraduate and legal studies, he was destined to be one of William and Mary's great contributors, also known for his achievements as an educator and scholar of Virginia history. Tyler guided the College to its 1906 ranking as a state institution, and to another milestone as the first state college to admit women. Tyler's writings on his family's history, on Virginia history, and on Williamsburg's past argued for their collective significance to the nation, and formed an important body of historical and genealogical information. Among his many works, Tyler also addressed the South's position in the Civil War. He wrote and published *A Confederate Catechism: The War of 1861–1865*. This small pamphlet, which had a third printing in 1929, provided answers to twenty questions about such controversial topics as the cause of Southern secession, slavery as the cause of the Civil War, and whether the firing on Fort Sumner began the war. Tyler's answer to the question "What did the South fight for?" began with a sentence in capital letters: "IT FOUGHT TO REPEL INVASION AND FOR SELF-GOVERNMENT, JUST AS THE FATHERS OF THE AMERICAN REVOLUTION HAD DONE." Throughout the rest of this response and others within the *Catechism*, Tyler's succinct arguments strongly contested Northern views of the war, the South, and President Lincoln's goals.[16]

Historian Peter Carmichael has written that the 1890s through the 1940s represented a time in which "Virginians looked to history to find sustenance, secure a collective identity, and along the way promote cultural tourism."[17] This search for significance manifested in diverse ways beyond historical discourse. During the waning decades of the 19th century, many white Southerners felt a need to justify the Confederate Army's defeat and the core principles leading to sectionalism and secession. Arguments for slavery and states' rights reemerged as the Old South and the New South interfaced.

William and Mary's history at this point intersects with the social and political promotion of racial purity, a product of the times. In the early 1900s, there was a growing national resistance to European immigration, particularly newer immigrants from southern and eastern Europe. These groups, it was charged, were not assimilating adequately into American society and also "diluted the purity of the nation's racial stock."[18] Former wartime adversaries found common ground in the combined legacy of Anglo-Saxon, Anglo-Nordic, and Teutonic races. This heritage, they felt, had been critical to founding America and forging its greatness.[19] Proponents of the eugenics movement such as Madison Grant (author of a popular 1916 book, *The Passing of the Great Race*) warned that to mix Nordic races with other "lower" races such as African American or American Indian jeopardized white civilization and would cause its decline.[20] The Ku Klux Klan re-emerged and by the 1920s, racial purists advanced a series of Jim Crow laws in Virginia to halt miscegenation and potential "passing" by non-whites.[21] In his inaugural address on October 19, 1921, William and Mary's incoming president J.A.C. Chandler asked:

> Who should be the constituents of the College? As I see it, this college should appeal to all types of our citizens, but there is one type that I am especially anxious to continue to enroll in the student body. It is that sturdy Anglo Saxon stock found in our state....[22]

The *Daily Press* in Newport News, Virginia, reflected the attitudes of many white Virginians in a March 15, 1924, editorial titled, "Integrity of the Anglo-Saxon Race." Editor-owner Walter S. Copeland stated, "The Anglo-Saxon race has no moral right to amalgamate with any colored race, for in doing so, it would destroy itself." Further, Copeland was adamant: "Rather than that we would prefer that every white child in the United States were sterilized and the Anglo-Saxon race left to perish in its purity."[23]

As the product of their times, such beliefs contributed to the development of eugenics-related coursework and organizations. Anglo-Saxon Clubs were founded at selected campuses and towns around Virginia by John Powell, noted composer and supporter of Virginia's racial integrity movement. In addition to a local chapter in Newport News established by W.S. Copeland and another chapter in Williamsburg, one of these clubs was organized at William and Mary, according to a February 15, 1924, announcement in its student newspaper, *The Flat Hat*.[24] Seeking new members, the announcement stated that chapters were already "in full operation" at the University of Virginia, Washington and Lee, Randolph-Macon College and other Virginia institutions of higher learning.[25] According to a previous *Flat Hat* article on May 18, 1923, a group of about twenty young men met in 1923 under the guidance of John Powell "and affected [the] tentative organization of a Post of the Anglo-Saxon Club of America." The clubs' emergence on college and university campuses mirrored political and cultural opinions of the white majority in Virginia. In 1926, President Julian Chandler faced a related decision: how to deal with the gift of a flagpole and United States flag from the revived Ku Klux Klan, which supported the racial purity movement. Although he accepted the flag and flagpole, Chandler did not fully acquiesce, refuting the KKK's position in his speech at the September 26 ceremony.[26] The president faced support and criticism regarding his handling of the situation. Afterward, the flagpole marked College Corner (at the intersection of Jamestown Road and South Boundary Street) until the late 1950s, but the tablet identifying its donors was removed in the 1940s.[27] In an interview conducted with former professor and administrator J. Wilfred Lambert about his student days and fifty-year career at the College, Lambert recalled that "shortly after" John Edward Pomfret became president of William and Mary in 1941, Pomfret asked at a staff meeting about the flagpole and the tablet attributing it to the Ku Klux Klan:

> He [Pomfret] remarked that he was not in favor of vandalism, but he would have no objection whatever if the bronze plaque were taken off that flagpole and disappeared forever. The next day the bronze plaque disappeared, and I have no way of knowing what on earth happened to it.[28]

Alumnus Thomas Lipscomb '61 wrote that President Alvin Duke Chandler was responsible for quietly moving the flagpole to the Marshall-Wythe Law School parking lot 33 years later.[29] Recent research by William and Mary professor Terry Meyers and the College's Lemon Project notes that the flagpole was "recycled" at James Blair Hall, where it flew the Virginia flag during Massive Resistance.[30]

In addition to a hardening stance on race issues in Virginia, sweeping changes in state public education policies, and the College's resulting revitalization, two other developments influenced William and Mary in the first decades of the new century. First, higher education marked a new phase in which colleges and universities viewed their pasts as unique institutional markers. In the 1870s, William and Mary was not the only colonial college with surviving 17th- and 18th-century structures; as John Thelin found in his research on American campuses between 1870 and 1930, period buildings at Princeton and Brown at the time reflected low degrees of institutional attention to their colonial legacies.[31] Yet as time went on, the onset of historic revivalism in American culture favored buildings that looked old, rather than modern, influencing campus construction. Similarly, colleges and universities infused tradition into campus life and their public personas, adding mascots, extracurricular traditions, and other markers of loyalty and heritage.[32]

Second, a cultural renaissance based on early American history and its preservation began in the late 1800s and flourished in the early 20th century, as demonstrated in the restoration of Virginia's colonial capital led by philanthropist John D. Rockefeller Jr. In his history of the restoration of Williamsburg, Anders Greenspan points out that the creation of the Colonial Williamsburg Foundation transformed a small town essentially neglected in the 1920s into "one of the United States' premier social history museums and tourist destinations."³³ Despite the perceived intrusion of the restoration effort, by Yankees at that, among some old-time residents, others felt pride and excitement in the Cinderella-like transformation underway in their town. Emotions were also tied to the prevailing social attitudes of the time. A 1930 *Virginia Gazette* editorial predicted, "Williamsburg will be the most attractive place in America for those who love old traditions and are proud of their Anglo-Saxon lineage and of the men and women who made America what it is today."³⁴ The emergence of such historical revivalist and nationalist sentiments helped to form broader American attitudes from the late 19th century into the 1920s. As their familiar 19th-century world was assaulted by rapid-fire change, many people felt a sense of uneasiness about what might be lost in the march toward modernity.³⁵ Recalling the Revolutionary War period's fight for independence and the Founding Fathers' philosophies was a reminder of core American values, and created a surge of nationalist pride.

> After philanthropist John D. Rockefeller agreed to fund the town's restoration in 1924, Williamsburg's colonial heritage increasingly overshadowed its nineteenth-century past. Some community members fought that development in public forums, while other community members advocated for (or acquiesced to) the transformation of their town. One retired Army officer, Major Samuel D. Freeman, spoke up in the 1928 community meeting in which Dr. W.A.R. Goodwin revealed the extent of Rockefeller's involvement in purchasing historic Williamsburg properties. Freeman disagreed with the proposed transformation of buildings, streets, and green spaces downtown, for the purposes of Restoration. Although he expressed trust in both Rockefeller and Goodwin, Freeman feared for the future: Dr. Goodwin has spoken very beautifully and very poetically. But is this a philanthropic enterprise? Is it altruistic? There is no doubt but that the contract will go through, but I want you to know that there is one man who has had something to say on the other side. We will reap dollars, but will we own our town? Will you not be in the position of a butterfly pinned to a card in a glass cabinet, or like a mummy unearthed in the tomb of Tutankhamen?³⁶

The growth of the Colonial Williamsburg Foundation into an internationally known living history museum would not have been possible without the accumulation of acres of public and private property. The College was almost immediately affected with the restoration of the Main Building in 1928–1931, and its renaming as the Sir Christopher Wren Building. Restoring the President's House and the Brafferton to an 18th-century appearance in 1931 visually reinforced William and Mary's colonial heritage. The city's social fabric also changed: African Americans had conducted successful businesses, held property, and experienced town life with their white neighbors prior to the restoration. However, the exclusionary atmosphere that developed echoed Virginia's racial stance in the early 20th century.[37] In the new interpretation that emerged through the restoration, Williamsburg's social history was predominantly white, male, and bound to its colonial past. Williamsburg's Civil War memories in turn became an anachronism. They were symbolically transferred in 1932 when the city's Confederate monument was moved from Palace Green (formerly Courthouse Green) in connection with the Governor's Palace reconstruction.[38] Erected by the United Daughters of the Confederacy and local citizens in 1908, the large obelisk was dedicated to the Confederate soldiers and sailors of Williamsburg and James City County. Moving it was the start of a public controversy and several relocations in the 20th century, including the monument's current placement in Williamsburg's Bicentennial Park. The monument, the Civil War, and those honored dead no longer occupied their former place in the city's public memory.

Other factors in this loss of memory were the dying off of Civil War veterans and their contemporaries, and losses of historical records through fire and time. Yet despite early researchers' primary focus on documenting Williamsburg's 18th-century history and buildings, they did capture important aspects of the Civil War past along the way. They interviewed residents who experienced the Civil War's impact on the town and College firsthand and often included stories and snippets of local and family history in their documentation. These eyewitness stories were documented and today form an important part of available primary resources on the period; they have informed this narrative. At William and Mary, Earl Gregg Swem Library's Special Collections has extensive related holdings such as the papers of Benjamin Ewell and Faculty Minutes for the College, with a comprehensive digital database. Area volunteers currently are transcribing handwritten period documents for digital accessibility to the past. These emerging resources, the Special Collections Research Center's "From Fights to Rights" exhibits, and ongoing research by faculty and students have created a significant new perspective on the College's history during the one hundred-fiftieth anniversary of the Civil War.

To question the College's traditional narrative is to acknowledge what many now view as a shadowed side of the past. Such re-examinations contest deeply embedded perspectives of William and Mary within its own community and in popular perceptions of American history, but the College is hardly alone in this process. In the larger arena of state and national history, many major institutions are exploring their historical narratives, and in some cases bringing past actions into alignment with 21st century social, political, and historical views. The board of the Virginia Press Association acted in 2000 to remove Walter S. Copeland's name from an award for journalistic integrity and community service established in 1949.[39] In 2010, Radford University's Board of Visitors voted unanimously to rename Powell Hall, originally named in 1968.[40] It had previously honored John Powell, a noted Virginia pianist and composer as well as an ardent white supremacist responsible in part for the successful passage of Virginia's Racial Integrity Act of 1924. In both cases, action was taken soon after contemporary researchers discovered these connections.

In 2009, William and Mary's Board of Visitors voted to acknowledge the College's part in owning and exploiting slave labor, and in later supporting the Jim Crow era. The College's "Lemon" Project, supported by the Board of Visitors and the Lyon G. Tyler Department of History, is a related research effort launched in 2009 "charged with exploring the College's past ties to slavery and to exclusionary Jim Crow practices."[41] This research has addressed multiple aspects of that history, including: antebellum defense of the institution of slavery; racial intolerance in the Jim Crow era; desegregation milestones in 1951, 1963, and 1967; and the establishment of the first African American academic program in 1997. Moreover, the Lemon Project has put a face on that history by acknowledging African Americans left out of the College's saga, such as George Greenhow, who as a free black custodian was taught to read and write by a student in the 1850s. The project received an Image Award from William and Mary's NAACP chapter and was also named Community Organization of the Year.

As noted earlier, William and Mary's Earl Gregg Swem Library undertook a major four-year project in 2011 to commemorate the one hundred fiftieth anniversary of the Civil War and the fiftieth anniversary of the Civil Rights movement. In 2011 and 2012, a major preservation initiative on the Historic Campus yielded significant evidence of Civil War–era features, including a well and defensive works thrown up in the vicinity of the Wren Building.[42] Archaeologists from the William and Mary Center for Archaeological Research also uncovered period artifacts such as uniform buttons, dishes, and rifle rounds.[43] These discoveries, like a recent pre–Civil War drawing of the Wren Building acquired by Special Collections, invite the prospect that more of the College's relationship to this period will be discovered and shared.

It is well to remember that when people examine the past, particularly one surrounded by conflict and controversy, they may succumb unawares to *presentism*, or historical analysis based on current beliefs and values. There is a temptation to judge the past harshly, to romanticize it, or otherwise view it anachronistically. Yet, if the voices of the past do not ring true to current social mores or values, that does not make them less relevant. Rather, it holds us accountable to seek a fuller, more inclusive understanding of those times and the people who lived them. For The College of William and Mary, this means seeking reconnection to those who went before.

In the generations since the Civil War, many people have reflected upon William and Mary's history in public, among them President Warren G. Harding. He participated in J.A.C. Chandler's formal inauguration as the College's nineteenth president on October 19, 1921.[44] In his address, Harding (an honorary degree recipient) referred to "the tragedy of fratricidal war, in which [William and Mary] escaped destruction only at the price of a baptism in fire."[45]

Some listeners in 1921 still knew firsthand what crises that trial by fire inflicted upon William and Mary and how many, especially Benjamin Ewell, strove to save it. Recognition is due those Civil War leaders who shaped the course of the war, just as we honor Revolutionary War figures from the College who led America to independence. It is past time to fully commemorate the William and Mary students, faculty, and alumni who served the Union or the Confederacy. As it had done before, William and Mary contributed its own: those who helped to shape the course of the Civil War, those who gave their lives, and those who committed themselves to the College and the nation as both sought to rebuild. These forgotten souls remind us that William and Mary's 19th-century struggles in war and peace were vital to today's modern university and to the history of higher education in the South. Their conflicts are controversial, often difficult to revisit, and in some ways have been masked by myth. Yet to look more deeply informs our understanding of how the College has endured these four centuries. In President Harding's words, "Its genius for drawing close to the spirit of the times, for always contributing greatly to the leadership of great affairs, has been the abiding glory of William and Mary."[46]

Military Service Table

The Civil War Military Service of William and Mary Students and Alumni by Class Year

(Categorized by military rank and years of attendance — grouped by decade for alumni)

Year	Total	Officers	Enlisted	Pvt.	Cpl.	Sgt.	Lt.	Capt.	Maj.	Col.	Gen.
1860–1861	59	17	42	30	6	6	10	6	1	—	—
1850–1859	142	84	58	42	2	14	27	44	4	8	1
1840–1849	74	45	29	23	2	4	6	17	13	8	—
1830–1839	45	27	19	16	2	1	3	11	2	10	1
1820–1829	6	4	2	1	—	1	—	1	1	2	—
1810–1819	1	1	—	—	—	—	—	—	1	—	—
1800–1809	1	1	—	—	—	—	—	—	—	—	1
	(328)	(178)	(150)	(112)	(12)	(26)	(46)	(79)	(22)	(28)	(3)

- There are some alumni who were identified as Confederate Army veterans in College publications for which specific military service could not be determined. They are therefore not included in this table.
- There were at least 32 alumni (not included on this table) who served as surgeons — all in the Confederate Army.
- Only seven individuals on this table, Lt. Gen. Winfield Scott, 1st Lt. Philip A. Johnson (29th Illinois Infantry), Pvt. James Beatty (1st Maryland Light Artillery), Pvt. H.B. Hammond (Maine), Pvt. Benjamin Howes (41st New York Infantry), Pvt. J.J.H. Newman (2nd Maryland Infantry), and Pvt. William Reynolds (1st Maryland Infantry), served in the Union Army. The rest served in the Confederate Army.
- There were at least five alumni (not included on this table) who enrolled at the College in the later 1860s, following service in the Confederate Army.

APPENDIX A

The Civil War Service of William and Mary Students, 1861–1865

* = *Confederate military service has not been determined (although the student is honored for Confederate military service on the memorial plaque in the Wren Building, no evidence to substantiate the claim has been found).*

Argyle, T.R. — Private, 4th VA Cavalry, CSA (Co. F). From Goochland, VA. Died in service (9/10/1861), Goochland, VA.

Armistead, Robert T. — Private, 3rd VA Cavalry, CSA. From Williamsburg, VA. With General Lee's Army at Appomattox.

Atkinson, R.C. — Private, 3rd VA Cavalry, CSA. From Smithfield, VA.

Ayres, Richard J., Jr. — 2nd Lieutenant, 39th VA Infantry, CSA. From Accomac, VA.

Barlow, T.J. — Sergeant, 32nd VA Infantry, CSA (Co. C). Captured at Antietam (9/17/62), Paroled at Shepherdstown, WV (9/25/62). Paroled at Appomattox CH, 4/9/65. Member — Portsmouth, VA, veteran camp. From Williamsburg, VA.

Bidgood, J.V. — Sgt. Major, 32nd VA Infantry, CSA (Co. C). Captured at Sailor's Creek (4/6/65), Took oath of allegiance and released 6/23/65. Became VP of J.W. Randolph publishers after war, also served as a colonel in VA Militia. Active in Confederate veterans' groups. From Williamsburg, VA. Living as of 1916.

Browne, William O. — Sergeant, 12th VA Infantry, CSA. Mortally wounded in action Malvern Hill, VA (7/1/62). Died in Richmond, VA, hospital (8/3/62). From Hicksford, VA.

Bush, John W. — Corporal, 9th VA Cavalry, CSA (Co. H). From Burnt Ordinary, VA.

Chandler, John H. — Captain, 40th VA Infantry, CSA (Co. K). Captured 4/6/65 at Sailor's Creek, VA, POW at Johnson's Island. Released on oath (6/19/65). From Westmoreland Co., VA.

Coke, J.A. — Captain, 1st VA Artillery, CSA. From Williamsburg, VA.

Day, William H. — Captain, 1st NC Infantry, CSA (Co. K). From Grove Hill, NC.

Deans, J.H. — Private, United Artillery, CSA. From Gloucester, VA.

Dix, Henry S. — Private, 32nd VA Infantry, CSA (Co. C). Later in Mathews Light

Artillery. Disabled and discharged due to "disease of spine." From Williamsburg, VA.
Dix, James H.— Private, 32nd VA Infantry, CSA (Co. C), Died of Typhoid. First "Junior Guard" Casualty (1861). From Accomac, VA.
Dix, John G.— Private, Mathews Light Artillery, CSA. From Williamsburg, VA.
Fosque, George B.— Sergeant, 39th and 46th VA Infantries, CSA. Captured at Roanoke 2/8/62, paroled 2/21/62 at Elizabeth City, NC. Captured 3/30/65. Took oath at Point Lookout prison (6/4/65). From Onancock, VA.
Galt, W.— Private, 4th VA Cavalry, CSA. From Fluvanna, VA.
Gee, Sterling H.— Captain, 1st NC Infantry, CSA (Co. K). Killed in action at Battle of Five Forks (1865). From Weldon, NC.
Gwynn, Worth O.— Corporal, 4th VA Cavalry, CSA. From Norfolk, VA.
Hardy, James — Private, 12th VA Infantry, CSA (Co. K). From Norfolk, VA.
Harrison, Charles S.— Captain, 10th Battalion, VA Heavy Artillery, CSA. From Prince George Co., VA.
Harrison, George E.— Private, 1st VA Artillery, CSA (Co. E). From Cabin Point, VA.
Hough, Gresham — Private, 1st MD Infantry and 1st MD Cavalry, CSA. From Baltimore, MD.
Hoxton, William —1st Lieutenant (Adjutant for Inspector of Artillery), CSA. From Washington, D.C.
Hubbard, Benjamin H.B.— Sergeant, 9th VA Cavalry, CSA. From Lancaster Co., VA.
Jones, Henley T., Jr.— 2nd Lieutenant, 32nd VA Infantry, CSA (Co. C). Paroled at Appomattox CH (4/9/65). Farmer and druggist in Williamsburg after war. Active in Confederate veterans' groups. Died 7/16/02.
Jones, Richard H.— Private, 40th VA Infantry, CSA (Co. G). From Hampton, VA.
Jordan, H.E.— Private, 34th VA Infantry, CSA. From Richmond, VA.
*Kellam, F.C.A., Jr.— CSA. From Accomac, VA.
Lawson, James S.—1st Lieutenant, 32nd VA Infantry, CSA (Co. G) and later 1st VA Artillery. From James City Co., VA.
*Lippitt, Armistead L.— CSA. From Alexandria, VA.
Macmurdo, Meriwether A.— Private, 4th VA Cavalry, CSA. Discharged 11/25/61. From Hanover Co., VA.
Mason, George — Corporal, 5th Battalion, VA Infantry, CSA. From Greensville, VA.
Meade, Henry J.— Corporal, 16th VA Cavalry, CSA. From Bedford, VA.
Mercer, Thomas H.— Private, 32nd VA Infantry, CSA (Co. C), later a Lt. of Artillery. From Williamsburg, Va. With Gen. Lee's Army at Appomattox. Died from pneumonia in 9/65.
Miller, George S.— 2nd Lieutenant, 26th VA Infantry, CSA (Co. D). From Mathews Co., VA.
Morecock, W.H.E.—1st Lieutenant, 32nd VA Infantry, CSA (Co. C). Died on 4/12/96. From Williamsburg, VA.
Myers, J.D.— Private, 32nd VA Infantry, CSA (Co. C). From Lexington, VA.
Newton, Norton C.— Private, 6th VA Infantry, CSA (Co. G.). Druggist pre/postwar from Norfolk. Substitute for a John H. Williams.
Page, Peyton N.— Major, Staff Officer, CSA. From Gloucester, VA.
Peachy, W.D.— Private, 3rd VA Infantry, CSA. From Williamsburg, VA.
Poindexter, Charles — Private, VA Light Artillery/Richmond Howitzer's (Anderson's Co.) CSA. From Richmond, VA.
Ponton, Henry D.— Private, 12th NC Infantry, CSA. From Weldon, NC.

Reese, William A.—Private, 53rd VA Infantry, CSA (Co. F). From Greensville, VA.
Reynolds, William—Private, 1st MD Infantry, USA, cousin of Benjamin S. Ewell. From Baltimore, MD.
Robertson, G.W.—Private, 53rd VA Infantry, CSA (Co. H). From Petersburg, VA.
Sharp, H.T.—Private, Signal Corps, CSA. From Norfolk, VA.
Sherwell, W.—Corporal, 32nd VA Infantry, CSA (Co. I). From Williamsburg, VA.
Slater, L.P.—Sergeant, 32nd VA Infantry, CSA (Co. C). From Williamsburg, VA.
Spratley, E.W.—Private, 12th VA Infantry, CSA (Co. I). Discharged 7/22/62. Furnished substitute, John L. Jeans. From Greensville, VA.
Stubbs, Thomas J.—Private, 34th VA Infantry, CSA (Co. A). From Gloucester, VA. Prof. of math at William and Mary after the war.
Stubbs, William C.—Corporal, 40th VA Cavalry Battalion and then 24th VA Cavalry Regiment, CSA. From Gloucester, VA.
Trueheart, W.C.—1st Lieutenant, 23rd VA Infantry, CSA. From Prince Edward, VA.
Tucker, John H.—Private, 3rd VA Cavalry, CSA (Co. I).
Tucker, Thomas S. Beverly—2nd Lieutenant, CSA. From Williamsburg, VA. Aide to Maj. Gen. Lafayette McClaws. Severely wounded at Fredericksburg. Reenrolled at W&M after war. Died in 1872 due to complications from wound.
Tunstall, Alexander, Jr.—1st Lieutenant, CSA. Staff Officer. From Norfolk, VA.
Wash, Alphonso A.—Private, 4th VA Cavalry, CSA. Was possibly in the 15th VA. Infantry first as a private. From Montpelier, VA.
Williams, James H.—Private, 16th VA Infantry, CSA (Co. C). From Northampton Co., VA.
Williams, John G.—Private, 13th VA Infantry, CSA (Co. A). From Orange Co., VA. Served as a courier for Lt. Gen. Jubal Early, surrendered at Appomattox (4/9/65). Later became a prominent lawyer and bank president in Orange—also served as commonwealth's attorney. Died 9/26/11.
Williams, John N.—Private, 6th VA Infantry, CSA (Co. G). From Norfolk, VA. Discharged for typhoid fever (4/16/63), later joined the Richmond Howitzers. Worked for his father (who was Norfolk's city treasurer) and was later a druggist after the war. Member of Pickett-Buchanan Camp, UCV. Died in 1914.
Wise, Richard A.—Captain, 10th VA Cavalry, CSA. Later resigned and enlisted as a private in 4th VA Cavalry. Served balance of war as a captain/asst. inspector general on his father's staff. Surrendered at Greensboro, NC, in 1865. Earned his MD at Med. College of VA in 1869. Professor at W&M in years after war. Headed Eastern State and served in the VA House of Delegates from 1885–87 and the U.S. House from 1898 to 1900. Died in 1900.
Wyman, F.M.—Private, 21st Mississippi Infantry, CSA (Co. A). From Vicksburg, MS.

APPENDIX B

The Civil War Service of William and Mary Faculty, 1861–1865

Ewell, Benjamin S.—Colonel, 32nd VA Infantry Regiment (CSA), later served on staffs of Gen. Joseph E. Johnston and Lt. Gen. Richard S. Ewell. President of William and Mary, 1848–1849 and 1854–1888.

Joynes, Edward S.—Civilian Administrator, Confederate War Department, Private–3rd VA Regiment/Local Defense Group, CSA. Later a prominent Southern educator.

McCandlish, Thomas P.—Captain, Quartermaster, 32nd VA Infantry, CSA. Professor of languages at W&M after the war.

Morris, Charles—Major, CSA. Initially served in the 4th Virginia Infantry. Later served on staffs of Maj. Gen. Lafayette McClaws and Brig. Gen. Alexander R. Lawton. Prominent Southern educator after the war.

Morrison, Robert J.—Captain, Quartermaster, 32nd VA Infantry, CSA. Died of typhoid (1861).

Snead, Thomas T. L.—Captain, CSA Engineering Corps. Served with Lt. Gen. Thomas "Stonewall" Jackson. Returned as math professor to W&M after war.

Taliaferro, Edwin—1st Lieutenant, 32nd VA Infantry, CSA. Later a captain on Maj. Gen. Lafayette McClaws's staff. Commanded the Confederate Arsenal in Macon, Georgia, as a major for the balance of the war. Returned to William and Mary as a Latin professor after the war. Died in 1867 from tuberculosis.

APPENDIX C

The Civil War Service of William and Mary Alumni, 1861–1865

If a degree is listed next to the person's name, he graduated in the year indicated. If no degree is listed the date is the year of enrollment. Degrees: A.B. = Bachelor of Arts; L.B. = Bachelor of Law; N.B. = Bachelor of Natural Science; B.P. = Bachelor of Philosophy; A.M. = Master of Arts; Ll.D. = Doctor of Laws, honorary degree.

1804

Scott, Winfield — Lt. General, USA. Served in the War of 1812 and commanded all U.S. forces during the Mexican War. Ran unsuccessfully for president in 1852. Commander of all Union forces in early stages of Civil War. Died in 1866 at age 79. From Dinwiddie Co., VA.

1805

Crittenden, John J. — U.S. Attorney General, U.S. Senator, gov. of KY, U.S. Rep. Served in the War of 1812. U.S. Attorney Gen. under Presidents William H. Harrison and Millard Fillmore. An anti-secessionist and Lincoln supporter, he worked to keep Kentucky in the Union. Died in 1863. From Versailles, KY.

1806

Tyler, John — 10th president of the United States, V.P., U.S. Senator, gov. of VA, U.S. Rep. Chairman of 1861 Peace Convention in Washington, D.C. Served in the Provisional Confederate Congress. Elected to the Confederate Congress, but died before he could take his seat in 1862. From Charles City Co., VA.

1809

Rives, William C. — U.S. Senator and U.S. Rep. for VA before the Civil War. Member of 1861 Peace Convention in Washington, D.C. Later a member of the Confederate Congress. Died in 1868. From Amherst Co., VA.

1810–1811

Edmund Ruffin — Southern rights activist. Supposedly fired first shot at Fort Sumter. From Prince George Co., VA.

1814-1815
Morton, Jackson — U.S. Senator for FL before the Civil War. Member of Confederate Congress. From FL.

1816-1817
Macfarland, William H. (Ll.D., 1870) — Member of Confederate Congress.

1817-1818
Lyons, James (Ll.D., 1870) — Member of Confederate Congress. From Hanover Co., VA.

1818-1819
Morton, Jeremiah — U.S. Rep. for VA. Member of 1861 Secession Convention (younger brother of Jackson Morton). From Culpeper Co., VA.
Sawyer, Samuel T. — U.S. Rep. for NC before the Civil War. Major — CSA. From NC.

1820
Mason, James M. — U.S. Senator and U.S. Rep. for VA before the Civil War. Served as Commissioner for the Confederacy to Great Britain and France during the war. One of the two diplomats at the center of the famous *Trent* Affair in 1861. Received Law Degree from W&M. Died in 1871. From Fairfax Co., VA.

1820-1821
Robertson, Wyndham — Gov. of VA. Member of Committee of Nine. From Richmond, VA.

1822-1823
Booker, George — Major, CSA. Staff Officer. From Hampton, VA.

1823-1824
Munford, George W. (L.B., 1824) — Secretary of the Commonwealth, VA. From Richmond, VA.

1824-1825
Brockenbrough, John W. — Member of Confederate Congress. From Hanover Co., VA.
Garland, Samuel — Member of VA Secession Convention (1861). Grandnephew of Patrick Henry. From Amherst Co., VA.

1825-1826
Garland, William H. (A.B., 1826) — Lt. Colonel, 4th LA Infantry, CSA. Grandnephew of Patrick Henry. From Amherst County, VA.
Stuart, Alexander H.H. — U.S. Secretary of the Interior. Member of the Committee of Nine. From Staunton, VA.

1826-1827
Jeffries, James M. — Captain, 24th VA Cavalry (Co. E). From King and Queen Co., VA.

1827-1828
Cunliffe, Edwin — Sergeant, 41st VA Infantry (Co. B). From Manchester, VA.
Selden, William A. — Surgeon, CSA. From Richmond, VA.

1828-1829
Douglass, Samuel — Colonel, CSA. From Petersburg, VA.
Robins, A.W. (L.B., 1829) — Private, 24th VA Cavalry (Co. D). From Gloucester Co., VA.

1829–1830
Chambliss, John R. (L.B., 1829) — Member of Confederate Congress. Father of Brig. Gen. John R. Chambliss, Jr., CSA. From Sussex County.

1830–31
Blow, George (A.B., 1831) — Lt. Colonel, 14th VA Infantry, CSA. Brig. General in Virginia Militia prior to the war. Captured during fall of Norfolk, 1862. Prominent judge after the war. From Sussex Co., VA.

Tompkins, C.Q. (A.B., 1831) — Colonel, 22nd VA Infantry, CSA. Served with Col. George S. Patton, CSA (ancestor of WWII Gen. George S. Patton). From Mathews Co., VA.

1831–1832
Bowden, Lemuel J. (L.B., 1832) — U.S. Senator (VA). From Williamsburg, VA.

Early, Samuel H. (A.B., 1832) — 2nd Lieutenant, CSA. Brother of Lt. Gen. Jubal Early, CSA. Staff Officer.

1832–1833
Taliaferro, A.G. (A.B., 1833) — Colonel, 23rd VA Infantry. From Gloucester Co., VA.

1834–1835
Crafford, William — Private, 32nd VA Infantry (Co. H), CSA. From Warwick Co., VA.

Henley, John A. — Captain, 32nd VA Infantry (Co. C), CSA. From Williamsburg, VA.

Segar, Richard — Private, 34th VA Infantry (Co. K), CSA. From Urbana, VA.

1835–1836
Leake, Walter D. (L.B., 1836) — Captain, Leake's Company, Virginia Light Artillery, CSA. From Goochland Co., VA.

1836–1837
Banister, Monro — Surgeon, CSA. From Amelia Co., VA.

Bayly, William P. — Private, 39th VA Infantry (Co. D), CSA. From Accomac Co., VA.

Carrington, George C. — Surgeon, 6th VA Cavalry, CSA. From Halifax Co., VA.

Harrison, John P. — Captain, 5th Battalion VA Infantry (Co. D), CSA. From Charles City Co., VA.

Mallory, Charles K. — Colonel, 115th Virginia Militia, CSA. From Hampton, VA.

McGowan, William J. — Private, 13th VA Cavalry (Co. F), CSA. From Petersburg, VA.

Richardson, George — Colonel, CSA. From Kentucky.

Robinson, Powhatan — Captain, Engineering Corps, CSA. From Petersburg, VA.

Tyler, John, Jr. (A.B., 1837) — Asst. Secretary of War, CSA (son of Pres. John Tyler). From Charles City Co., VA.

Tyler, Robert (L.B., 1837) — Registrar, Confederate Treasury (son of Pres. John Tyler). From Charles City Co., VA.

1837–38
Clarke, James L. — Private, 40th VA Infantry (Co. C), CSA. From Gloucester, Co., VA.

Dew, Benjamin F. (A.B., 1838) — 1st Lieutenant, 9th VA Militia (Co. B), CSA. From King and Queen Co., VA.

Faulcon, Jacob — Captain, 5th VA Cavalry (Co. E), CSA. From Surry Co., VA.

Galt, John M. (A.B., 1838) — Major, CSA. Staff Officer. From Williamsburg, VA.

Grigsby, John W. (L.B., 1838) — Colonel, CSA. From Rockbridge Co., VA.
McRae, Duncan — Colonel, 5th NC Infantry, CSA. From North Carolina.
Pollard, William G. — Captain, 53rd VA Infantry (Co. H), CSA. From King William Co., VA.
Steger, John O. (A.B., 1838) — Private, 3rd VA Infantry (Co. B), CSA. From Amelia Co., VA.
Yerby, William H. — Corporal, 32nd VA Infantry (Co. C), CSA. From Lancaster Co., VA.

1838-39

Cary, John B. (A.B., 1839) — Lt. Colonel, 32nd VA Infantry, CSA. Later a colonel on staff of Maj. Gen. John B. Magruder. From Hampton, VA.
Claiborne, Herbert A. (L.B., 1839) — Captain, CSA (Staff Officer). From Richmond, VA.
Coke, John A. (A.B., 1839) — 2nd Lieutenant, 32nd VA Infantry (Co. G), CSA. From Williamsburg, VA.
Crump, William W. (L.B., 1839) — Private, 12th VA Infantry (Co. G), CSA. From Richmond, VA.
Glenn, W.W. — Corporal, 4th MD Infantry (Co. F), USA. From Baltimore, MD.
Jones, James F. — Colonel, CSA. From Frederick Co., VA.
Montague, Charles W. (A.B., 1839) — Private, 5th VA Cavalry (Co. A), CSA. From Gloucester Co., VA.
Radford, Winston — Captain, 2nd VA Cavalry (Co. G), CSA. From Lynchburg, VA.
Stanard, John B. — Captain, CSA. From Fredericksburg, VA. Staff Officer.
Street, Waddy — Private, 9th VA Cavalry (Co. G), CSA. Lunenburg Co., VA.
Trible, Austin M. (L.B., 1839) — VA State Senator. Elected to the Confederate Congress. From Essex Co., VA.

1839-40

Beatty, James — Private, 1st Regiment, MD Light Artillery (Co. B), USA. From Baltimore, MD.
Field, Thomas W. — Private, 34th VA Infantry (Co. A), CSA. From Gloucester Co., VA.
Howes, Benjamin — Private, 41st New York Infantry (Co. B, C), USA. From New York, NY.
Jones, Walker F. — Private, 21st VA Militia (Co. C), CSA. From Gloucester Co., VA.
Jones, Warner T. (A.B., L.B., 1840) — Colonel, 21st VA Militia, CSA. Judge. From Gloucester Co., VA.
Meade, Peyton — Private, Richmond Howitzers, CSA. From Amelia Co., VA.
Old, William (L.B., 1840) — Captain, 4th VA Cavalry, CSA. From Powhatan, VA.
Pendleton, James P. — Private, 34th VA Infantry (Co. H), CSA. From King & Queen Co., VA.
Seawell, M. (L.B., 1840) — Private, 21st VA Militia (Co. C), CSA. Prominent lawyer. From Gloucester Co., VA.
Sims, William H. (A.B., 1840) — Private, 18th VA Infantry (Co. C, H), CSA. From Halifax Co., VA.
Skinner, Tristham L. (A.B., 1840) — Major, 1st NC Infantry, CSA. Killed in action during Battle of Seven Pines. From NC.
Wright, George T. — Sergeant, 9th VA Cavalry (Co. F), CSA. From Essex Co., VA.

1840-41

Dejarnette, Daniel C. — U.S. Rep. (1859-1861). Member of Confederate Congress. From Caroline Co., VA.

Drinkard, William R. (A.B., 1841) — Captain, 1st VA State Reserves (Co. E, I), CSA. From Petersburg, VA.

Finney, Oswold B. — Surgeon, CSA. Later a VA State Senator. From Accomac Co., VA.

Haymond, A.F. — Major, CSA. Staff Officer.

Taliaferro, William B. (A.B., 1841) — Major General, CSA. Nephew of James A. Seddon, CSA Sec. of War. Fought in Mexican War and served in the VA House of Delegates before and after the Civil War. Served under CSA Gen. "Stonewall Jackson" in 1861-62 and held commands in SC and FL in war's later stages. Served as a Judge after the war. Died in 1898. From Gloucester, VA.

Warren, John D. (A.B., 1841) — Captain, 15th VA Infantry (Co. G), CSA. From Richmond, VA.

1841-1842

Bayly, Edmund W. — Captain, 39th VA Infantry (Co. C), CSA. From Northampton Co., VA.

Custis, John T. — Private, 39th VA Infantry (Co. C), CSA. From Accomac Co., VA.

Montague, Robert L. (L.B., 1842) — Member of Confederate Congress. Lt. Gov. of VA (1860-1864). (Granduncle of Wallis Simpson). From Middlesex Co., VA.

Moon, John S. (L.B., 1842) — Private, 56th VA Infantry (Co. G), CSA.

Ould, Robert (L.B., 1842) — Colonel, Prisoners Commissioner, CSA. From Washington, D.C.

Power, Robert H. — Asst. Surgeon, 115th VA Militia, CSA. From Yorktown, VA.

Riddick, Washington C. — Captain, CSA. Staff Officer. From Suffolk, VA.

1842-43

Douglas, Beverley B. (N.B., 1843) — Major, CSA. 1st Lt./Captain, 9th VA Cavalry (Co. H), CSA. U.S. Rep. in the 1870s. From New Kent, VA.

Peace, Pleasant P. (L.B., 1843) — 1st Lieutenant, 47th NC Infantry (Co. G), CSA. From NC.

White, Chastain — Captain, CSA. Staff Officer.

1843-44

Berkeley, Edmund (A.B., 1844) — Lt. Colonel, 8th VA Infantry (Co. C), CSA. From Loudoun Co., VA.

Douthat, Fielding L. — Private, 3rd VA Cavalry (Co. D), CSA. From Charles City Co., VA.

Eppes, Richard — Private, 5th VA Cavalry (Co. F), CSA. From Prince George Co., VA.

Selden, Miles (A.B., 1844) — Captain, 10th Battalion, VA Heavy Artillery. Staff Officer. From Charles City Co., VA.

Smith, Sydney (A.B., 1844) — Private, 3rd VA Cavalry (Co. I), CSA. From York Co., VA.

Tinsley, Thomas — Captain, 32nd VA Infantry (Co. F), CSA. From Richmond, VA.

Vaiden, Henry M. (A.B., 1844) — 2nd Lieutenant, 5th Battalion VA Infantry (Co. A), CSA. From Williamsburg, VA.

Wingo, Edward T. (L.B., 1844) — Private, 3rd VA Reserves (Co. G), CSA. From Cumberland Co., VA.

1844-45

Armistead, Robert B. (A.B., 1845) — Major, 22nd Alabama Infantry, CSA. Killed in action during Battle of Shiloh. From Alabama.

Berkeley, William N. — Major, 8th VA Infantry (Co., D), CSA. From Loudoun Co., VA.

Christian, James S. (A.B., 1845, A.M., 1847) — 2nd Lieutenant, 3rd VA Cavalry (Co. F), CSA. From Williamsburg, VA.

Coupland, John R. — Private, 3rd VA Infantry Local Defense (Co. D), CSA. From Petersburg, VA.

Flewellen, J.F. — Corporal, 21st Texas Cavalry (Co. E), CSA. From Georgia.

Latane, Thomas — Sergeant, 9th VA Militia (Co. A), CSA. From Essex Co., VA.

Mayo, Joseph C. (A.B., 1845) — Private, 34th VA Infantry, CSA. From Norfolk, VA.

McClaws, Abraham H. (A.B., 1845) — Major, CSA. From Georgia.

Peachy, Beverley St. George T. — Surgeon, CSA. From Williamsburg, VA.

Scott, Charles L. — Major, 4th Alabama Infantry, CSA. Congressman and Resident in California prior to the war. From Richmond, VA.

Staples, Waller R. — Member of Confederate Congress. From Patrick Co., VA.

Thompson, George G. (A.B., 1845) — Captain, 13th VA Infantry, CSA. From Culpeper, VA.

1845-1846

Cary, Richard M. (A.B., 1846) — Major, CSA. From Hampton, VA.

Curtis, William H. — Corporal, 32nd VA Infantry (Co. A), CSA. From Warwick Co., VA.

Dejarnette, Joseph S. (A.B., 1846) — 1st Lieutenant, 47th VA Infantry (Co. H), CSA. From Caroline Co., VA.

Foster, Daniel H. (L.B., 1846) — Private, 61st VA Militia (Co. G, I), CSA. From Mathews Co., VA.

McAlpine, Charles R. — Captain, 41st VA Infantry (Co. 1G), CSA. From Portsmouth, VA.

Shield, Charles H. (A.B., 1846) — Private, 41st VA Infantry (Co. E), CSA. From Norfolk, VA.

Thompson, George G. (L.B., 1846) — Captain, CSA. From Culpeper, VA. Staff Officer.

Urquhart, Thomas — Major/Surgeon, 6th VA Infantry, CSA. From Southampton Co., VA.

Vaughan, William R. — Captain, 3rd VA Cavalry (Co. B), CSA. From Hampton, VA.

1846-47

Bernard, Jesse T. — Captain, CSA. Staff Officer. From Portsmouth, VA.

Christian, Robert (A.B., 1847, A.M., 1850) — Private, 3rd VA Cavalry (Co. F), CSA. From Williamsburg, VA.

Clarke, Joseph S.R. (L.B., 1847) — Private, 40th VA Infantry (Co. C), CSA. From Williamsburg, VA.

Coles, Peyton (A.B., 1847) — Surgeon, 59th VA Infantry, CSA. Albemarle Co., VA.

Councill, William J. — Private, 59th VA Militia (Hunter's Co.), CSA. From Suffolk, VA.

Crenshaw, Miles (A.B., 1847) — Captain, 16th VA Infantry (Co. F, S), CSA. Staff Officer. From Fluvanna Co., VA.

Fleming, Thomas M. — Private, 4th VA Cavalry (Co. F), CSA. From Goochland, VA.

Friend, John E. — Private, VA Second Class Militia (Wolff's Co.), CSA. From Chesterfield Co., VA.

Haile, William J. (A.B., 1847) — Lt. Colonel, CSA.
Hairston, Samuel H. (L.B., 1847) — Major, 11th MS Infantry, CSA. From Mississippi.
Harrison, Julian (A.B., 1847) — Colonel, CSA. From Goochland, VA.
Hope, James B. (L.B., 1847) — Major, CSA. Staff Officer. From Norfolk, VA.
Jones, George B. — Captain, 3rd VA Cavalry (Co. B), CSA. From Hampton, VA.
Jones, William B. (L.B., 1847) — Captain, 32nd VA Infantry, CSA. From Warwick Co. (Newport News), VA.
Kent, James — Colonel, CSA. From Petersburg, VA.
Mitchell, William H. — Sergeant, 9th VA Cavalry (Co. H), CSA From Richmond, VA.
Motley, John (L.B., 1847) — Captain, CSA. Staff Officer. From Williamsburg, VA.
Taliaferro, P.A. — Surgeon, CSA. Brother of Maj. Gen. William B. Taliaferro, CSA. From Gloucester, VA.
Waller, Hugh M. (A.B., 1847, A.M., 1850) — Captain, 32nd VA Infantry, CSA. From Williamsburg, VA.
Watson, Thomas N. (A.B., 1847) — Private, 3rd VA Cavalry, Co. K From Richmond, VA.
Weisiger, Junius L. — CSA. From Goochland, VA.

1847–48

Botts, Benjamin B. — Major, CSA. Staff Officer. From Richmond, VA.
Coke, Richard (L.B., 1848) — Captain, 15th Texas Infantry, CSA. Also a staff officer and later a governor of Texas. From Williamsburg, VA.
Dudley, W.A. — Private, 5th VA Cavalry (Co. D), CSA. From Petersburg, VA.
Edwards, Joseph — Private, 9th VA Infantry (Co. E), CSA. From Surry Co., VA.
Eubank, Richard (A.B., 1848) — Private, 9th VA Cavalry (Co. G), CSA. From Essex Co., VA.
Harris, Robert E. — Color Sergeant, 19th VA Infantry (Co. H), CSA. From Nelson Co., VA.
Murdaugh, Claudius W. (A.B., 1848) — 2nd Lieutenant, 41st VA Infantry (Co. G), CSA. From Portsmouth, VA.
Priddy, William H. — Surgeon, CSA. From Hanover Co., VA.
Redwood, Leroy H. — 1st Sergeant, Murphy's Battalion, AL Cavalry (Co. B), CSA. From Alabama.
Tucker, St. George (L.B., 1848) — Lt. Colonel, 15th VA Infantry, CSA. From Winchester, VA.

1849–1850

Fauntleroy, William H. — Private, 9th VA Cavalry (Co. F), CSA. From King and Queen Co., VA.
Hammond, H.B. — Private, unidentified Maine regiment, USA. From Maine.
Harrison, Randolph — Colonel, CSA. From Goochland, VA.
Neblett, Colin — 1st Lieutenant, 20th VA Infantry (Co. C), CSA. From Lunenburg Co., VA.
Tyler, Tazewell — Surgeon, CSA. Asst. Surgeon, 22nd Battalion VA Infantry. Son of U.S. President John Tyler. From Charles City Co., VA.

1850–51

Atkinson, William E. — Private, 3rd VA Cavalry (Co. F), CSA.
Blane, William (L.B., 1851) — Private, 3rd VA Cavalry (Co. C), CSA. From Halifax Co., VA.

Christian, Isaac H. (L.B., 1851) — Private, 3rd VA Cavalry (Co. D), CSA. From Charles City Co., VA.
Douglas, William M. — Surgeon, CSA. From Williamsburg, VA.
Napier, Lemuel (L.B., 1851) — Private, 11th AL Infantry (Co. A), CSA. From Alabama.
Fleming, William R. — 2nd Lieutenant, 4th VA Cavalry (Co. F), CSA. From Goochland, VA.
Rudd, John S. — 2nd Lt., CSA. Staff Officer.

1851-52
Amiss, John B. — Private, 97th VA Militia (Co. H), CSA. From Rappahannock Co., VA.
Clowes, John W. — Private, 32nd VA Infantry (Co. C), CSA. From Williamsburg, VA.
Johnson, Philip A. (A.B., 1852) — 1st Lieutenant, 29th IL Infantry (Co. K), USA. From Illinois.
Kellam, E.E. — Private, 39th VA Infantry (Co. C), CSA. Accomac Co., VA.
Kirkland, Samuel S. — Captain, 6th NC Infantry (Co. A), CSA. From North Carolina.
Lee, Edwin G. — Brigadier General, CSA. Cousin of Gen. Robert E. Lee, CSA. Son-in-law of Brig. Gen. William N. Pendleton. From "Leeland," VA.
Todd, Westwood A. (A.B., 1852) — 2nd Lieutenant, CSA. Staff Officer. From Norfolk, VA.
Winn, Walter — Captain, CSA. Staff Officer. From Louisiana.

1852-53
Berkeley, C.F. — Captain, 8th VA Infantry (Co. D), CSA. From Loudoun Co., VA.
Bowyer, Edmund F. — Captain, Botetourt Artillery, CSA. From Fincastle, VA.
Coke, George H. — Surgeon, CSA. From Williamsburg, VA.
Donovan, John B. (L.B., 1853) — Private, 26 VA Infantry (Co. A), CSA. From Gloucester, VA.
Harris, S.G. (A.B., 1853) — Surgeon, CSA. From Mecklenburg, VA.
May, D.F. — Surgeon, CSA. From Petersburg, VA.
May, James — Captain, 14th VA Militia, CSA. From Petersburg, VA.
Parramore, T.C. — Private, 3rd VA Infantry — Local Defense (Co. D), CSA. State judge. From Accomac Co., VA.
Pettitt, John M. — CSA. From Williamsburg, VA.
Shield, W.H. — Surgeon, CSA. From York Co., VA.
Shorter, George H. — Captain, CSA. Staff Officer. From Georgia.
Sutton, Philip T. — Captain, CSA. Staff Officer. From Hanover, VA.
Stubblefield, Alexander (L.B., 1853) — Private, 26th VA Infantry (Co. A), CSA. From Charles City Co., VA.
Watkins, Warren — Private, 5th VA Cavalry (Co. H), CSA. From Williamsburg, VA.
Wise, James M. (A.M., 1853) — Captain, CSA. Staff Officer. From Washington DC.
Wise, George D. (A.B., 1853, L.B., 1855) — Captain, CSA. Killed in action before Battle of Petersburg. Relative of VA Gov./CSA Gen. Henry Wise. From Accomac Co., VA.
Wise, Obadiah J. (L.B., 1853) — Captain, 46th VA Infantry (Co. A), CSA. Killed in action at Roanoke Island. Son of VA Gov./Brig. Gen. Henry A. Wise, CSA. From Accomac Co., VA.

1853-54
Ashby, Henry M. — Colonel, CSA. From Fauquier Co., VA.
Ball, M.D. (A.B., 1854) — Lt. Colonel, 11th VA Cavalry, CSA. Also a Captain in the 5th VA Cavalry (Co. F), CSA. From Fairfax, VA.

Coke, Alexander (B.P., 1854, L.B., 1856)—Captain, 6th VA Infantry (Co. F), CSA. Initially enlisted as a Private. From Williamsburg, VA.
Coleman, H.E.—Colonel, CSA. From Halifax Co., VA.
Gilliam, J.S. (A.M., 1854)—Surgeon, CSA. From Petersburg, VA.
Grandy, Charles R. (A.B., 1854)—Captain, 16th VA Infantry (Co. H), CSA (also in Artillery Unit). From Norfolk, VA.
Lamb, William (B.P., 1854, L.B., 1855)—Colonel, CSA. Commanding Officer—Fort Fisher, NC. Served as Mayor of Norfolk in 1880s. From Norfolk, VA.
Lomax, T.L.—Private, 30th VA Infantry (Co. K), CSA. From King George Co., VA.
Paul, D'Arcy—1st Lt., 12th VA Infantry (Co. K), CSA. From Norfolk, VA.
Scarburgh, George T.—Surgeon, CSA. From Williamsburg, VA.
Slade, W.S.O.—Captain, CSA. From Washington, D.C.
Taliaferro, Van—Private, 11th VA Infantry (Co. G), CSA. From Lynchburg, VA.
Tayloe, B.T. (B.P., 1854)—Surgeon, CSA. From Prince George Co., VA.
Tayloe, Henry A.—CSA. From Richmond, VA.
Williamson, Thomas G.—Captain, 7th NC Infantry (Co. F) CSA. From Portsmouth, VA.
Winston, William D.—Private, 15th VA Infantry (Co. C), CSA. From Hanover Co., VA.
Wise, George D.—Captain, CSA. Staff Officer. From Washington, D.C.
Withers, Andrew F.—Sergeant, 17th VA Infantry (Co. K), CSA. From Fauquier Co., VA.
Wynne, Thomas (A.B., 1854)—Private, 5th VA Cavalry (Co. H), CSA. From Williamsburg, VA.

1854–55

Ball, Thomas—2nd Lieutenant, 47th VA Infantry (Co. F), CSA. From Richmond Co., VA.
Bell, A. Taylor (A.B., 1855)—Surgeon, CSA. From Norfolk, VA.
Bloxham, William D. (L.B., 1855)—Captain, 5th FL Infantry (Co. C), CSA. Staff Officer. From Florida.
Bright, Robert A.—Captain, 53rd VA Infantry and 1st VA Artillery, CSA. Also served as 2nd Lt. in 32nd VA Infantry (Co. I), CSA. From Williamsburg, VA.
Carter, Hill M., Jr. (A.B., 1855)—2nd Lieutenant, 3rd VA Cavalry (Co. C), CSA. Descendant of Robert "King" Carter and member of the prominent Carter family. Killed in action during the Battle of the Wilderness (1864). From Charles City Co., VA.
Chilton, John R.—Corporal, 9th VA Cavalry (Co. D), CSA. From Lancaster, VA.
Clark, John A. (L.B., 1855)—CSA. From Charles City Co., VA.
Clarke, John A.—Private, 32nd VA Infantry (Co. E), CSA. From Charles City Co., VA.
Davidson, A.S.—Asst. Surgeon, CSA. From Louisiana.
Gee, E.C.—Surgeon, CSA. From Brunswick Co., VA.
Gilliam, Joseph P.—Captain, Johnston Artillery, CSA. From Dinwiddie, VA.
Grandy, Cyrus W. (B.P., 1855)—Major, CSA. Staff Officer. From North Carolina.
Gwynn, Henry (B.P., 1855)—Captain, 9th VA Infantry (Co. F), CSA. From Raleigh, NC.
Hunter, F.C.S. (B.P., 1855)—Captain, 30th VA Infantry (Co. K), CSA. From King George Co., VA.

Jett, J.B. (L.B., 1855) — Captain, 40th VA Infantry (Co. C), CSA. From Westmoreland Co., VA.
Jones, Parke — Sergeant, 32nd VA Infantry (Co. C), CSA. From James City Co., VA.
Lively, Edward H. — Private, 32nd VA Infantry (Co. C), CSA. From Williamsburg, VA.
Marks, Junius E. — Sergeant, 5th VA Cavalry, CSA. Also a Private in the 12th VA Infantry, CSA. From Prince George Co., VA.
Morrissett, E. — Private, 18th VA Infantry (Co. F,C), CSA. From Chesterfield, VA.
Nowlin, Abner W.C. (B.P., 1855) — Captain, 24th VA Infantry (Co. C), CSA. From Wytheville, VA. VA State Senator.
Perrin, John T. — Major, CSA. Also Captain in 26th VA Infantry (Co. E), CSA. From Gloucester, VA.
Robertson, J.R. (A.B., 1855) — Sergeant, 12th VA Infantry (Co. H), CSA. From Petersburg, VA.
Sands, Johnson H. — Captain, 1st VA Artillery (Co. 2c), CSA. From Williamsburg, VA.
Shands, Thomas E. — 3rd Lieutenant, 5th Battalion, VA Infantry (Co. C), CSA. From Prince George Co., VA.
Smith, A.S. — CSA. From Norfolk, VA.
Smith, J.R. — CSA. From Norfolk, VA.
Southall, Joseph W. — Private, 1st VA Cavalry (Co. G), CSA. From Amelia, VA.
Stringfellow, Charles S. (A.B., 1855) — Major, CSA. From Petersburg, VA.
Sullivan, John S. — CSA. From Lancaster Co., VA.
Sully, Edwin — Private, 4th VA Cavalry (Co. H), CSA. From Alexandria, VA.
Vest, Walker W. (A.M., 1855) — Served in Confederate War Department. From Williamsburg, VA.
Warren, H.B. — Private, 5th VA Cavalry (Co. H), CSA. From James City Co., VA.

1855-56

Beckwith, Julian R. — Private, 12th VA Infantry (Co. E), CSA. From Prince George Co., VA.
Bowyer, Woodville — Private, 28th VA Infantry (Co. K), CSA. From Fincastle, VA.
Breckenridge, P.G. — Captain, CSA. Pvt./Sgt., 2nd VA Cavalry (Co. C), CSA. From Botetourt Co., VA.
Clay, William H. — Private, Nottoway Light Artillery, CSA. From Amelia Co., VA.
Coke, Alexander — Captain, 6th VA Infantry (Co. F), CSA. From Williamsburg, VA.
Delk, Samuel D. — Private, 9th VA Infantry (Co. E), CSA. From Isle of Wight, VA.
Gatewood, W.K. — Asst. Surgeon, CSA. From Middlesex Co., VA.
Graves, William H. (A.B., 1856) — Captain, CSA. From Wythe Co., VA.
Green, John W. — CSA. Killed in battle. From Culpeper Co., VA.
Hough, Samuel J. (B.P., 1856) — Private, 1st MD Cavalry (Co. A), CSA. From Baltimore, MD.
Jerdone, John — CSA. From Orange Co., VA.
Lindsay, Roswell — CSA. From Williamsburg, VA.
Lively, William E. — CSA. From Williamsburg, VA.
Mitchell, Goodrich — 1st Lieutenant, 49th VA Infantry (Co. C), CSA. From Fauquier Co., VA.
Montague, Edgar (L.B., 1856) — Colonel, 32nd VA Infantry, CSA. From Middlesex Co., VA.

Page, Richard M.—Captain, 26th VA Infantry (Co. A), CSA. From Gloucester Co., VA.
Pannill, James B. (L.B., 1856)—Captain, CSA. Staff Officer. From Patrick Co., VA. Cousin of Maj. Gen. J.E.B. Stuart, CSA.
Payne, Alexander D. (A.M., 1856)—Colonel, CSA. 2nd Lt./Captain, 4th VA Cavalry (Co. H), CSA. From Fauquier Co., VA.
Payne, William W. (A.B., 1856)—Surgeon, CSA. From Fauquier Co., VA.
Pettitt, William H.—Sergeant, 32nd VA Infantry (Co. I), CSA. Died in service. From Williamsburg, VA.
Smith, P. Bell (A.M., 1856)—Lt. Colonel, CSA. Son of VA Gov./Maj. Gen. William "Extra Billy" Smith, CSA. Staff Officer. From Fauquier Co., VA.
Smith, Thomas P. (A.M., 1856)—Colonel, CSA. Son of VA Gov./Maj. Gen. William "Extra Billy" Smith, CSA. From Fauquier Co., VA.
Snead, Thomas T.L. (A.M., 1856)—Captain, CSA. W&M faculty member. From Accomac Co., VA.
Spencer, Robert M.—Private, 3rd VA Cavalry (Co. I), CSA. From Greensville, VA.
Walke, W. Talbot (A.M., 1856)—1st Lieutenant, 39th VA Cavalry Battalion, CSA. Staff Officer. From Norfolk, VA.
White, Isaiah W.—Surgeon, CSA. From Accomac Co., VA.
Williamson, Thomas G.—Captain, CSA. From Caroline Co., VA.

1856-57

Arnold, Philip M. (A.B., 1857)—2nd Lieutenant, 15th VA Cavalry (Co. E), CSA. From King George Co., VA.
Arnold, Thomas T. (A.B., 1857)—2nd Lieutenant, 15th VA Cavalry (Co. E), CSA. From King George Co., VA.
Baptist, Edward L. (A.B., 1857)—Private, 3rd VA Cavalry (Co. A), CSA. From Mecklenburg Co., VA.
Barlow, John H.—1st Lieutenant, 32nd VA Infantry (Co. C), CSA. From Williamsburg, VA.
Barziza, D.U. (A.M., 1857)—Captain, 4th Texas Infantry (Co. C), CSA. From Williamsburg, VA.
Bayly, Josiah L.—Captain, CSA. From Accomac Co., VA.
Bowry, Robert A.—Private, James City Artillery, CSA. From Williamsburg, VA.
Clopton, W.I. (A.B., 1857)—Captain, CSA. 2nd Lt./1st Lt., 1st VA Artillery (Co. I-H), CSA. From Williamsburg, VA.
Edmunds, Paul C. (L.B., 1857)—1st Lieutenant, 53rd VA Infantry (Co. A), CSA. From Halifax Co., VA.
Graves, W.H. (A.B., L.B., 1857)—Captain, CSA. Died 7/29/1931. From Wytheville, VA.
Griswold, Joseph G. (A.B., 1857)—Major, CSA. Captain, 1st VA Infantry (William's Rifles), CSA. From Richmond, VA.
Jones, Jesse S. (A.B., 1857)—Captain, 3rd VA Cavalry (Co. B), CSA. From Hampton, VA.
Lamb, Robert W. (A.M., 1857)—Captain, CSA. Staff Officer. From Norfolk, VA.
Lawson, John W.—Surgeon, CSA. Later a VA State Senator. From Williamsburg, VA.
Mason, Edmunds (A.B., 1857)—Surgeon, CSA. From Greensville Co., VA.
McCandlish, T.P. (A.M., 1857)—Captain/Quartermaster, 32nd VA Infantry, CSA. Faculty member at W&M. From Williamsburg, VA.

The Civil War Service of William and Mary Alumni, 1861–1865 185

Newman, J.J.H. — Private, 2nd MD Infantry (Co. E), USA. From Baltimore, MD.
Parham, William C. (A.B., 1857) — Captain, CSA. From Brunswick Co., VA.
Spencer, J.S. — 2nd Lieutenant, 12 VA Infantry (Co. F), CSA. From Greensville Co., VA.
Stone, G.W. (A.M., L.B., 1857) — Private, 18th VA Inf. (Co. B) CSA. From Brunswick Co., VA.
Walke, Richard (A.M., 1857) — Captain, CSA. Staff Officer. From Norfolk, VA.

1857–58
Beale, John H. (A.B., 1858) — Private, Fredericksburg Artillery, CSA. From Fredericksburg, VA.
Clay, Charles E. — Private, 2nd VA Cavalry (Co. A), CSA. From Bedford, VA.
Coke, Octavius — Captain, 32nd VA Infantry (Co. C), CSA. Wounded at Battles of Antietam (1862) and Five Forks (1865). Moved to NC after the war and served as a NC State Senator and NC Secretary of State. Died in 1895. Originally from Williamsburg, VA.
Foreman, C.W. — Private, 6th VA Infantry (Co. G), CSA. From Princess Anne, VA.
Furcron, A.S. (A.B., 1858) — Sergeant, 4th VA Cavalry (Co. B), CSA. From Chesterfield, VA.
Garnett, W.J. — 2nd Lieutenant, 1st VA Artillery (Co. K), CSA. From Richmond, VA.
Garrett, William R. (A.M., 1858) — Captain, CSA. From Williamsburg, VA.
Hamilton, P. — 1st Lieutenant, CSA. Staff Officer. From Halifax Co., VA.
Hunton, Henry — Private, 4th VA Cavalry (Co. H), CSA. From Prince William Co., VA.
James, R.W. — CSA. From Williamsburg, VA.
Mann, George E. — CSA. Later a judge in Galveston, Texas. Originally from Gloucester, VA.
Marshall, William — Captain, 38th Battalion VA Light Artillery. Grandson of U.S. Chief Justice John Marshall. From Fauquier Co., VA.
Mason, Thomas W. (A.B., 1858) — CSA. From Greensville Co., VA.
May, Benjamin H. — Ensign, 12th VA Infantry (Co. F, S), CSA. From Petersburg, VA.
Parker, R.A. — Private, 5th VA Cavalry (Co. C), CSA. From Sussex Co., VA.
Pierce, John — Private, 32nd VA Infantry (Co. C), CSA. From Williamsburg, VA.
Snead, Charles W. — Asst. Surgeon, CSA. From Accomac Co., VA.
Stringfellow, H.M. (A.B., 1858) — Captain, CSA. Staff Officer. From Hanover, VA.
Taliaferro, William R. (B.P., 1858) — Private, 13th VA Infantry (Co. A), CSA. From Orange Co., VA.
Taylor, Robert G. (L.B., 1858) — CSA. From Gloucester, VA.
Tucker, B. St. George (A.M., 1858) — Surgeon, CSA. From Williamsburg, VA.
Wools, Charles S. (B.P., 1858) — Private, 5th LA Infantry, CSA. From Vicksburg, MS.

1858–1859
Bagwell, Edmund R. — 2nd Lieutenant, 46th Virginia Infantry, CSA. Later served in VA House of Delegates (1870s). From Onancock, VA.
Barlow, Thomas J. — QM Sergeant, 32nd VA Infantry (Co. C), CSA. From Williamsburg, VA.
Belvin, James W. — Surgeon, CSA. From Yorktown, VA.
Camm, Edward — Surgeon, CSA. From Williamsburg, VA.
Carrington, Thomas C. — Private, 32nd VA Infantry (Co. C), CSA. Died in Jan. 1863 after the Battle of Fredericksburg. From Williamsburg, VA.

Claiborne, Felix G.—1st Lieutenant, 38th VA Infantry (Co. E), CSA. From Halifax Co., VA.
Davis, W.S.—CSA. From Brunswick Co., VA.
Fornis, Thadeous K.—Private, 4th AL Infantry (Co. D), CSA. Killed in battle. From Alabama.
Gary, S.W.—CSA. From Norfolk, VA.
Harrison, T.R.—1st Lieutenant CSA. Staff Officer, From Richmond, VA.
Hurt, R.T.—Surgeon, CSA. From Petersburg, VA.
Kincheloe, Wickliffe—Sergeant, 8th VA Infantry (Co. B), CSA. Killed in battle.
Lindsay, George W.—Sergeant, 23rd VA Infantry (Co. H), CSA. From Richmond, VA.
May, George H.—Private, 12th VA Infantry (Co. A), CSA. From Petersburg, VA.
McCandlish, H.S.—Private, 32nd VA Infantry (Co. C), CSA. From Williamsburg, VA.
Neblett, Norman M.—2nd Lieutenant, 9th VA Cavalry (Co. G), CSA. From Williamsburg, VA.
Phifer, D.R.—Private, 33rd NC Infantry (Co. A, D), CSA. From NC.
Poindexter, George H.—2nd Lieutenant, CSA. Staff Officer, From Richmond, VA.
Robinson, T.V.—CSA. From Richmond, VA.
Smith, L.H.—CSA. From NC.
Worthen, James E.—CSA. From Richmond, VA.
Wynn, Robert E.—CSA. From Petersburg, VA.
Wynn, W.G.—CSA. From Petersburg, VA.
Young, William L.—1st Lieutenant, 32nd VA Infantry (Co. K), CSA. From Warwick Co., VA.

1859-60
Alfriend, Frank H. (A.B., 1860)—CSA. From Richmond, VA.
Atkinson, Robert C.—Private, 5th and 13th VA Cavalry, CSA. From Smithfield, VA.
Brister, R.A.—Sgt. Major, 3rd VA Infantry (Co. D), CSA. From Southampton Co., VA.
Causey, William N.—Sergeant, 3rd VA Cavalry (Co. B), CSA. From Hampton, VA.
Clarke, A.T.—CSA.
Harrell, Moses R., Jr.—Sergeant, 5th VA Cavalry (Co. H), CSA. From Williamsburg, VA.
Harrison, G.B.—CSA. From Cabin Point, VA.
Hubard, J.R.—CSA. From Norfolk, VA.
Hubbard, J. Filmer (A.B., 1860)—Private, 32nd VA Infantry, CSA. From James City Co., VA.
Jones, William Ap C.—Corporal, 34th VA Infantry (Co. A) CSA. From Gloucester, VA.
Lewis, Robert B.—Sergeant, 9th VA Cavalry (Co. C), CSA. From Westmoreland Co., VA.
Lindsay, J.S.—CSA. From Williamsburg, VA.
Southgate, John—CSA. From Norfolk, VA.
Stubbs, T. Jefferson (A.B., 1860)—Private, 34th VA Infantry (Co. H), CSA. Later a faculty member at W&M. From Gloucester, VA.
Tayloe, William (B.P., 1860)—CSA. From King George Co., VA.
Weir, Walter E. (A.M., 1860)—Captain, CSA. From Prince William Co., VA.
Wilkinson, John—CSA.

Chapter Notes

Preface

1. Anne W. Chapman, *Benjamin Stoddert Ewell: A Biography* (Ph.D. diss., College of William and Mary, 1984), 301.
2. E.J. Harvie, Benjamin Stoddert Ewell Obituary Notice, (report of the) Twenty-Sixth Annual Reunion of the Associates of the Graduates of the United States Military Academy, June 10, 1895.
3. Charles Edwards Lester, *Lester's History of the United States, Illustrated in Its Five Great Periods: Colonization, Consolidation, Development, Achievement, Advancement*, vol. 1 (New York: P.F. Collier, 1883), 202. (Google eBook)

Introduction

1. Burton Clark, *The Distinctive College: Antioch, Reed, and Swarthmore* (Chicago: Aldine, 1975), 280. Quoted in Russell T. Smith, "Distinctive Traditions of the College of William and Mary and Their Influence on the Modernization of the College, 1865 to 1919" (Ph.D. diss., College of William and Mary, 1980), 4.
2. Ibid.
3. Burton Clark, "The Organizational Saga in Higher Education," *Administrative Science Quarterly* 17:2 (June 1972): 178.
4. "Cool Facts," William and Mary History and Traditions, College of William and Mary.
5. "Traditions and Legends," Swem Special Collections Research Center Wiki, Swem Library, College of William and Mary.
6. "Sunset Ceremony," Swem Special Collections Research Center Wiki, Special Collections Research Center, Swem Library, College of William and Mary.
7. David F. Riggs, "Jamestown During the Civil War," Historic Jamestowne, National Park Service.

Chapter 1

1. Considered the oldest college building in the United States, this iconic structure was known as the "College Building" or "Main Building" before the twentieth-century restoration of Williamsburg. It was renamed to acknowledge Sir Christopher Wren (1632–1723), the English architect traditionally credited with its design.
2. J.E. Morpurgo, *Their Majesties' Royall Colledge: William and Mary in the Seventeenth and Eighteenth Centuries* (Washington, D.C.: Hennage, 1976), 5.
3. "Historical Chronology of the College of William and Mary: William & Mary 1618–1699," College of William and Mary.
4. Robert Beverly, *The History and Present State of Virginia, in Four Parts*, vol. 1 (1705), in "Documenting the American South."
5. Susan H. Godson, Ludwell H. Johnson, Richard B. Sherman, Thad Tate, and Helen C. Walker. *William and Mary: A History, 1693–1888*, 2 vols. (Williamsburg, VA: King & Queen Press, The Society of the Alumni, 1993), "Foundations: The Royal Charter of 1693," I: 3.
6. Morpurgo, 45–48.
7. Godson et al., I: 38.
8. The grammar school emphasized the study of Latin and Greek, while the school of moral and natural philosophy focused on the study of mathematics and science.
9. Wilford Kale, *Hark Upon The Gale: An Illustrated History of The College of William*

and Mary (Williamsburg, VA: Botetourt Press, 2007), 48–49. George Washington and Thomas Jefferson were also involved with the College in their later careers. Washington served as William and Mary's first American chancellor in the 1790s. Jefferson was active in reorganizing the College's curriculum while serving as governor of Virginia during the American Revolution.

10. Kale, 49; Godson et al., I: 110.

11. Kale, 49–53. Plans for building an addition to the Main (Wren) Building were drawn up around 1772. Work began on the project shortly thereafter, but was discontinued with the outbreak of the American Revolution.

12. *The History of the College of William and Mary: From Its Foundation, 1660, to 1874* (Richmond, VA: J.W. Randolph & English, 1874), 47.

13. "Historical Chronology of the College of William and Mary: William & Mary 1750–1799," College of William and Mary.

14. Ibid.

15. Godson et al., I: 120–125; Kale, 57–60.

16. It was believed that a British invasion of southeast Virginia was imminent, prompting concern that British forces would overrun Williamsburg. Virginia legislators felt that Richmond would be a safer place to conduct business. As it turned out, a British force led by Brig. Gen. Benedict Arnold raided Richmond before going into camp at Portsmouth. Williamsburg was never attacked but was occupied briefly by British forces.

17. Kale, 60. Efforts to move the College to Richmond were particularly strong in the 1820s, as a response to the creation of the University of Virginia. Future U.S. President John Tyler (W&M class of 1807), who was at the time a member of the Virginia General Assembly, was one of the strongest opponents of the proposed move.

18. Charles W. Elliot, *Winfield Scott: The Soldier and the Man* (New York: Macmillan, 1937).

19. Robert Polk Thompson, "Colleges in the Revolutionary South: The Shaping of a Tradition," in *History of Education Quarterly* (Winter 1970): 399.

20. Thompson, 402.

21. "Report of the President and Directors of the Literary Fund, to the General Assembly, in December 1816," in *Sundry Documents on a System of Public Education*, 18–34, quoted in Ruby O. Osbourne, "The College of William and Mary, 1800–1827" (Ph.D. diss., College of William and Mary, 1981, 311–312.

22. Godson et al., I: 218–219; Kale, 70–71. The movement to create the University of Virginia began in 1816, when it was referred to as "Central College." The General Assembly authorized the use of the name "The University of Virginia" on January 25, 1819.

23. Thomas Jefferson to Sidney Morse, March 9, 1823. Manuscripts Collection, The College of William and Mary, quoted in Osbourne, 410.

24. Godson et al., I: 218–219; Kale, 73.

25. William H. Garland to Sarah A. Garland, November 6, 1823, quoted in "Letters of Wm. H. Garland and Samuel M. Garland, Students at William and Mary College, 1823–1824," in *William and Mary Quarterly* 11:2 (April 1931): 136–137.

26. David Sacks, "The History of the William and Mary Campus" (B.A. honors thesis, College of William and Mary, 1984), 34.

27. Osbourne, 458–459.

28. Osbourne, 463.

29. Lyon G. Tyler, *The College of William and Mary in Virginia: Its History and Work, 1693–1907*, quoted in Sacks, 34.

30. Letter of resignation of Professor George Frederick Holmes, dated January 22, 1848, entered into the Faculty Assembly Minutes, April 3, 1848, William & Mary Digital Archive, Special Collections Research Center, The College of William and Mary.

31. Godson et al., I: 285; Chapman, *Benjamin Stoddert Ewell*, 106.

32. Kale, 74–77. Benjamin Ewell first came to William and Mary in 1848 as acting president and professor of mathematics. He was appointed president in 1854 and served until 1888, giving him one of the longest tenures of any William and Mary president.

33. Ewell and the board members argued over several issues in the 1850s, including a proposed move of the campus to Virginia's Eastern Shore as well as whether or not to maintain the grammar and law schools at the College. Ewell was successful in keeping the College in Williamsburg and dropping the grammar school, which he considered a distraction.

34. William and Mary alumnus and former president John Tyler was scheduled to be the event's keynote speaker. Tyler was also appointed the College's first chancellor since George Washington around this time.

35. "Historical Sketch of the College of William and Mary," in *The History of the Col-*

lege of William and Mary: From Its Foundation, 1693, to 1870 (Baltimore: John Murphy), 3–4

36. "Historical Sketch of the College of William and Mary," 49. Included here is an account of the 1859 fire dated February 12, 1859, by Professor Robert J. Morrison, whose writing formed much of this historical section of the William and Mary catalogue.

37. Extract from letter from St. George Tucker to Professor Morrison, February 9, 1859, in "Historical Sketch of the College of William and Mary," 49.

38. Ibid, 49.

39. Extract from the 166th anniversary address by alumnus and ex-President John Tyler, in "Historical Sketch of the College of William and Mary," 50.

40. Godson et al., I: 287–288; Kale, 81–82.

41. "Historical Sketch of the College of William and Mary," 51.

42. Michael David Cohen, *Reconstructing the Campus: Higher Education and the American Civil War* (Charlottesville: University of Virginia Press, 2012), 21–24.

43. Mary Elizabeth Massey, "The Civil War Comes to the Campus," in *Education in the South* (Farmville, VA: Longwood College Press, 1959).

44. E.B. Long, *The Civil War Day by Day: An Almanac, 1861 1865*, quoted in Brian Steel Wills, *The War Hits Home: The Civil War in Southeastern Virginia* (Charlottesville: University Press of Virginia, 2001), 10.

45. Wills, 10.

46. James McPherson, *Battle Cry of Freedom: The Civil War Era* (Oxford: Oxford University Press, 1988), 276.

47. Ibid.

48. James I. Robertson Jr., *Civil War Virginia: Battleground for a Nation* (Charlottesville: University Press of Virginia, 1991), vii.

49. Robertson, *Civil War Virginia*, 38.

50. Robert F. Pace, *Halls of Honor: College Men in the Old South* (Baton Rouge: Louisiana State University Press, 2004), 98–102.

51. Ewell Autobiography, date unknown, Special Collections Research Center, Swem Library, College of William and Mary.

52. Godson et al., I: 289.

53. Only two 1861 William and Mary students did not ultimately serve in the Confederate Army — William Reynolds of Maryland (who has been mentioned) and Thomas R. Bowden, the son of Lemuel Bowden, a prominent Unionist who later served as mayor of Williamsburg during the Federal occupation and then as a United States Senator. There is no evidence that Thomas Bowden served in either the Union or Confederate armies.

54. Thirty-five of the college's seventy students formally petitioned the faculty for the creation of a military company on January 8, 1861. Richard A. Wise to Henry A. Wise, January 9, 1861, Special Collections Research Center, Swem Library, College of William and Mary

55. Deposition of William Reynolds, February 27, 1872, Special Collections Research Center, Swem Library, College of William and Mary.

56. Carol K. Dubbs, *Defend This Old Town: Williamsburg during the Civil War* (Baton Rouge: Louisiana State University Press, 2002), 8–9, 13; Deposition of William Reynolds, February 27, 1872. Ewell forbade the students from raising the flag on the College Building itself. Secession vote from Wills, 15.

57. Peter Wallenstein, "The Struggle to Learn: Higher Education in Civil War Virginia," in *Virginia at War, 1864* (Lexington, KY: University of Kentucky Press, 2009), 101–105.

58. Pace, *Halls of Honor*, 20–21.

59. "Extracts from the Laws of the College of William and Mary," *The History of William and Mary College*, 157.

60. Pace, 4–5, 12–13.

61. Pace, 8–9.

62. Pace, 4–5. See Bertram Wyatt-Brown, *Southern Honor: Ethics and Behavior in the Old South* (New York: Oxford, 1982).

63. "Extracts from the Laws of the College of William and Mary," *The History of William and Mary College*, 156-157.

64. Michael Sugrue, "We Desired Our Future Rulers to be Educated Men," in *The American College in the Nineteenth Century*, ed. Roger L. Geiger (Nashville: Vanderbilt University Press), 98.

65. Sugrue, "We Desired Our Future Rulers to be Educated Men," 99.

66. This study draws upon many comparisons between Southern students at William and Mary and those at other Southern colleges. These comparisons are valid because of the common experiences shared by young males of this generation in the South. However, in some respects William and Mary was different from its counterparts in Virginia and in other Southern states. At the time, Southern colleges were generally either "state" insti-

tutions or those affiliated with a particular religious denomination. Since it was originally chartered by the English Crown, William and Mary does not completely fit into either category. Its history and lineage make the College unique among its peers.

67. Peter Carmichael, *The Last Generation: Young Virginians in Peace, War, and Reunion* (Chapel Hill: University of North Carolina Press, 2005), 8–9.

68. Ibid. Although Carmichael studied college students at many Virginia colleges prior to the Civil War, including the University of Virginia and Randolph-Macon College, William and Mary itself was not examined. However, it can be argued that the sentiments of most Virginia college students at the time were relatively common.

69. Ibid., 8–9, 37–39.

70. Ibid., 12–13.

71. Ibid.

72. Deposition of William Reynolds, February 27, 1872.

Chapter 2

1. "Historical Chronology of the College of William and Mary: William & Mary 1750–1799," College of William and Mary, http://www.wm.edu/about/history/chronology/1750to1799/index.php (accessed May 12, 2011).

2. The actions of the French government had long-lasting effects, as its acknowledgment of damages to the College was cited as a critical argument for the United States government to make reparations for similar wartime destruction during the Civil War.

3. Sacks, 37–38.

4. Faculty Committee Report, The College of William and Mary, February 8, 1860, Book 5, 1847–1883, William & Mary Digital Archive, Swem Library, College of William and Mary, http://hdl.handle.net/10288/13457 (accessed May 31, 2011).

5. Ibid.

6. *Weekly Gazette*, April 6, 1859, in Dearstyne, *Architectural History of the Wren Building of the College of William and Mary* (Colonial Williamsburg Foundation Library Research Report Series, 1951), 60.

7. Faculty Assembly Minutes, 1846–1879, The College of William and Mary, in Dearstyne, 64.

8. Anne W. Chapman, "The College of William and Mary, 1849–1859: The Memoirs of Silas Totten" (Master's thesis, 1978, 185.

Totten also pointed out that although the 1859 fire was too big and fast-moving to be contained, a newspaper reporter noted in the March 16, 1859 *Weekly Gazette* that Williamsburg did not have a fire engine — and that when asked by the Williamsburg Council in 1850, the William and Mary faculty voted not to support the establishment of a fire company and purchase of a community fire engine. See Chapman's Notes for Chapter 17, footnote 7, 200.

9. Carmichael, 2.

10. Samuel Eliot Morison, *Three Centuries of Harvard, 1636–1936* (Cambridge and London: Belknap Press of Harvard University, 1946), 303.

11. John R. Thelin, *A History of American Higher Education* (Baltimore and London: Johns Hopkins University Press, 2004), 74–75.

12. Charles F. Thwing, *A History of Higher Education in America* (New York: D. Appleton, 1906), 252–257.

13. Thwing, 257.

14. Ervin L. Jordan Jr., *Charlottesville and the University of Virginia in the Civil War*, 2nd ed. (Lynchburg: H.E. Howard, 1988), 6.

15. Ibid.

16. The College of William and Mary Matriculation Book, entries for 1849–1859, Special Collections Research Center, Swem Library, College of William and Mary.

17. Ibid., 41.

18. Ibid., 28.

19. Silas Totten, quoted in Chapman, "The College of William and Mary, 1849–1859," 154.

20. Thwing, 254–255. Charles F. Thwing was president of Western Reserve University and Adelbert College at the time of his book's publication. He conducted the research over the course of 25 years, particularly acknowledging librarians at Harvard, Yale, Brown and Dartmouth for their assistance. Thwing included enrollment figures for Washington, D.C., and Maryland in his totals for Southern students enrolled at Harvard, Princeton, and Yale; the D.C. and Maryland totals were subtracted for the purposes of this chapter.

21. *The Catalogue of The College of William and Mary*, 1858–1859, 98.

22. Ibid., 100.

23. *Richmond Daily Republican*, February 27, 1852, in Chapman, "The College of William and Mary 1849–1859," 28; also footnote 57, 41.

24. Alexander T. Stewart letter dated September 28, 1859, in Faculty Assembly Minutes, October 17, 1859. Alexander Turney Smith, of Scotch descent, studied at Trinity College in Dublin and immigrated to the United States. He later pioneered in New York retailing, ultimately becoming known as a philanthropist and as one of the nation's three wealthiest men by his death in 1876. See "Picture History," http://www.picturehistory.com/product/id/18312, (accessed May 18, 2011), and also "Alexander Turney Stewart" in All Biographies, http://www.all-biographies.com/politicians/alexander_turney_stewart.htm (accessed May 18, 2011).

25. Henry A. Wise statement recorded in the December 23, 1859, *Richmond Daily Dispatch*, quoted in Chapman, "The College of William and Mary, 1849–1859," footnote 3, 163.

26. According to "Proceedings of a Meeting of the Students of William and Mary College" on May 31, 1853, students established a committee that prepared unanimous resolutions in defense of Totten's character and conduct, writing to the *Richmond Examiner* editor. See the "Proceedings," 29, in the Totten Folder, Faculty-Alumni Files, William and Mary Special Collections.

27. Silas Totten left William and Mary with his family and became the second president of the University of Iowa. William and Mary's loss was Iowa's gain, as that university was struggling to survive financially and academically. After his election to the presidency in 1859, the university's Board of Trustees empowered Totten to reorganize the institution. He reinvigorated it with a new plan creating independent departments with separate programs of study. Unfortunately for Totten, Civil War sentiments again cast a long shadow. In 1862, he was criticized for his pro-Southern sympathies. Totten's son, a university student and Confederate sympathizer, escaped an angry crowd and left for good. Totten resigned his presidency due to a conflict with the Methodist governor of Iowa. He moved to Illinois, and later establishing a female seminary in Kentucky. "Biographical Note," Papers of Silas Totten, The University of Iowa Libraries Special Collections & University Archives, http://www.lib.uiowa.edu/spec-coll/archives/guides/RG05/RG05.01.02.htm (accessed May 16, 2011); Chapman, "The College of William and Mary, 1849–1859," 13.

28. *Catalogue of The College of William and Mary*, 1858–1859, 96.

29. Chapman, "The History of William and Mary College: 1849–1859," 143.

30. Ibid., 161.

31. Sharon E. Knapp, "Benjamin Sherwood Hendrick," in *Dictionary of North Carolina Biography*, William S. Powell, ed. (Chapel Hill: University of North Carolina Press, 1979–1996). In Documenting the American South, http://docsouth.unc.edu/browse/bios/pn0000708_bio.html (accessed May 16, 2011).

32. Biographical note, John Brown White Papers, Z. Smith Reynolds Library, Wake Forest University, http://zsr.wfu.edu/collections/special/archives/presidentspapers#white (accessed May 16, 2011).

33. "Proceedings at the Inauguration of Frederick A. P. Barnard, S.T.D., Ll.D., as President of Columbia College on Monday, October 3, 1864," 15, in http://books.google.com/books?id=ej1AAAAAYAAJ&printsec=frontcover#v=onepage&q&f=false (accessed May 16, 2011).

34. *The Catalogue of the College of William and Mary*, 1860–1861, 4, Special Collections Research Center, Swem Library, College of William and Mary.

35. Ibid., 5.

36. Ibid., 19.

37. Ibid., 18.

38. Harvard College Catalogues, cited in John S. Goff, *Robert Todd Lincoln: A Man in His Own Right* (Norman: University of Oklahoma Press, 1969), 45.

39. Goff, 44–45.

40. Goff, 60–61. According to Goff, evidence indicates that Robert Todd Lincoln wanted to enter the service according to period sources, but that his mother acknowledged her reluctance for him to do so, even to her husband. Goff cites Elizabeth Keckley, *Behind the Scenes* (New York: G.W. Carleton, 1868), 119.

41. Morison, 303; Jason Emerson, "Edwin Booth Saved Robert Todd Lincoln's Life," *Civil War Times* (June 12, 2006), in HistoryNet.com, http://www.historynet.com/edwin-booth-saved-robert-todd-lincolns-life.htm (May 15, 2011)

42. Morison, 303.

43. Thomas Jefferson Wertenbaker, *Princeton 1746–1896* (Princeton: Princeton University Press, 1946), 265–266.

44. *Princeton Standard*, August 9, 1861, quoted in Wertenbaker, 270–271.

45. *Princeton Alumni Weekly*, May 23, 1917, quoted in Wertenbaker, 267.

46. Wertenbaker, 268.

47. Ibid., 270.

48. Ewell was appointed professor of mathematics in 1848, acting president in 1848–49, professor of natural philosophy in 1869, and president in 1854. Joynes had been professor of Greek, Greek literature, and German since 1858, the same year that Morrison had been appointed professor of history and political economy. See *The History of William and Mary College, From Its Foundation, 1693, to 1870*, 70–71.

49. Faculty Minutes, May 10, 1861, Book 5, 1847–1883, William & Mary Digital Archive, Swem Library, College of William and Mary, http://hdl.handle.net/10288/13457 (accessed May 31, 2011).

50. Ibid.

51. Robertson, *Civil War Virginia*, 89.

52. Faculty Minutes, 28 September 1861, Book 5, 1847–1883, William and Mary Digital Archive, Swem Library, College of William and Mary, http://hdl.handle.net/10288/13457 (accessed May 31, 2011). Edwin Taliaferro was Professor of Latin, Latin literature, and the Romance languages.

53. McPherson, 426–427.

54. Faculty Minutes, December 1860, Book 5, 1847–1883, http://hdl.handle.net/10288/13457 (accessed May 31, 2011). Founded in 1838 by bookseller George Westermann, Westermann and Co. published dictionaries, books on history, books on travel, and scientific dissertations. In the 1920s and '30s, Westermann and Co. extended its scope in light of the pedagogical reform movement to education. After the war it continued to publish textbooks, other education-oriented books, atlases, and books on geography and history (http://www.euroarchiveguide.org/database/archives_sourcesd_209.htm, (accessed May 22, 2011). Westermann and Co. was located on West Forty-Eighth Street in New York City in the 1930s, and at that time imported books from Germany. It was shut down during World War II. See "New York City Bookshops in the 1930s and 1940s: The Recollections of Walter Goldwater [interview], *DLB Yearbook* 166, 139–172 (http://www.autodidactproject.org/other/goldwat3.html (accessed May 22, 2011).

55. Faculty Minutes, December 1860, Book 5, 1847–1883, http://hdl.handle.net/10288/13457 (accessed May 31, 2011).

56. "The College in the Years 1861–1865," Report by President Benjamin S. Ewell to the Board of Visitors and Governors of the College of William and Mary, Richmond, Virginia, July 5, 1865. In Prentice Duell, *Literary References to the Wren Building*, Colonial Williamsburg Research Report (1931), John D. Rockefeller Jr. Library, The Colonial Williamsburg Foundation, 151.

57. Faculty Assembly Minutes, September 28, 1861, Book 5, 1847–1883, William and Mary Digital Archive, Special Collections Research Center, Swem Library, College of William and Mary.

58. Ibid., September 30, 1861.

59. Ibid., January 20, 1862.

60. John S. Charles, "Recollections of Williamsburg: as it appeared at the beginning of the Civil War and just previously thereto, with some incidents on the life of its citizens," 1928, TR-90, Special Collections, John D. Rockefeller Jr. Library, The Colonial Williamsburg Foundation, 1–2.

61. Charles, 2–3.

62. Dubbs, *Defend This Old Town*, 21.

63. Ibid., 23.

64. Victoria King Lee with Penticolas Lee, "Williamsburg in 1861," Special Collections, John D. Rockefeller Jr. Library, The Colonial Williamsburg Foundation, 1.

65. Lee, "Williamsburg in 1861," 14.

66. Ibid., 15.

67. Dubbs, *Defend This Old Town*, 27.

68. Account found among the Randolph Shotwell Papers and printed in the *William and Mary Quarterly* 13, 26–27, in Dearstyne, 69. An excellent account of wartime medical treatment in Williamsburg is found in Dubbs's history, *Defend This Old Town*.

69. Benjamin S. Ewell's report to the Board of Visitors and Governors of the College of William and Mary, July 5, 1865, in Duell, 151.

70. Charles H. Buttz to the Hon. Legrande W. Perce, February 6, 1872, ID No. 1980.130. Series 1, Box 2, Folder 1, Office of the President, Benjamin Stoddert Ewell Papers, Special Collections Research Center, Swem Library, College of William and Mary.

71. David Edward Cronin, "The Vest Mansion: Its Historical and Romantic Associations as Confederate and Union headquarters (1862–1865) in the American Civil War" (typescript copy of original manuscript in the Collection of the New-York Historical Society), Special Collections, John D. Rockefeller Jr. Library, Colonial Williamsburg Foundation, copy 2, 214. In this account, Cronin describes how Union pickets, as relic hunters, had removed silver coffin plates before being discovered, and that one such piece sent to New York was identified and returned to

William and Mary by a "sensible Northern merchant."
72. Frank H. Taylor, *Philadelphia in the Civil War 1861–1865* (Philadelphia: City of Philadelphia, 1913), 160.
73. Edward J. Longacre, "The Most Inept Regiment of the Civil War," *Civil War Times Illustrated* 8:7 (November 1969): 4–7; William L. Burton, *Melting Pot Soldiers: The Union's Ethnic Regiments* (New York: Fordham University Press, 1998), 103.
74. Robert Hunt Rhodes, ed., *All for the Union: The Civil War Diary and Letters of Elisha Hunt Rhodes* (New York: Orion, 1991).
75. Taylor, 160.
76. Ibid., 160–161.

Chapter 3

1. "The Rebel Retreat a Necessity–Their Supplies [sic] Running Short–Treatment of the Negroes–Search for Concealed Weapons," *New York Times*, May 12, 1862, http://www.nytimes.com/1862/05/18/news/rebel-retreat-necessity-their-suppiles-running-short-treatment-negroes-search.html?scp=4&sq=William%20and%20Mary%20college%2018 62&st=cse (accessed 14 July 2011).
2. Dubbs, *Defend This Old Town*, 268.
3. Cronin, preface, i; Parke Rouse Jr., *Remembering Williamsburg: A Sentimental Journey through Three Centuries* (Richmond, VA: Dietz, 1989), 26
4. *The Union Army: A History of Military Affairs in the Loyal States 1861–65 — Records of the Regiments in the Union Army — Cyclopedia of Battles — Memoirs of Commanders and Soldiers* (Madison, WI: Federal Publishing, 1908), 400. http://openlibrary.org/books/OL6564135M/Philadelphia_in_the_Civil_War_1861-1865 (accessed May 22, 2011).
5. Cronin, 25.
6. William Oliver Stevens, *Old Williamsburg and Her Neighbors* (New York: Dodd, Mead, 1938), 255.
7. Cronin, 90.
8. Cronin, preface, ii.
9. Ibid.
10. Cronin, 25–26, in Mary A. Stephenson, "The Palmer House Historical Report, Block 9 Building 24 Lot 27, Colonial Williamsburg Foundation Library Research Report Series —1131," Colonial Williamsburg Foundation Library, Williamsburg, Virginia, January 1960, 31–32.
11. Dubbs, *Defend This Old Town*, 270.

Later, Campbell was exchanged and resigned his commission on October 13, 1862, replaced by Lt. Col. William Lewis.
12. Dubbs, *Defend This Old Town*, 270.
13. Maj. Gen. H.W. Halleck to Maj. Gen. John A. Dix, September 10, 1862, *Index to Miscellaneous Documents of the House of Representatives for the Session of the Fiftieth Congress, 1887-88* (Washington, D.C.: U.S. Government Printing Office, 1889), 11.
14. Maj. Gen. John A. Dix to Maj. Gen. H.W. Halleck, September 10, 1862, *Index to Miscellaneous Documents of the House of Representatives*, 11.
15. Ibid.
16. According to *The Encyclopaedia Britannica*, *cashiering* is dismissal for an offense committed by officers only that is "scandalous conduct unbecoming to the character of an officer and a gentleman." This punishment is an alternative to imprisonment. See Thomas Spencer Baynes, "Military Law," in *The Encyclopedia Britannica*, vol. 16, H.G. Allen, ed., 1888, k298., http://books.google.com/books?id=BZ0MAAAAYAAJ&pg=PA298&lpg=PA298&dq=cashiering+soldiers&source=bl&ots=PKPCN_8KIf&sig=mA0Pg-EQnrPlbJCbCCctDhScZcw&hl=en&ei=KCTgTY3yEOL10gHi86yoCg&sa=X&oi=book_result&ct=result&resnum=10&sqi=2&ved=0CFgQ6AEwCQ#v=onepage&q=cashiering%20soldiers&f=false (accessed May 27, 2011).
17. Maj. Gen. H.W Halleck, War Department, to Maj. Gen. John A. Dix, Fort Monroe, September 11, 1862, *Index to Miscellaneous Documents of the House of Representatives*, 11.
18. United States War Dept., John Sheldon Moody, Calvin D. Cowles, Frederick C. Ainsworth, Robert N. Scott, Henry M. Lazelle, George Breckenridge, *The War of the Rebellion: A Compilation of the Official Records of the Union and Confederate Armies*, Series 1, vol. 18 (Washington, D.C.: U.S. Government Printing Office, 1887), 391.
19. Maj. Gen. H.W. Halleck, War Department, to Maj. Gen. John A. Dix, Fort Monroe, September 11, 1862, *Index to Miscellaneous Documents of the House of Representatives*, 12.
20. Maj. Wilson was discharged from military service on October 13, 1862, as were Maj. Edward Boteler and Maj. William C. Heuser. See Samuel P. Bates, *History of Pennsylvania Volunteers, 1861–5: Prepared in Compliance with Acts of the Legislature*, vol. 2 (Harrisburg: B. Singley, State Printer), 578.
21. Maj. Gen. H.W Halleck, War Department, to Maj. Gen. John A. Dix, Fort Mon-

roe, September 11, 1862, *Index to Miscellaneous Documents of the House of Representatives*, 13.

22. Ibid.
23. Ibid.
24. Bates, 578.
25. Roger D. Hunt, *Colonels in Blue: Union Army Colonels of the Civil War* (Mechanicsburg, PA: Stackpole Books), 44.
26. Bates, 569.
27. J.L. Slater, "Burning of the College in 1862," in *William and Mary Quarterly* 11:179, Earl Gregg Swem, ed.
28. Dubbs, *Defend This Old Town*, 271–272.
29. Edward P. McKinney, *Life in Tent and Field, 1861–1865* (Boston: Richard G. Badger, Gorham, 1922), 65.
30. *Annual report of the Adjutant-General of the State of New York for the Year 1894*, vol. 2: *Registers of the 5th, 6th, 7th and 8th Regiments of Cavalry, N.Y. Vols., in the War of the Rebellion*, Adjutant General's Office (Albany: James B. Lyon, State Printer, 1895), 485.
31. *Obituary Record of Graduates of Yale College Deceased from July, 1858, to July 1870. Presented at the Annual Meetings of the Alumni, 1860–70* (New Haven, CT: Tuttle, Morehouse & Taylor, 1870), 109.
32. "The Roll of Honor," General City News, *New York Times*, 2.
33. McKinney, 33.
34. Speech by James Lanman Harmar, Yale University, Class of 1861 Triennial Meeting July 27, 1864), 27–28. Winthrop D. Shelton, Secretary. November 25, 1864, New Haven, Connecticut.
35. McKinney, 62.
36. McKinney, 63.
37. McKinney, 64.
38. McKinney, 63–65.
39. Charles, 6.
40. Charles Almanzo Babcock, *Venango County, Pennsylvania: Her Pioneers and People*, vol. 2 (Franklin: PA: J.H. Beers, 1919), 806.
41. Ibid.
42. Ibid.
43. Ibid., 807.
44. *History of the College of William and Mary from Its Foundation, 1693, to 1870*, 52–3.
45. Ibid.
46. Carol K. Dubbs, "Fortress Williamsburg: Preserving a Treasure through Four Years of War," in *Williamsburg Virginia, 1699–199: A City before the State*, Robert O. Maccubbin, ed. Commissioned and produced by Martha Hamilton-Phillips, 300th Anniversary Commission, City of Williamsburg (Richmond: Carter), 101.

47. McPherson, 435–436.
48. Brig. Gen. Henry A. Wise to Maj. Gen. Arnold Elzey, February 10, 1863, *The War of the Rebellion*: v. 1–53 [ser. No. 1–111], 152.
49. Victoria King Lee, 16.
50. Carson O. Hudson, *Civil War Williamsburg* (Williamsburg, VA: Colonial Williamsburg Foundation, 1997), 34.
51. J. Clarence Stonebraker, *The Unwritten South: Cause, Progress, and Result of the Civil War; Relics of Hidden Truth after Forty Years*, 4th ed. (Hagerstown, MD: Hagerstown Bookbinding and Printing, 1903), 121.
52. Cronin, 219–220.
53. Ibid., 221–223; Dubbs, *Defend This Old Town*, 338.
54. Ibid.
55. Carson Hudson, "We Bow Our Heads to Yankee Despotism: Occupied Williamsburg in the War Between the States," in *The Colonial Williamsburg Journal* (Summer 2000).
56. Lyon G. Tyler, *Williamsburg: The Old Colonial Capital* (Richmond: Whittet & Shepperdson, 1903), 93.

Chapter 4

1. Although most of these individuals never returned to William and Mary after the onset of the war, they will still be referred to as "students" in this section for ease of identification.
2. L.A. Wilmer, J.H. Jarrett, and G.W.F. Vernon, *History and Roster of Maryland Volunteers, War of 1861–5*, vol. 1 (Baltimore: Guggenheimer, Weil, 1898), 34. According to this source, William Reynolds deserted in February 1862.
3. Godson et al., 289; Deposition of William Reynolds, 27 February 1872.
4. Jordan, 23, 26.
5. The eastern theater was defined as the region around Virginia. The western theatre was considered Tennessee, Kentucky, western Georgia, etc.
6. Louis H. Manarin, *North Carolina Troops 1861–1865: A Roster*, vol. 3: *Infantry* (Raleigh: North Carolina Office of Archives and History, 1971), 245.
7. Robert E.L. Krick, *Staff Officers in Gray: A Biographical Register of the Staff Officers in the Army of Northern Virginia* (Chapel Hill: University of North Carolina Press, 2003), 136. Sterling H. Gee was mistakenly shot by men of the 26th South Carolina Infantry.
8. Manarin, 245.

9. Ezra J. Warner, *Generals in Gray: Lives of the Confederate Commanders* (Baton Rouge, LA, 1959), 341.
10. Warner, *Generals in Gray,* 342.
11. Richard A. Wise to Henry A. Wise, January 9, 1861, Special Collections Research Center, Swem Library, College of William and Mary.
12. Krick, 308.
13. Rosewell Mansion was destroyed by a fire in 1916. Its ruins are now a historic site that is undergoing archeological study.
14. Online Biographical Directory of the United States Congress, 1771–present.
15. Thomas A. Glenn, *Some Colonial Mansions and Those Who Lived in Them: With Genealogies of the Various Families Mentioned* (Philadelphia: Henry T. Coates, 1899), 195–200; Page L. Warden, *The Kin Patch: A Path to the Past* (White Stone, VA, 1997), 141. John Page and Thomas Jefferson were related both biologically and through marriage.
16. Florence T. Carlton, *A Genealogy of the Known Descendants of Robert Carter of Corotoman* (Richmond, VA: Whittet & Shepperdson, 1982), 215.
17. Krick, 236.
18. Dubbs, *Defend This Old Town*, 3.
19. St. George Tucker was an acquaintance of Thomas Jefferson, who also studied law under George Wythe.
20. Dubbs, *Defend This Old Town*, 14.
21. Thomas Tucker to Cynthia Washington, 16 April 1863, Special Collections Research Center, Swem Library, College of William and Mary.
22. Krick, 289.
23. Ibid., 220.
24. Les Jensen, *32nd Virginia Infantry* (Lynchburg, VA: H.E. Howard, 1990), 194.
25. Dubbs, *Defend This Old Town*, 6, 27, 74; *Official Records*, Series 1, vol. 11, Chapter 23, Part 1, 578; Krick, 220.
26. Krick, 220.
27. Jensen, 2–4. Ewell later became a full colonel in the Confederate Army.
28. These students were Sgt. T.R. Barlow, Sgt. Maj. J.V. Bidgood, Pvt. James H. Dix, Pvt. Henry S. Dix, 2nd Lt. Henley T. Jones Jr., Pvt. Thomas H. Mercer, 1st Lt. W.H.E. Morecock, Pvt. J.D. Myers, and Sgt. L.P. Slater; Dubbs, *Defend This Old Town*, 6–7. The Williamsburg Junior Guard was mustered into Confederate service on April 28, 1861; Jensen, 6–7.
29. Thomas P. Nanzig, *3rd Virginia Cavalry* (Lynchburg, VA: H.E. Howard, 1989), 3.

30. Jensen, 173–209.
31. Components of the 32nd Virginia were also present at the Battle of Antietam in 1862.
32. National Park Service Online Civil War Soldiers and Sailors System, http://www.itd.nps.gov/cwss.
33. Jensen, 196.
34. Richard M. McCurry, *Virginia Military Institute Alumni in the Civil War: In Bello Praesidium* (Lynchburg, VA: H.E. Howard, 1999), 178.
35. David F. Riggs, *13th Virginia Infantry* (Lynchburg, VA: H.E. Howard, 1988), 148.
36. Judge Nathaniel Beverly Tucker was known in Southern political circles for his 1836 novel, *Partisan Leader*, which advocated Southern secession from the Union; Dubbs, *Defend This Old Town*, 22–23.
37. In the early stages of the war, it was common in both the Union and Confederate armies for men to elect their officers. Due to problems resulting from incompetence and inexperience, the Union army abandoned this policy and developed stricter promotion standards. In many cases, the Confederates continued to elect their officers.
38. One source referred to Richard A. Wise as a colonel in the Confederate Army. However, there is no known evidence to support this claim.
39. Strong evidence suggests that the lone Union student, William Reynolds, served in the 1st Maryland Infantry, USA. There are no known students who served in either the Union or Confederate Navies or Marine Corps.
40. "Ground-pounder" was an old military term for an infantryman.
41. "The Burg" is short for Williamsburg, VA.
42. Thomas Tucker to Cynthia Washington, December 6, 1862, Special Collections Research Center, Swem Library, College of William and Mary.
43. Thomas Tucker to Cynthia Washington, November 24, 1862, Special Collections Research Center, Swem Library, College of William and Mary.
44. Thomas Tucker to Cynthia Washington, April 16, 1863, Special Collections Research Center, Swem Library, College of William and Mary.
45. Lyon G. Tyler, ed., *Encyclopedia of Virginia Biography*, vol. 4 (New York: Lewis Historical, 1915), 261–262.
46. Robert J. Driver Jr., *10th Virginia Cavalry* (Lynchburg, VA: H.E. Howard, 1992),

176; Caroline B. Sinclair, *Gloucester's Past In Pictures*, 2nd ed. (Virginia Beach, VA: Walsworth, 2005), 60.

47. Jensen, 173–209; Darrell L. Collins, *46th Virginia Infantry* (Lynchburg, VA: H.E. Howard, 1992), 109; Sgt. George Fosque also served in the 46th Virginia Infantry Regiment.

48. Jensen, 174.

49. Thomas Tucker to Cynthia Washington, April 16, 1863, Special Collections Research Center, Swem Library, College of William and Mary.

50. Kenneth L. Stiles, *4th Virginia Cavalry* (Lynchburg, VA: H.E. Howard, 1985), 97; William D. Henderson, *12th Virginia Infantry* (Lynchburg, VA: H.E. Howard, 1984), 114; *The History of the College of William and Mary from its Foundation, 1660, to 1874*, 152.

51. Dubbs, *Defend This Old Town*, 40.

52. Jensen, 181.

53. Michael A. Cavanaugh, *6th Virginia Infantry* (Lynchburg, VA: H.E. Howard, 1988), 136; Lee A. Wallace Jr., *The Richmond Howitzers* (Lynchburg, VA: H.E. Howard, 1993), 135.

54. Furnishing substitutes was a common method for the affluent in the North and South to get out of military service. Since it was a relatively expensive procedure, it was generally done only by the upper class. See Henderson, 158.

55. Cavanaugh, 133. One source indicates that Newton later served as a second lieutenant and drillmaster in the Confederate Army. However, this information has not been confirmed.

56. Jensen, 174.

57. Brig. Gen. Montgomery Dent Corse, CSA (1816–1895).

58. Col. Edgar B. Montague, CSA (1832–1885). Colonel Montague was also a William and Mary alumnus.

59. Maj. Baker P. Lee, CSA (1830–1901).

60. Joseph V. Bidgood, "Further Reflections of Second Cold Harbor," in *Southern Historical Society Papers*, vol. 37 (Richmond, VA: Southern Historical Society, 1909), 319–320.

61. Carlton, 215.

62. Krick, 236.

63. Krick, 308; Kale, 93.

64. "Memorial Addresses on the Life and Character of Richard Alsop Wise," Fifty-Sixth Congress, Second Session (Washington, D.C.: U.S. Government Printing Office, 1901), 8.

65. Driver, 176; "Congressman Wise Dead," *New York Times*, December 22, 1900.

66. "Memorial Addresses on the Life and Character of Richard Alsop Wise," 10.

67. Frederick Johnston, *Memorials of Old Virginia Clerks* (Lynchburg, VA: J.F. Bell, 1888), 228.

68. Deposition of William Reynolds, February 27, 1872.

69. McCurry, 178.

70. Ibid.

71. Tyler, *Encyclopedia of Virginia Biography*, 262.

72. P.P. Barbour, "John G. Williams," in *Report of the Twenty-Fourth Annual Meeting of the Virginia State Bar Association*, vol. 25 (Richmond, VA: Virginia State Bar Association, 1912), 81–82; Riggs, 148.

73. Jensen, 174; the state militias would later be renamed the National Guard in the early twentieth century.

74. Robert Page Waller Diary, September 22, 1865; October 10, 1865, Special Collections Research Center, Swem Library, College of William and Mary.

75. Cynthia Beverly Tucker Coleman, "Peninsula Campaign," Tucker-Coleman Collection, Special Collections Research Center, Swem Library, College of William and Mary.

76. Jensen, 189.

77. "General Brander of the Virginia Division and his Staff," *Atlanta Journal-Constitution*, July 23, 1898, 15; Jensen, 174, 189.

78. "Congressman Wise Dead," *New York Times*, December 22, 1900.

79. Jensen, 189.

80. Lyon G. Tyler, ed., *William and Mary Quarterly* 11 (Richmond, VA: Whittet & Shepperdson, 1903), 179.

Chapter 5

1. Peter Wallenstein, "Higher Education in Civil War Virginia" (Blacksburg, VA: Virginia Tech, 2007), 9, 13.

2. "Autobiography," President's Papers—Benjamin S. Ewell, Special Collections, Swem Library; Chapman, "Benjamin Stoddert Ewell," 141–42; Deposition of William Reynolds, February 27, 1872; Dubbs, *Defend This Old Town*, 14.

3. Yates Snowden, ed., *History of South Carolina*, vol. 5 (Chicago: Lewis, 1920), 322; E.T. Crowson, "Edward S. Joynes: A Masterful Southern Educator," *William and Mary Alumni Magazine* (Winter 1986), 13–14.

4. Edwin A. Alderman and Joel C. Harris, eds., *Library of Southern Literature*, vol. 7

(Atlanta: Martin and Hoyt, 1907), 2859–2860.

5. Edward S. Joynes to John Tyler, May 29, 1860, Special Collections Research Center, Swem Library, College of William and Mary; "Edward S. Joynes" (pamphlet), Joynes Center for Continuing Studies, Winthrop College, 1981; Dubbs, *Defend This Old Town*, 49, 59, 319.

6. Faculty/Alumni File: Thomas P. McCandlish, Special Collections Research Center, Swem Library, College of William and Mary; Dubbs, *Defend This Old Town*, 27; Jensen, 193; Krick, 205.

7. Miller-Morris Collection, University of Georgia Libraries, University of Georgia, Athens; "Professors at William and Mary College: Charles Morris," *Tyler's Quarterly* 4 (1922), 130–33; Krick, 225–226.

8. Miller-Morris Collection, University of Georgia Libraries, University of Georgia, Athens; "Professors at William and Mary College: Charles Morris," *Tyler's Quarterly* 4 (1922), 130–33; 225–226.

9. Krick, 226; Louise P. du Bellet, *Some Prominent Virginia Families*, vol. 2 (Lynchburg, VA: J.P. Bell, 1907), 525.

10. Du Bellet, 535.

11. Krick, 226. Robert J. Morrison Papers, Special Collections Research Center, Swem Library, College of William and Mary; Dubbs, *Defend This Old Town*, 19, 29–30; Lafayette McClaws to his wife, July 2, July 30–August 1, 1861, McClaws Papers; Cynthia Washington to Charles W. Coleman, July 20, 1861, September 7, 1861, Tucker-Coleman Collection, Special Collections Research Center, Swem Library, College of William and Mary.

12. Robert J. Morrison Papers, Special Collections, Swem Library; Dubbs, *Defend This Old Town*, 19, 29–30; Faculty Minutes, September 28, 1861, Special Collections Research Center, Swem Library, College of William and Mary; Cynthia Washington to Charles W. Coleman, October 31, 1861, Tucker-Coleman Collection, Special Collections Research Center, Swem Library, College of William and Mary.

13. Du Bellet, 536.

14. Krick, 271.

15. Faculty/Alumni File: Thomas T.L. Snead, Special Collections Research Center, Swem Library, College of William and Mary; Lyon G. Tyler, ed., *William and Mary Quarterly* 10 (Richmond, VA: Whittet & Shepperdson, 1902), 126; Dubbs, *Defend This Old Town*, 17, 20, 22, 49, 371; Krick, 271.

16. Du Bellet, 741; Krick, 279–280.

17. Edwin Taliaferro to F. Bland B. Tucker, February 6, 1861, White-Wellford-Taliaferro-Marshall Family Papers, Southern Historical Center, University of North Carolina.

18. Carmichael, 128.

19. Edwin Taliaferro, *An Address Delivered before the Masonic Fraternity of Williamsburg, Virginia, November 15, 1860* (Richmond, VA: Macfarlane & Ferguson, 1861), 28–29.

20. Dubbs, *Defend This Old Town*, 14, 22, 25, 27, 39–40, 43, 49, 57, 63, 69, 73, 88, 347, 367; Jensen, 203; Krick, 279–280.

21. Faculty/Alumni File: Edwin Taliaferro, Special Collections Research Center, Swem Library, College of William and Mary.

22. Ibid.

23. Dubbs, *Defend This Old Town*, 14, 22, 25, 27, 39–40, 43, 49, 57, 63, 69, 73, 88, 347, 367; Jensen, 203.

24. Chapman, "Benjamin Stoddert Ewell," 30–39, 125–58.

25. Robert E. Lee was in his final year of West Point when Benjamin Ewell entered the Academy. Although they were acquaintances for years thereafter, they were never close friends.

26. Chapman, "Benjamin Stoddert Ewell," ix, 41–44, 125–128. The Virginia Peninsula consists of the stretch of land between the James and York Rivers. The city of Williamsburg and the modern-day cities of Newport News and Hampton are located in this area.

27. Chapman, "Benjamin Stoddert Ewell," 129–131.

28. Ibid.

29. Chapman, "Benjamin Stoddert Ewell," 131–135. Fort Magruder was named for Confederate General John B. Magruder.

30. Chapman, "Benjamin Stoddert Ewell," 134–36.

31. Joseph E. Johnston to Robert E. Lee, May 23, 1862, Joseph E. Johnston Papers, Special Collections Research Center, Swem Library, College of William and Mary; Jensen, 68–70, 194; Steven H. Newton, *Joseph E. Johnston and the Defense of Richmond* (Lawrence: University of Kansas Press, 1998).

32. Joseph E. Johnston to Robert E. Lee, May 23, 1862, Joseph E. Johnston Papers, Special Collections Research Center, Swem Library, College of William and Mary; Chapman, "Benjamin Stoddert Ewell," 137–41.

33. Chapman, "Benjamin Stoddert Ewell," 137–141; Warner, *Generals in Gray*, 161; General Johnston was upset that President

Davis placed him in seniority as a full general below Samuel Cooper, Albert Sidney Johnston, and Robert E. Lee, even though Johnston had attained the highest rank (brigadier general) among the group in the antebellum U.S. Army.

34. Chapman, "Benjamin Stoddert Ewell," 137–41.

35. Ibid.

36. Chapman, "Benjamin Stoddert Ewell," 141–44.

37. Chapman, "Benjamin Stoddert Ewell," 144–149.

38. Craig L. Symonds, *Joseph E. Johnston: A Civil War Biography* (New York: W.W. Norton, 1992), 252; Chapman, "Benjamin Stoddert Ewell," 144–150.

39. Benjamin S. Ewell to Braxton Bragg, April 13, 1864, Special Collections Research Center, Swem Library, College of William and Mary; Chapman, "Benjamin Stoddert Ewell," 151–56.

40. Chapman, "Benjamin Stoddert Ewell," 151–156; Bragg was a former student of Ewell's at West Point in the mid-1830s, and Ewell tried to help him whenever he could.

41. Report of Benjamin S. Ewell to General Samuel S. Cooper, August 5, 1864, Johnston Papers, Special Collections Research Center, Swem Library, College of William and Mary.

42. Dispatch Book and "Report of Benjamin S. Ewell, February 20, 1865," Johnston Papers, Special Collections Research Center, Swem Library, College of William and Mary.

43. Chapman, "Benjamin Stoddert Ewell," 156–58.

44. A species of worm had attacked and destroyed many of the pre-existing campus trees either before or during the Civil War.

45. Tyler, *William and Mary Quarterly* 10, 126; Edward S. Griffing, ed., *Sixth Catalogue of Theta Delta Chi* (Boston: Chapple, 1911), 71.

46. Edwin Taliaferro to Benjamin S. Ewell, June 13, 1865, Special Collections Research Center, Swem Library, College of William and Mary; Faculty/Alumni File: Thomas P. McCandlish, Special Collections Research Center, Swem Library, College of William and Mary; Dubbs, *Defend This Old Town*, 371, 373.

47. Crowson, 14.

48. Charles B. Flood, *Lee: The Last Years* (New York: Mariner, 1998), 145–146.

49. Alderman and Harris, 2859; Crowson, 14–15.

50. Crowson, 15.

51. Faculty/Alumni File: Edward S. Joynes, Special Collections Research Center, Swem Library, College of William and Mary; Crowson, 15.

52. A.L. Hull, *A Historical Sketch of the University of Georgia* (Atlanta: Foote & Davies, 1894), 137–138.

53. Faculty/Alumni File: Charles Morris, Special Collections Research Center, Swem Library, College of William and Mary; Gwen Y. Wood, *A Unique and Fortuitous Combination: An Administrative History of the University of Georgia School of Law* (Athens: University of Georgia Press, 1998), 18.

54. Jordan, *Charlottesville*, 23; Virginius Dabney, *Mr. Jefferson's University: A History* (Charlottesville: University of Virginia Press, 1981), 26; Wallenstein, "The Struggle to Learn," 105–106.

55. Wallenstein, "The Struggle to Learn," 104–108.

56. Jon L. Wakelyn, "Civilian Higher Education in the Making of Confederate Army Leaders," in *The Confederate High Command and Related Topics*, Lawrence L. Hewitt and Roman J. Heleniak, eds. (Shippensburg, PA: White Mane, 1990), 80; Wallenstein, "Higher Education in Civil War Virginia," 4–5.

Chapter 6

1. Alumni are considered here to be those who attended and/or graduated from the college.

2. Chapman, "Benjamin Stoddert Ewell," 205. Of the 1,356 students who attended William and Mary between 1825 and 1861, about 1,154 were Virginia residents.

3. Jordan, *Charlottesville*, 23.

4. Wallenstein, "Higher Education in Civil War Virginia," 13.

5. High political office is defined here as service as a member of Congress, ambassador, etc.

6. Allan Peskin, *Winfield Scott and the Profession of Arms* (Kent, OH: Kent State University Press, 2003), 3; Ezra J. Warner, *Generals in Blue: Lives of the Union Commanders* (Baton Rouge: Louisiana State University Press, 1964), 429; John S. Bowman, *Who Was Who in the Civil War* (Avenel, NJ: Crescent, 1994), 183; William A. DeGregorio, *The Complete Book of U.S. Presidents: From George Washington to Bill Clinton* (New York: Gramercy, 1997), 201–202.

7. Elliott, 714; Bowman, 183; Warner, *Generals in Blue*, 430.
8. Doris Kearns Goodwin, *Team of Rivals: The Political Genius of Abraham Lincoln* (New York: Simon & Schuster, 2005), 371–372; Bowman, 183; Warner, *Generals in Blue*, 430.
9. E.G. Swem, "Kentuckians at William and Mary College before 1861 with a Sketch of the College before that Date," in *Filson Quarterly* 23 (1949): 173–198.
10. Albert D. Kirwin, *John J. Crittenden: The Struggle for Union* (Lexington: University of Kentucky Press, 1962), 11–13.
11. Online Biographical Directory of the U.S. Congress; Bowman, 56.
12. Kirwin, v.
13. Ibid., v.
14. *Encyclopedia of the Civil War* (Princeton: Gramercy, 1997), 91–92; Bowman, 56.
15. Parke Rouse Jr., *Cows on the Campus: Williamsburg In Bygone Days* (Richmond, VA: Dietz, 1973), 57–59.
16. Ibid., 60.
17. Ibid.
18. Henry Wilson later served as vice-president under Ulysses S. Grant.
19. Rouse, *Cows on the Campus*, 60.
20. Maj. Gen. J.E.B. Stuart was his first cousin, once removed; Susan R. Hull, *Boy Soldiers of the Confederacy* (New York: Neale, 1905), 125–126.
21. Alexander F. Robertson, *Alexander Hugh Holmes Stuart, 1807–1891: A Biography* (Richmond, VA: William Byrd, 1925), 11–14, 18–34, 51–55, 179–204.
22. "Monthly Record of Current Events," *Harper's New Monthly Magazine* 32 (December 1865 to May 1866): 128; Robertson, *Alexander Hugh Holmes Stuart*, 205–208.
23. "Monthly Record of Current Events," 128.
24. Ibid.
25. Online Biographical Directory of the U.S. Congress; Flood, 80–82; David J. Eicher, *Dixie Betrayed: How the South Really Lost the Civil War* (Lincoln: University of Nebraska Press, 2006), 294–299.
26. Austin M. Trible's great-great-grandnephew is Paul S. Trible Jr., a former member of the U.S. House of Representatives and the U.S. Senate, and current president of Christopher Newport University in Newport News, Virginia.
27. Paul S. Trible Jr., "Austin Meredith Trible and John Trible Thomas Hundley II," in the *Essex County Historical Society Newsletter* 24:2 (May 1984): 2; Bruce S. Allardice, *Confederate Colonels: A Biographical Register* (Columbia: University of Missouri Press, 2008), 203–204.
28. DeGregorio, 150; Thomas T. Munford was appointed brigadier general in November 1864, though it was never officially confirmed.
29. Allardice, *Confederate Colonels*, 296.
30. Norman B. Ferris, *The Trent Affair: A Diplomatic Crisis* (Knoxville: University of Tennessee Press, 1981), 4–6; Online Biographical Directory of the U.S. Congress.
31. Craig L. Symonds, *Lincoln and His Admirals: Abraham Lincoln, the U.S. Navy, and the Civil War* (New York: Oxford University Press, 2008), 80–81; *Encyclopedia of the Civil War*, 363–365; Online Biographical Directory of the U.S. Congress.
32. Tyler played a major role in operating the college for decades through letters and interaction with several college officials, including Benjamin Ewell.
33. Oliver P. Chitwood, *John Tyler: Champion of the Old South* (New York: D. Appleton, 1939), 426; DeGregorio, 149–152.
34. Max J. Skidmore, *After the White House: Former Presidents as Private Citizens* (New York: Palgrave-Macmillan, 2004), 56–57; DeGregorio, 158–159.
35. DeGregorio, 158–159; Skidmore, 56–57.
36. *The History of the College of William and Mary*, 110–153.
37. Ibid.
38. Ibid.
39. Ibid.
40. Krick, 210, 237; Bruce S. Allardice, *Confederate Colonels*, 46.
41. Allardice, *Confederate Colonels*, 185–186.
42. Krick, 119.
43. Samuel H. Early to Jubal A. Early, March 23, 1834, Jubal A. Early Papers, vol. I, Library of Congress; Charles C. Osborne, *Jubal: The Life and Times of General Jubal A. Early, CSA, Defender of the Lost Cause* (Chapel Hill, NC: Algonquin, 1992), 13–14.
44. The eastern theater is defined here as the area including most of Virginia, North Carolina, South Carolina, Maryland, and Pennsylvania.
45. *The History of the College of William and Mary*, 110–153; Nanzig, 100; Jensen, 178.
46. Allardice, *Confederate Colonels*, 185–186, 276.
47. Allardice, *Confederate Colonels*, 231; Lyon G. Tyler, *Men of Mark in Virginia, Ideals*

of American Life: A Collection of Biographies of Leading Men in the State, vol. 1 (Washington, D.C., Men of Mark, 1906), 190–191.

48. Jensen, 159, 194; Allardice, *Confederate Colonels*, 231; Tyler, *Men of Mark in Virginia*, 191.

49. Alexandra L. Levin, *"This Awful Drama": General Edwin Gray Lee, C.S.A., and His Family* (New York: Vantage, 1987), 4–12; Warner, *Generals in Gray*, 177–178.

50. Levin, *"This Awful Drama,"* 20–21.

51. Warner, *Generals in Gray*, 177–178; Alexandra L. Levin, "The Canada Contact: Edwin Gray Lee," *Civil War Times* 18:3 (June 1979): 4–8.

52. Levin, "The Canada Contact," 42–47; Levin, *"This Awful Drama,"* 122–123.

53. Levin, "The Canada Contact," 42–47.

54. Warner, *Generals in Gray*, 297–298; Bowman, 204; Helen P. Trimpi, *Crimson Confederates: Harvard Men Who Fought for the South* (Knoxville, TN: University of Tennessee Press, 2010), 296.

55. Trimpi, 297.

56. Bowman, 204; Warner, *Generals in Gray*, 340; Trimpi, 298–300.

57. Taliaferro's promotion to major general is disputed by historians. Although he was listed in his official parole as a major general, no Confederate records are known to exist that acknowledge his promotion to that rank. In her book *Crimson Confederates*, Helen P. Trimpi argues that Taliaferro was approved for promotion to major general in January 1865, but the promotion was contingent upon whether an appropriate command could be made available. However, in the chaotic final months of the war, such a position was never found, leaving Taliaferro in an administrative limbo concerning his military rank. For the purposes of this book, he is referred to as a major general.

58. Bowman, 204; *Official Records*, Series 1, vol. 35, Chapter 47, Part 1, 620; Ludwell L. Montague, *Gloucester County in the Civil War*, 37–40; Trimpi, 300–305.

59. Bruce S. Allardice, *More Generals in Gray* (Baton Rouge: Louisiana State University Press, 2006), 1–14.

60. Ibid., 22–23.

61. Ibid., 23.

62. Ibid., 108–109.

63. Ibid.

64. Ibid.

65. *The History of the College of William and Mary*, 110–153; Jensen, 178; "Richard Coke," *The Biographical Encyclopedia of Texas* (New York: Southern Publishing, 1880), 17.

66. "William Dunnington Bloxham," *The National Cyclopaedia of American Biography*, vol. 11 (New York: J.T. White, 1901), 382.

67. Wyndham Robertson, *Pocahontas and Her Descendants* (Richmond, VA: J.W. Randolph & English, 1887), 81–83; Jacob N. Breneman, *A History of Virginia Conventions* (Richmond, VA: J.L. Hill, 1902), 78.

68. "Beverly Browne Douglas," Online Biographical Directory of the United States Congress; Trimpi, 305; *The History of the College of William and Mary*, 110–153.

69. Elizabeth City County was later merged into the City of Hampton, Virginia.

70. Sara E. Bearss, ed., *Dictionary of Virginia Biography*, vol. 3 (Richmond: Library of Virginia, 2006), 107–108.

71. Ibid.

72. Bearss, 108–109; Trimpi, 305; Tyler, *Men of Mark in Virginia*, 191–192.

73. Edmund Ruffin attended the College between 1810 and 1812.

Chapter 7

1. "The Civil War and the University of Richmond," The University of Richmond, http://urhistory.richmond.edu/milestones/civilWar.html (accessed June 9, 2011).

2. Pace, 104–105.

3. Pace, 115.

4. "The Civil War and the University of Richmond."

5. "Custer marker at UVa. Removed; error cited," *Washington Times*, C4, May 11, 2001, http://www.garryowen.com/uva.htm (accessed June 9, 2011). There has been some controversy over whether or not city and town officials actually surrendered; see Ervin L. Jordan, Jr., "Charlottesville During the Civil War," *Encyclopedia Virginia*, http://www.encyclopediavirginia.org/Charlottesville_During_the_Civil_War (accessed June 9, 2011).

6. Dan R. Frost, *Thinking Confederates*, Knoxville, TN: University of Tennessee Press, 2000, 30.

7. Pace, 115.

8. Ibid.

9. Benjamin Ewell to Hugh Blair Grigsby, October 1864, quoted in Chapman, "Benjamin Stoddard Ewell," 166.

10. Report by President Benjamin S. Ewell to the Board of Visitors and Governors, The

Notes—Chapter 7

College of William and Mary, July 5, 1861, in Duell, 155–156.

11. Chapman, "Benjamin Stoddert Ewell," 167.

12. L.N. Holly and J.P. Martin, "Leadership in Crisis: A Historical Analysis of Two College Presidencies in Reconstruction Virginia," *Higher Education in Review* 9 (2012): 50–51.

13. Eric Foner, *A Short History of Reconstruction*, New York: Harper & Row, 1990, 164.

14. Chapman, 230–232.

15. Ibid., 233.

16. Ibid., 234–235.

17. Ibid., 248–249.

18. Benjamin Ewell, Report to the Board, July 5, 1865, in Duell, 161.

19. Ibid.

20. Faculty Assembly Minutes, August 2, 1865, in Duell, 163.

21. Letter from Robert. E. Lee to the Trustees of Washington College, August 24, 1865, in Douglas Southall Freeman, *R.E. Lee: A Biography* (New York: Charles Scribner's Sons, 1934), 318.

22. Freeman, 224.

23. As a state-supported institution, Washington College had previously received interest from bonds guaranteed by the state.

24. Freeman, 248.

25. Holly and Martin, p. 47.

26. Gen. Robert E. Lee to Mrs. Cynthia B. Tucker Coleman, January 21, 1867, MS. Tucker-Coleman Papers, Photostat in Department of Research and Record, Colonial Williamsburg Incorporated, in Dearstyne, 74.

27. Allen Brinkley, *The Unfinished Nation: A Concise History of the American People*, 5th ed. (Boston: McGraw-Hill, 2008), 404–405.

28. "Address of Colonel William Lamb in receiving the tablet, on behalf of the Visitors of the College," *Addresses delivered at the Unveiling of the Tablet erected by the Alumni to the Memory of Benjamin Stoddert Ewell, LLD, late President of the College of William and Mary, College Chapel, June 21, 1899*. Published by the Alumni Association, Richmond, VA: Whittet & Shepperdson, 1988, 14. ID No. 1980.130, Series 1, Series 1, Box 2, Folder 6, Office of the President, Benjamin Stoddert Ewell Papers, Special Collections Research Center, Earl Gregg Swem Library, The College of William and Mary.

29. Report to the Board of Visitors and Governors of The College of William and Mary, September 14, 1866, in Duell, 164; Chapman, "Benjamin Stoddert Ewell," 178.

30. Ulysses Simpson Grant, John Y. Simon, *The Papers of Ulysses S. Grant*, January 1–September 30, 1867 (Carbondale: Southern Illinois University Press, 1991), 135.

31. Chapman, "Benjamin Stoddert Ewell," 178.

32. Ibid., 183.

33. Report from Benjamin Ewell to the Board of Visitors, March 27, 1887, as cited in Lisa Heuvel, "The Peal That Wakes No Echo: Benjamin Ewell and the College of William and Mary," *Virginia Cavalcade* 28:2 (Autumn 1978): 77.

34. *Weekly Gazette*, Williamsburg, VA, March 28, 1860, in Duell, 146.

35. "Honorary Degree Recipients," The College of William and Mary.

36. Holly and Martin, p. 55.

37. "Honorary Degree Recipients," The College of William and Mary.

38. Ibid.

39. Ibid.

40. Ibid.

41. Jennifer Green, "Virginia Military Institute during the Civil War," *Encyclopedia Virginia*, http://www.encyclopediavirginia.org/Virginia_Military_Institute_During_the_Civil_War.

42. Chapman, "The College of William and Mary, 1849–59," 77, 81.

43. Ibid., 79.

44. Chapman, "Benjamin Stoddert Ewell," 97–98.

45. Ibid., 98.

46. Chapman, "The College of William and Mary, 1849–59," 80.

47. Ibid.

48. Letter from George E. Dabney to Fleming B. Miller, June 8, 1854, Ewell Family Papers, Folder 2, Special Collections, Swem Library, College of William and Mary.

49. Chapman, 187.

50. Parke Rouse Jr., "'Old Buck': A Hero in Spite of Himself," *William and Mary Alumni Gazette* 50:6 (Winter 1983): 20.

51. "George Washington Custis Lee," Arlington House, the Robert E. Lee Memorial (National Park Service).

52. Frost, 73.

53. Smith, *Distinctive Traditions*, 34–35,

54. Ibid., 37.

55. Letter from Benjamin S. Ewell to the editor of the *Richmond Whig*, September 16, 1868, ID No. 1980.130, Series 1, Box 2, Folder 4, Office of the President, Benjamin Stoddert Ewell Papers, Special Collections Research Center, Swem Library, College of William and Mary.

56. Letter from Benjamin S. Ewell to Elizabeth S. Ewell Scott, January 4, 1868. ID No. 1980.130, Series 1, Box 2, Folder 4, Office of the President, Benjamin Stoddert Ewell Papers, Special Collections Research Center, Swem Library, College of William and Mary.

57. Letter from Benjamin Stoddert Ewell to the editor of the *New York Times*, January 5, 1869. ID No. 1980.130, Box 2, 1868–1874, Folder 4, Office of the President, Benjamin Stoddert Ewell Papers, Special Collections Research Center, Swem Library, College of William and Mary.

58. Ibid.

59. Letter from Thomas Dunn English to Benjamin S. Ewell, March 2, 1869, ID No. 1980.130, Series 1, Box 1, Folder 4, Office of the President, Benjamin Stoddert Ewell Papers, Special Collections Research Center, Swem Library, College of William and Mary.

60. Letter from Frederick Barnard to Rev. Dr. B.L. Haight, December 13, 1869, ID No. 1980.130, Series 1, Box 2, Folder 5, Office of the President, Benjamin Stoddert Ewell Papers, Special Collections Research Center, Swem Library, College of William and Mary.

61. Letter from Benjamin S. Ewell to Hugh Blair Grigsby, August 21, 1867, Single Transcript TR 00, 1800–1933 and no date, Special Collections, John D. Rockefeller Jr. Library, The Colonial Williamsburg Foundation.

62. Joseph M. Stetar, "In Search of a Direction: Southern Higher Education after the Civil War," *History of Education Quarterly* 25:3 (Autumn 1985): 341.

63. Peter Wallenstein, *Cradle of America: Four Centuries of Virginia History* (Lawrence: University of Kansas Press, 2007), 224–225.

64. Chapman, "Benjamin Stoddert Ewell," 204.

65. Ibid., 230.

66. Ibid., 229.

67. Chapman, "Benjamin Stoddert Ewell," 238.

68. Cronin, 258.

69. Letter of Maj. Gen. Ambrose Burnside to Benjamin S. Ewell, January 16, 1869, Benjamin S. Ewell Papers, 1980.130, Box 1, Folder 4, ID No. 1980.130, Series 1, Box 2, Folder 4 Office of the President, Benjamin Stoddert Ewell Papers, Special Collections Research Center, Swem Library, College of William and Mary. Office of the President, Benjamin Stoddert Ewell Papers, Special Collections Research Center, Swem Library, College of William and Mary.

70. Herbert Baxter Adams, *The History of the College of William and Mary: A Contribution to the History of Higher Education, With Suggestions for Its National Promotion* (Washington, D.C.: U.S. Government Printing Office, 1887), 54, http://books.google.com/books?id=WpgaAAAAYAAJ&pg=PA54&lpg=PA54&dq=benjamin+ewell+joseph+e.+johnston&source=bl&ots=BO5cHI3oDi&sig=BkBxKu6CCYjqIJ0TtDkYna08ZRs&hl=en&ei=zNDJTb2hLIXagQfBq8DxBQ&sa=X&oi=book_result&ct=result&resnum=1&ved=0CBsQ6AEwADgK#v=onepage&q=benjamin%20ewell%20joseph%20e.%20johnston&f=false (accessed 27 June 2011), 65.

71. Letter from Henry A. Wise to the Rector, Visitors and Faculty of William and Mary College, July 22, 1870. ID No. 1980.130. Series 1, Box 2, Folder 5, Office of the President, Benjamin Stoddert Ewell Papers, Special Collections Research Center, Swem Library, College of William and Mary.

72. Ibid.

73. Chapman, "Benjamin Stoddert Ewell," 210–211.

74. *Congressional Globe*, February 24, 1872, 98, http://books.google.com/books?id=qkMFAAAAYAAJ&dq=%22fifth+pennsylvania+cavalry%22&q=William+and+Mary+College#v=snippet&q=William%20and%20Mary%20College&f=false (accessed June 28, 2011).

75. Ibid.

76. Ibid., 95.

77. Ibid.

78. Ibid., 217.

79. John Esten Cooke, "William and Mary College," in *Scribner's Monthly* (November 1875), 14, http://books.google.com/books?id=4q3PAAAAMAAJ&pg=PA1&dq=Scribner%27s+Monthly+November+1875&hl=en&ei=GEcmTtzBFcPLgQfflNFc&sa=X&oi=book_result&ct=result&resnum=1&ved=0CC8Q6AEwAA#v=onepage&q=Scribner%27s%20Monthly%20November%201875&f=false, (accessed June 27, 2011).

80. Ibid.

81. Ibid., 15.

82. John J.W. O'Donoghue and E.A. Hewitt, eds., "Fires in College Buildings," *The Chronicle: A Weekly Insurance Journal* 19:6 (Feb. 8, 1877): 81, http://books.google.com/books?id=9XwoAAAAYAAJ&printsec=frontcover#v=onepage&q&f=false (accessed June 25, 2011).

83. McKinney, 66.

84. Ibid., 67–73.

85. Ibid., 237–238.

86. Russell Smith, "The Second Founding of William and Mary," *The Alumni Gazette of the College of William and Mary* 17:6 (January–February 1980), 10–11.

87. Chapman, "Benjamin Stoddert Ewell," 36.

88. "Alma Mater," a poem by Charles Washington Coleman, in *Two hundredth anniversary of the charter of the College of William and Mary, 1693–1883* (Richmond, VA: Whittet & Shepperdson, 1894), 18. http://books.google.com/books?id=uwoTAQAAMAAJ&dq=Benjamin+Ewell&q=Coleman#v=snippet&q=Coleman&f=false (accessed June 18, 2011).

89. Ibid., 22. Coleman's biography may be found in http://myweb.wvnet.edu/~jelkins/lp-2001/coleman.html, (accessed June 18, 2011).

90. Chapman, "Benjamin Stoddert Ewell," 258.

91. Frost, 82.

92. Smith, "Distinctive Traditions," 47.

93. Frost, 90. According to Frost, a study conducted near the end of the 19th century found that scientific equipment at nine Northern schools averaged $211,000 per institution, in comparison to nine Southern schools with comparable equipment averaging $41,587 each.

94. Adams, 62.

95. Ibid., 88.

96. Ibid., 67.

97. Ewell to the Visitors and Governors, November 26, 1885, as quoted in Sacks, 45.

98. Smith, "The Second Founding of William and Mary," 9.

99. Ibid.,12.

100. Ibid., 13.

101. Letter from H.N.R. Dawson to Col. B.S. Ewell, May 11, 1887, in *Letters, Etc., Relating to the College of William and Mary*, printed by Benjamin Long, *Gazette* Office, Williamsburg, VA (n.d.), 4. ID No. 1980.130. Series 1, Box 2, Folder 6. 1872–1899, Office of the President, Benjamin Stoddert Ewell Papers, Special Collections Research Center, Swem Library, College of William and Mary.

102. Letter from D.C. Gilman, Ll.D., President of Johns Hopkins University, to Col. Benjamin Ewell, May 28, 1887, in *Letters, Etc., Relating to the College of William and Mary*, 1.

103. Letter from Charles F. Richardson, Secretary, Phi Beta Kappa, Alpha of New Hampshire, to President Ewell, Williamsburg, Va. June 10, 1887, in *Letters, Etc., Relating to the College of William and Mary*, 2.

104. Letter from Hugh Blair Grigsby to Benjamin S. Ewell, January 28. 1868.

Epilogue

1. Kale, 91.

2. "William and Mary Chronology," The College of William and Mary; Kale, 91.

3. Smith, "The Second Founding of William and Mary," 15.

4. Godson et al., II: 442.

5. Godson et al., II: 441–442, 454.

6. "Historical Chronology of William and Mary," College of William and Mary.

7. Smith, "Distinctive Traditions," 113.

8. Ibid.

9. Ibid.

10. "Historical Chronology of William and Mary," The College of William and Mary.

11. J. Allen Watts, "An address delivered before the society of the alumni of the college of William and Mary on the occasion of the celebration of the two hundredth anniversary of the charter, June 21, 1893," *Two Hundredth Anniversary of the College of William and Mary 1693* (Richmond, VA: Whittet & Shepperdson, 1894), 40. Like his father, Senator Watts attended William and Mary. He then attended law school at the University of Virginia, practiced law in Roanoke, Virginia, and was acknowledged as one of the leaders of the Virginia Bar.

12. Frost, 38.

13. Ibid., 58.

14. "Lyon G. Tyler," Biographical Sketch, Swem Library Special Collections Research Center Wiki, College of William and Mary.

15. "John Tyler," Biographical Sketch, Swem Library Special Collections Research Center Wiki, College of William and Mary.

16. Lyon G. Tyler, *A Confederate Catechism: The War of 1861–1865*, 3rd ed. (Holdcroft, VA: Lyon G. Tyler, 1930), 5.

17. Wallenstein, *Cradle of America*, 271.

18. Brinkley, 575.

19. Frost, 57–58.

20. Paul Lombardo, "Eugenic Laws against Race Mixing," Image Archive on the American Eugenics Movement, http://www.eugenicsarchive.org/html/eugenics/essay7text.html (accessed July 15, 2011).

21. Richard Sherman, "The Last Stand: The Fight for Racial Integrity in Virginia in the 1920s," *The Southern Historical Association* 54:1 (February 1988): 69–70.

22. Julian Alvin C. Chandler, "Installa-

tion Address of Dr. J.A.C. Chandler," *The William and Mary Quarterly* 14:4 (October 1934), 290–294.

23. Tony Gabriele, "'To Perish in Its Purity': *Daily Press* editorial urged further racial separation in extreme terms," *Daily Press*, Newport News, Virginia, http://www.dailypress.com/news/black-history/dp-09955sy0may30,0,6566289.story (accessed July 10, 2011).

24. Terry L. Meyers, "A First Look at the Worst: Slavery and Race Relations at the College of William and Mary," *William & Mary Bill of Rights Journal* 16:4 (2008), 1158. http://scholarship.law.wm.edu/wmborj/vol16/iss4/8/ (accessed November 10, 2012) ; *The Flat Hat*, College of William and Mary, February 15, 1924.

25. *The Flat Hat*, College of William and Mary, February 15, 1921.

26. "Ku Klux Klan," Special Collections Research Center Database, Swem Library, College of William and Mary.

27. Godson et al., II: 612–613.

28. J. Wilfred Lambert, Oral History. Williamsburg, Virginia, January 8, 1975, 34. William & Mary Digital Archive, Swem Library Special Collections, Swem Library, College of William and Mary.

29. Thomas Lipscomb, "Two, Four, Six, Eight. We Want to Integrate,'" *William and Mary Alumni Magazine* 75:2 (Winter 2009). William and Mary Alumni Association.

30. "African Americans and the College: A Historical Timeline," The Lemon Project, College of William and Mary.

31. John Thelin, "Alma Mater, Lost and Found: The American Campus Restored, 1880 to 1930," *The Alumni Gazette of The College of William and Mary* 50:6, 9.

32. Thelin, 11.

33. Anders Greenspan, *Creating Colonial Williamsburg: The Restoration of Virginia's Eighteenth-Century Capital*, 2nd ed. (Chapel Hill: University of North Carolina Press, 2009), 1.

34. Greenspan, 25.

35. Greenspan, 13.

36. Roseanne Thaiss Butler, "The Man Who Said No," *Civil War Journal* (Autumn, 2011), history.org/foundation/journal/autumn 11/man.cfm (accessed August 17, 2012).

37. Kelly Brennan, Ben Bromley, Zach Hilpert, Kim Lincoln, Maggie McDonald, Salar Mohandesi, Caroline Murray, Vanessa Ponton, Cherie Seise, Constance Sisk, and Sam Walsh, "Integration at Work: The First Labor History of the College of William and Mary" (Unpublished paper, College of William and Mary, 2008), 13–14.

38. Butler, ibid.

39. "Copeland's name stricken from award," *Washington Times*, July 26, 2000.

40. Colin Daileda, "Powell Hall renamed," *The Tartan* (Radford University's student newspaper), September 7, 2010.

41. Erin Zagursky, "Lemon Project wins Image award, gears up for events," *The William and Mary News*, April 26, 2011.

42. Joseph McClean, "Archaeologists uncover the remains of a Civil War well," *William and Mary Ideation*, August 23, 2012.

43. Ibid.; Brock Vergakis, "William and Mary Civil War Remnants Discovered," *Huffington Post*, August 19, 2012.

44. Warren G. Harding, *Address of the President of the United States at the College of William and Mary, Williamsburg, Virginia, October 19, 1921* (Washington, D.C.: no publisher, 1921), 10.

45. Ibid.

46. Ibid.

Bibliography

Manuscripts

Swem Library, College of William and Mary, Williamsburg, Virginia

Special Collections Research Center:
Ewell Family Papers.
Joseph E. Johnston Papers.
Robert P. Waller Diaries, 13 vols., 1858–1872.
Richard A. Wise Papers.
Robert J. Morrison Papers.
Tucker-Coleman Collection.
Chronology File, Subject File College.
College Matriculation Book, Bursar.
Faculty Assembly Minutes.
President's Papers — Benjamin S. Ewell.

John D. Rockefeller, Jr., Library, Colonial Williamsburg Foundation, Williamsburg, Virginia

Special Collections:
Charles, John S. "Recollections of Williamsburg: as it appeared at the beginning of the Civil War and just previously thereto, with some incidents on the life of its citizens" (1928).
Cronin, David Edward. "The Vest Mansion, Its Historical and Romantic Associations as Confederate and Union Headquarters (1862–1865) in the American Civil War" (1908–1910). (Typescript copy of original manuscript in the Collection of the New-York Historical Society.)
Lee, Victoria King, with Penticolas Lee. "Williamsburg in 1861."

Public Services:
Dearstyne, Howard. "Architectural History of the Wren Building of the College of William and Mary." Colonial Williamsburg Foundation Library Research Report Series (1951).
Duell, Prentice. "Literary References to the Wren Building." Colonial Williamsburg Foundation Library Research Report Series (1931).
Stephenson, Mary A. "The Palmer House Historical Report, Block 9 Building 24 Lot 27, Colonial Williamsburg Foundation Library Research Report Series — 1131." Williamsburg, VA: Colonial Williamsburg Foundation Library, January 1960, 31–32. Reports\RR1131.xml (accessed June 2, 2011).

The Library of Congress, Washington, D.C.

Library Manuscripts Collection:
Jubal A. Early Papers.

University of Georgia Libraries, Athens, Georgia

Library Manuscripts Collection:
Miller-Morris Collection.

Wilson Library, University of North Carolina, Chapel Hill, North Carolina

Southern Historical Collection:
Lafayette McClaws Papers, 472.
White-Wellford-Taliaferro-Marshall Papers.

Thomas Cooper Library, University of South Carolina, Columbia, South Carolina

Caroliniana Library:
Edward S. Joynes Papers.

Virginia Historical Society, Richmond, Virginia

Library Manuscripts Collection:
Thomas S. Place Scrapbook, 1862–1899.

Online Primary Sources

Adams, Herbert Baxter. *The History of the College of William and Mary: A Contribution to the History of Higher Education, With Suggestions for Its National Promotion*. Washington, D.C.: U.S. Government Printing Office, 1887. http://books.google.com/books?id=WpgaAAAAYAAJ&pg=PA54&lpg=PA54&dq=benjamin+ewell+joseph+e.+johnston&source=bl&ots=BO5cHI3oDi&sig=BkBxKu6CCYjqIJ0TtDkYna08ZRs&hl=en&ei=zNDJTb2hLIXagQfBq8DxBQ&sa=X&oi=book_result&ct=result&resnum=1&ved=0CBsQ6AEwADgK#v=onepage&q=benjamin%20ewell%20joseph%20e.%20johnston&f=false (accessed 27 June 2011).

Babcock, Charles Almanzo. *Venango County, Pennsylvania: Her Pioneers and People*, vol. 2. Franklin, PA: J.H. Beers, 1919. (accessed June 4, 2011).

Bates, Samuel P. *History of Pennsylvania Volunteers, 1861–5: Prepared in Compliance with Acts of the Legislature*, vol. 2. Harrisburg: B. Singley, State Printer. (accessed June 1, 2011).

Beverly, Robert. *The History and Present State of Virginia, in Four Parts*, vol. 1 (1705). In "Documenting the American South." http://docsouth.unc.edu/southlit/beverley/beverley.html, 91 (accessed May 11, 2011). http://docsouth.unc.edu/southlit/beverley/beverley.html, 91 (accessed May 11, 2011).

Coleman, Charles Washington. "Alma Mater," a poem. In *Two hundredth anniversary of the charter of the College of William and Mary, 1693–1883*. Richmond, VA: Whittet & Shepperdson, 1894. http://books.google.com/books?id=uwoTAQAAMAAJ&dq=Benjamin+Ewell&q=Coleman#v=snippet&q=Coleman&f=false (accessed June 18. 2011).

Congressional Globe, February 24, 1872. http://books.google.com/books?id=qkMFAAAAYAAJ&dq=%22fifth+pennsylvania+cavalry%22&q=William+and+Mary+College#v=snippet&q=William%20and%20Mary%20College&f=false (accessed June 28, 2011).

Cooke, John Esten. "William and Mary College." In *Scribner's Monthly* (November 1875). http://books.google.com/books?id=4q3PAAAAMAAJ&pg=PA1&dq=Scribner%27s+Monthly+November+1875&hl=en&ei=GEcmTtzBFcPLgQffNFc&sa=X&oi=book_result&ct=result&resnum=1&ved=0CC8Q6AEwAA#v=onepage&q=Scribner%27s%20Monthly%20November%201875&f=false (accessed June 27, 2011).

Harmar, James Lanman. Speech, Yale University, Class of 1861 Triennial Meeting July 27, 1864), 27–28. Winthrop D. Shelton, Secretary. November 25, 1864, New Haven, CT. http://www.ebooksread.com/authors-eng/yale-university-class-of-1861 Duell1-/triennial-meeting-goo/1-triennial-meeting-goo.shtml

"Joseph Edward Choate." In 1911 *Encyclopaedia Britannica*: http://www.1911encyclopedia.com/Joseph_Hodges_Choate (accessed May 31, 2011).

Lambert, J. Wilfred. Oral History. Williamsburg, Virginia, January 8, 1975, 34. William and Mary Digital Archive, Swem Library Special Collections, Swem Library, College of William and Mary. https://digitalarchive.wm.edu/handle/10288/3481.

O'Donoghue, John J.W., and E.A. Hewitt, eds. "Fires in College Buildings." In *The Chronicle: A Weekly Insurance Journal* 19:6 (Feb. 8, ewitt, EdsHewitt, 1877): 81. http://books.google.com/books?id=9XwoAAAAYAAJ&printsec=frontcover#v=onepage&q&f=false (accessed June 25, 2011).

"The Rebel Retreat a Necessity–Their Suppiles [sic] Running Short–Treatment of the Negroes–Search for Concealed Weapons," *New York Times*, May 12, 1862. http://www.nytimes.com/1862/05/18/news/rebel-retreat-necessity-their-suppiles-running-short-treatment-negroes-search.html?scp=4&sq=William%20and%20Mary%20college%201862&st=cse (accessed July 14, 2011).

Rhodes, Robert Hunt, ed. *All for the Union: The Civil War Diary and Letters of Elisha Hunt Rhodes*. New York: Orion, 1991.

http://www.wwnorton.com/college/history/archive/resources/documents/ch17_04.htm, paragraph 17 (accessed May 31, 2011).

"The Roll of Honor," General City News, *New York Times*, September 14, 1862, 2. http://www.nytimes.com/1862/09/14/news/general-city-news.html?scp=2&sq=South%20Presbyterian%20Church%20+%20September%2014,%201862&st=p&pagewanted=2, (accessed June 1, 2011).

Slater, J.L. "Burning of the College in 1862." In *William and Mary Quarterly*, 11:179, Earl Gregg Swem, ed. http://books.google.com/books?id=GSYjAQAAIAAJ&pg=PA178&dq=henley+t.+jones&hl=en&ei=PSjVTeTMAob2gAeLgLGDDA&sa=X&oi=book_result&ct=result&resnum=2&ved=0CEQQ6AEwAQ#v=onepage&q=henley%20t.%20jones&f=false, (accessed May 22, 2011).

United States War Dept., John Sheldon Moody, Calvin D. Cowles, Frederick C. Ainsworth, Robert N. Scott, Henry M. Lazelle, George Breckenridge. *The War of the Rebellion: A Compilation of the Official Records of the Union and Confederate Armies*, Series 1, vol. 18. Washington;, D.C.: U.S. Government Printing Office, 1887. http://ebooks.library.cornell.edu/m/moawar//text/waro0026.txt (accessed May 27, 2011).

William and Mary Digital Archive: Faculty Assembly Minutes, Book 5 (1846-1855). https://digitalarchive.wm.edu/bitstream/handle/10288/13457/FM51846-1855.pdf?sequence=1.

Wise, Brig. Gen. Henry A., letter to Maj. Gen. Arnold Elzey, February 10, 1863, *The War of the Rebellion*: v. 1–53 [ser. No. 1–111], 152, http://books.google.com/books?id=ed4OAQAAMAAJ&pg=PA152&dq=Henry+A.+Wise++%22rascally+Germans&hl=en&ei=YujqTf2EGZG0sAPQzbXoDQ&sa=X&oi=book_result&ct=result&resnum=2&ved=0CC8Q6AEwAQ#v=onepage&q=Henry%20A.%20Wise%20%20%22rascally%20Germans&f=false (accessed June 4, 2011).

Published Primary Sources (Letters, Memoirs, Reports and Speeches)

Annual report of the Adjutant-General of the State of New York for the Year 1894, vol. 2: Registers of the 5th, 6th, 7th, and 8th Regiments of Cavalry, N.Y. Vols., in the War of the Rebellion. Adjutant General's Office. Albany: James B. Lyon, State Printer, 1895.

Bidgood, Joseph V. "Further Reflections of Second Cold Harbor." In *Southern Historical Society Papers*, vol. 37, ed. R.A. Brock. Richmond, VA: Southern Historical Society, 1909.

Chandler, Julian Alvin C. "Installation Address of Dr. J.A.C. Chandler." In *The William and Mary Quarterly* 14:4 (October 1934): 290–294.

Columbia University. "Proceedings at the Inauguration of Frederick A.P. Barnard, S.T.D., Ll.D., as President of Columbia College on Monday, October 3, 1864." New York: Hurd and Houghton, 1865.

The Flat Hat. College of William and Mary, February 15, 1921.

Garland, William H., and Samuel Garland. "Letters of Wm. H. Garland and Samuel M. Garland, Students at William and Mary College, 1823–1824." In *William and Mary Quarterly* 11:2 (April 1931): 136–145.

Grant, Ulysses Simpson, and John Y. Simon. *The Papers of Ulysses S. Grant*, January 1–September 30, 1867. Carbondale: Southern Illinois University Press, 1991. http://books.google.com/books?id=Mk7a6J79RO0C&printsec=frontcover#v=onepage&q=Benjamin%20Ewell&f=false (accessed June 10, 2011).

Harvie, E. J. Benjamin Stoddert Ewell Obituary Notice, (report of the) Twenty-Sixth Annual Reunion of the Associates of the Graduates of the United States Military Academy, June 10, 1895. http://penelope.uchicago.edu/Thayer/E/Gazetteer/Places/America/United_States/Army/USMA/AOG_Reunions/26/Benjamin_S_Ewell*.html (accessed November 19, 2012).

Index to Miscellaneous Documents of the House of Representatives for the Session of the Fiftieth Congress, 1887–88. Washington, D.C.: U.S. Government Printing Office, 1889.

Keckley, Elizabeth. *Behind the Scenes*. New York: G.W. Carleton, 1868.

Lester, Charles Edwards. *Lester's History of the United States, Illustrated in Its Five Great Periods: Colonization, Consolidation, Development, Achievement, Advancement*, vol. 1. New York: P.F. Collier, 1883. Google eBook, https://play.google.com/store/books/details?id=5XJBAAAAIAAJ&rdid=book-5XJBAAAAIAAJ&rdot=1 (accessed November 19, 2012).

Letters, Etc., Relating to the College of William and Mary. Printed by Benjamin Long,

Gazette Office, Williamsburg, VA (n.d.). ID No. 1980.130. Series 1, Box 2, Folder 6. 1872–1899, Office of the President, Benjamin Stoddert Ewell Papers, Special Collections Research Center, Swem Library, College of William and Mary.

McKinney, Edward P. *Life in Tent and Field, 1861–1865.* Boston: Richard G. Badger, Gorham, 1922.

"Memorial Addresses on the Life and Character of Richard Alsop Wise." Fifty-Sixth Congress, Second Session. Washington D.C.: U.S. Government Printing Office, 1901.

"Monthly Record of Current Events." *Harper's New Monthly Magazine* 32 (1866).

Northrup, Cyrus, Ll.D. "Yale's Relation to the Development of the Country: An Address delivered at the Yale Bicentennial Celebration, New Haven, Connecticut, October 22, 1901." Minneapolis: Printed privately, 1901.

Obituary Record of Graduates of Yale College Deceased from July 1858 to July 1870. Presented at the Annual Meetings of the Alumni, 1860–70. New Haven, CT: Tuttle, Morehouse & Taylor, 1870.

Taliaferro, Edwin. *An Address Delivered before the Masonic Fraternity of Williamsburg, Virginia, November 15, 1860.* Richmond, VA: Macfarlane & Ferguson, 1861.

Tyler, Lyon G. *A Confederate Catechism: The War of 1861–1865*, 3rd ed. Holdcroft, VA: Lyon G. Tyler, 1930.

———. *Williamsburg: The Old Colonial Capital.* Richmond, VA: Whittet & Shepperdson, 1903.

Watts, J. Allen. "An address delivered before the society of the alumni of the college of William and Mary on the occasion of the celebration of the two hundredth anniversary of the charter, June 21, 1893." In *Two Hundredth Anniversary of the College of William and Mary, 1693–1893.* Richmond, VA: Whittet & Shepperdson, 1894.

Unpublished Secondary Sources (Academic Papers)

Chapman, Anne W. "Benjamin Stoddert Ewell: A Biography." Ph.D. diss., College of William and Mary, 1984.

———. "The College of William and Mary, 1849–59: The Memoirs of Silas Totten." Master's thesis, College of William and Mary, 1978.

Heuvel, Sean M. "The Old College Goes to War: The Civil War Experiences of William and Mary Students, Faculty, and Alumni." Master's thesis, University of Richmond, 2006.

Osborne, Ruby O. "The College of William and Mary in Virginia, 1800_1827." Ph.D. diss., College of William and Mary, 1981.

Sacks, David A. "The History of the William and Mary Campus." Bachelor's honors thesis, College of William and Mary, 1984.

Smith, Russell T. "Distinctive Traditions at the College of William and Mary and Their Influence on the Modernization of the College, 1865 to 1919." Ph.D. diss., College of William and Mary, 1980.

Wallenstein, Peter. "Higher Education in Civil War Virginia." Lecture given during Civil War Weekend (March 10, 2007), Virginia Tech, Blacksburg, VA, 2007.

Published Secondary Sources (Articles, Documents, Newspapers, and Periodicals)

Atlanta Journal-Constitution

Barbour, P.P. "John G. Williams." In *Report of the Twenty-Fourth Annual Meeting of the Virginia State Bar Association*, vol. 25. Richmond, VA: Virginia State Bar Association, 1912.

Catalogue of the Alumni and Alumnae for the Years 1865–1923, vol. 18, no. 5. Williamsburg, VA: College of William and Mary, 1923.

Crowson, E.T. "Edward S. Joynes: A Masterful Southern Educator." In *William and Mary Alumni Magazine* (Winter 1986).

Davis, William C. "Edwin Gray Lee." In *The Confederate General* 4 (1990).

Dubbs, Carol K. "Fortress Williamsburg: Treasure through Four Years of War." In *Williamsburg, VA, 1699–1999: A City Before the State.* Robert O. Maccubbin, ed. Commissioned and produced by Martha Hamilton-Phillips, 300th Anniversary Commission, City of Williamsburg. Richmond, VA: Carter, 1999.

"Edward S. Joynes" (pamphlet). Joynes Center for Continuing Studies, Winthrop College, 1981.

Emerson, Jason. "Edwin Booth Saved Robert Todd Lincoln's Life." In *Civil War Times* (June 12, 2006).

Harper's Weekly

The Harvard Crimson

Heuvel, Lisa. "The Peal That Wakes No Echo: Benjamin Ewell and the College of William and Mary." In *Virginia Cavalcade* 28:2 (Autumn 1978).

Heuvel, Sean M. "The Old College Goes to War: The Civil War Service of William and Mary Students," *Virginia Social Science Journal* 42 (2007): 32–48.

The History of the College of William and Mary from its Foundation, 1660, to 1874. Richmond, VA: J.W. Randolph & English, 1874.

Holly, L.N., and J.P. Martin. "Leadership in Crisis: A Historical Analysis of Two College Presidencies in Reconstruction Virginia." *Higher Education in Review* 9 (2012): 37–48.

Knapp, Sharon E. "Benjamin Sherwood Hendrick." In *Dictionary of North Carolina Biography*. William S. Powell, ed. Chapel Hill: University of North Carolina Press, 1979–1996.

Levin, Alexandra L. "The Canada Contact: Edwin Gray Lee." In *Civil War Times* 18:3 (June 1979): 4–8, 42–47.

Longacre, Edward J. "The Most Inept Regiment of the Civil War." In *Civil War Times* 8:7 (November 1969): 4–7.

Massey, Mary Elizabeth. "The Civil War Comes to the Campus." In *Education in the South*. Farmville, VA: Longwood College Press, 1959.

Morrison, Robert. "Historical Sketch of the College of William and Mary." In *The History of the College of William and Mary: From Its Foundation, 1693, to 1870*. Baltimore: John Murphy, 1870.

The New York Times

"Professors at William and Mary College: Charles Morris." In *Tyler's Quarterly* 4 (1922): 130–33.

"Richard Coke." In *The Biographical Encyclopedia of Texas*. New York: Southern Publishing, 1880.

Rouse, Parke, Jr., "'Old Buck': A Hero in Spite of Himself." In *The Alumni Gazette of the College of William and Mary* 50:6 (Winter 1983): 18–20.

Sherman, Richard. "The Last Stand: The Fight for Racial Integrity in Virginia in the 1920s." In *The Southern Historical Association* 54:1 (February 1988), 69–70.

Smith, Russell. "The Second Founding of William and Mary." In *The Alumni Gazette of The College of William and Mary*, 17:6 (January–February 1980), 9–15.

Stetar, Joseph M. "In Search of a Direction: Southern Higher Education after the Civil War." In *History of Education Quarterly* 25:3 (Autumn 1985): 341–367.

Sugrue, Michael. "We Desired Our Future Rulers to Be Educated Men." In *The American College in the Nineteenth Century*. Roger L. Geiger, ed. Nashville: Vanderbilt University Press, 2000.

Swem, E.G. "Kentuckians at William and Mary College before 1861 with a Sketch of the College before that Date." In *Filson Quarterly* 23 (1949).

Thelin, John. "Alma Mater, Lost and Found: The American Campus Restored, 1880 to 1930." In *The Alumni Gazette of the College of William and Mary* 50:6, 9.

Thompson, Robert P. "Colleges in the Revolutionary South: The Shaping of a Tradition." In *History of Education Quarterly* (Winter 1970): 399–412.

Trible, Paul S. "Austin Meredith Trible and John Trible Thomas Hundley II." In *Essex County Historical Society Newsletter* 24:2 (1984).

The Union Army: A History of Military Affairs in the Loyal States 1861–65 — Records of the Regiments in the Union Army — Cyclopedia of Battles — Memoirs of Commanders and Soldiers. Madison, WI: Federal Publishing, 1908.

Wakelyn, Jon L. "Civilian Higher Education in the Making of Confederate Army Leaders." In *The Confederate High Command & Related Topics*. Lawrence L. Hewitt and Roman L. Heleniak, eds. Shippensburg, PA: White Mane, 1990.

Wallenstein, Peter. "The Struggle to Learn: Higher Education in Civil War Virginia." In *Virginia at War, 1864*. William C. Davis and James I. Robertson, eds. Lexington: University of Kentucky Press, 2009.

"William Dunnington Bloxham." In *The National Cyclopaedia of American Biography*, vol. 11. New York: J.T. White, 1901.

Published Secondary Sources (Books)

Alderman, Edwin A., and Joel C. Harris, eds. *Library of Southern Literature*, vol. 7. Atlanta: Martin and Hoyt, 1907.

Allardice, Bruce S. *Confederate Colonels: A Biographical Register*. Columbia: University of Missouri Press, 2008.

_____. *More Generals in Gray*. Baton Rouge: Louisiana State University Press, 2006.

Barrett, Walter. *The Old Merchants of New York*, vol. 5. New York: John W. Lovell, 1885.

Bearss, Sara B., ed. *Dictionary of Virginia Biography*, vol. 3. Richmond: Library of Virginia, 2006.

Bowman, John S. *Who Was Who in the Civil War*. Avenel, NJ: Crescent, 1994.

Brenaman, Jacob N. *A History of Virginia Conventions*. Richmond, VA: J.L. Hill, 1902.

Brinkley, Allen. *The Unfinished Nation: A Concise History of the American People*. 5th ed. Boston: McGraw-Hill, 2008.

Brooks, Robert P. *The University of Georgia Under Sixteen Administrations, 1785–1955*. Athens: University of Georgia Press, 1955.

Burton, William L. *Melting Pot Soldiers: The Union's Ethnic Regiments*. New York: Fordham University Press, 1998.

Carlton, Florence T. *A Genealogy of the Known Descendants of Robert Carter of Corotoman*. Richmond, VA: Whittet & Shepperdson, 1982.

Carmichael, Peter. *The Last Generation: Young Virginians in Peace, War, and Reunion*. Chapel Hill: University of North Carolina Press, 2005.

Cavanaugh, Michael A. *6th Virginia Infantry*. Lynchburg, VA: H.E. Howard, 1988.

Chitwood, Oliver P. *John Tyler: Champion of the Old South*. New York: D. Appleton, 1939.

The Civil War Society. *Encyclopedia of the Civil War*. Princeton: Gramercy, 1997.

Cohen, Michael David. *Reconstructing the Campus: Higher Education and the American Civil War*. Charlottesville: University of Virginia Press, 2012.

Collins, Darrell L. *46th Virginia Infantry*. Lynchburg, VA: H.E. Howard, 1992.

Cushman, Henry W. *A Historical and Biographical Genealogy of the Cushmans: The Descendants of Robert Cushman, the Puritan, from 1617 to 1855*. Boston: Little, Brown, 1855.

Dabney, Virginius. *Mr. Jefferson's University: A History*. Charlottesville: University of Virginia Press, 1981.

DeGregorio, William A. *The Complete Book of U.S. Presidents: From George Washington to Bill Clinton*. New York: Gramercy, 1997.

Driver, Robert J., Jr. *10th Virginia Cavalry*. Lynchburg, VA: H.E. Howard, 1992.

Dubbs, Carol K. *Defend This Old Town: Williamsburg during the Civil War*. Baton Rouge: Louisiana State University Press, 2002.

Du Bellet, Louise P. *Some Prominent Virginia Families*, vol. 2. Lynchburg, VA: J.P. Bell, 1907.

Eicher, David J. *Dixie Betrayed: How the South Really Lost the Civil War*. Lincoln: University of Nebraska Press, 2006.

Elliott, Charles W. *Winfield Scott: The Soldier and the Man*. New York: Macmillan, 1937.

Ferris, Norman B. *The Trent Affair: A Diplomatic Crisis*. Knoxville: University of Tennessee Press, 1977.

Flood, Charles B. *Lee: The Last Years*. New York: Mariner, 1998.

Foner, Eric. *A Short History of Reconstruction*. New York: Harper & Row, 1990.

Frost, Dan R. *Thinking Confederates*. Knoxville: University of Tennessee Press, 2000.

Glenn, Thomas A. *Some Colonial Mansions and Those Who Lived in Them: With Genealogies of the Various Families Mentioned*. Philadelphia: Henry T. Coates, 1899.

Godson, Susan, Ludwell H. Johnson, Richard B. Sherman, Thad W. Tate, and Helen C. Walker. *The College of William and Mary: A History*, vol. 1: *1693–1888*. Williamsburg, VA: King and Queen Press, 1993.

Goff, John S. *Robert Todd Lincoln: A Man in His Own Right*. Norman: University of Oklahoma Press, 1969.

Goodwin, Doris Kearns. *Team of Rivals: The Political Genius of Abraham Lincoln*. New York: Simon & Schuster, 2005.

Govan, Gilbert E., and James W. Livingood. *A Different Valor: The Story of General Joseph E. Johnston, C.S.A.* New York: Bobbs-Merrill Company, 1956.

Greenspan, Anders. *Creating Colonial Williamsburg: The Restoration of Virginia's Eighteenth-Century Capital*. 2nd ed. Chapel Hill: University of North Carolina Press, 2009.

Griffing, Edward S. *Sixth Catalogue of Theta Delta Chi*. Boston: Chapple, 1911.

Harding, Warren G. *Address of the President of the United States at the College of William and Mary, Williamsburg, Virginia, October 19, 1921*. Washington, D.C.: no publisher, 1921.

Hastings, Earl C., Jr., and David Hastings. *A Pitiless Rain: The Battle of Williamsburg, 1862*. Shippensburg, PA: White Mane, 1997.

Henderson, William D. *12th Virginia Infantry*. Lynchburg, VA: H.E. Howard, 1984.

Hudson, Carson O. *Civil War Williamsburg*.

Williamsburg, VA: Colonial Williamsburg Foundation, 1997.
Hughes, Robert M. *General Johnston.* New York: D. Appleton, 1893.
Hull, A.L. *A Historical Sketch of the University of Georgia.* Atlanta: Foote & Davies, 1894.
Hull, Susan R. *Boy Soldiers of the Confederacy.* New York: Neale, 1905.
Hunt, Roger D. *Colonels in Blue: Union Army Colonels of the Civil War (The Mid-Atlantic States).* Mechanicsburg, PA: Stackpole Books, 2007.
Jensen, Les. *32nd Virginia Infantry.* Lynchburg, VA: H.E. Howard, 1990.
Johnston, Frederick. *Memorials of Old Virginia Clerks.* Lynchburg, VA: J.F. Bell, 1888.
Jordan, Ervin L., Jr. *Charlottesville and the University of Virginia in the Civil War.* Lynchburg, VA: H.E. Howard, 1988.
Kale, Wilford. *Hark Upon The Gale: An Illustrated History of The College of William and Mary.* Williamsburg, VA: Botetourt Press, 2007.
Kirwin, Albert D. *John J. Crittenden: The Struggle for the Union.* Lexington: University of Kentucky Press, 1962.
Krick, Robert E.L. *Staff Officers in Gray: A Biographical Register of the Staff Officers in the Army of Northern Virginia.* Chapel Hill: University of North Carolina Press, 2003.
Levin, Alexandra L. *"This Awful Drama": General Edwin Gray Lee, C.S.A., and His Family.* New York: Vantage, 1987.
McCurry, Richard M. *Virginia Military Institute Alumni in the Civil War: In Bello Praesidium.* Lynchburg, VA: H.E. Howard, 1999.
McPherson, James M. *Battle Cry of Freedom: The Civil War Era.* Oxford: Oxford University Press, 1988.
Manarin, Louis H. *North Carolina Troops 1861–1865: A Roster,* vol. 3: *Infantry.* Raleigh: North Carolina Office of Archives and History, 1971.
Miller, Richard F. *Harvard's Civil War: A History of the Twentieth Massachusetts's Volunteer Infantry.* London: University of New England Press, 2005.
Morison, Samuel Eliot. *Three Centuries of Harvard, 1636–1936.* Cambridge and London: Belknap Press of Harvard University, 1946.
Morpurgo, J.E. *Their Majesties' Royall Colledge: William and Mary in the Seventeenth and Eighteenth Centuries.* Washington, D.C.: Hennage, 1976.
Murphy, Terrence. *10th Virginia Infantry.* Lynchburg, VA: H.E. Howard, 1989.
Nanzig, Thomas. *3rd Virginia Cavalry.* Lynchburg, VA: H.E. Howard, 1989.
Newton, Steven H. *Joseph E. Johnston and the Defense of Richmond.* Lawrence: University of Kansas Press, 1998.
Osborne, Charles C. *Jubal: The Life and Times of General Jubal A. Early, CSA, Defender of the Lost Cause.* Chapel Hill, NC: Algonquin, 1992.
Pace, Robert F. *Halls of Honor: College Men in the Old South.* Baton Rouge: Louisiana State University Press, 2004.
Peskin, Allan. *Winfield Scott and the Profession of Arms.* Kent, OH: Kent State University Press, 2003.
Pfanz, Donald C. *Richard S. Ewell: A Soldier's Life.* Chapel Hill: University of North Carolina Press, 1998.
Riggs, David. *13th Virginia Infantry.* Lynchburg, VA: H.E. Howard, 1988.
Robertson, Alexander F. *Alexander Hugh Holmes Stuart, 1807–1891: A Biography.* Richmond, VA: William Byrd, 1925.
Robertson, James I., Jr. *Civil War Virginia: Battleground for a Nation.* Charlottesville: University of Virginia Press, 1991.
Robertson, Wyndham. *Pocahontas and Her Descendants.* Richmond, VA: J.W. Randolph & English, 1887.
Rouse, Parke Jr. *Cows on the Campus: Williamsburg In Bygone Days.* Richmond, VA: Dietz, 1973.
_____. *Remembering Williamsburg: A Sentimental Journey through Three Centuries.* Richmond, VA: Dietz, 1989.
Sinclair, Caroline B. *Gloucester's Past in Pictures.* Virginia Beach: Walsworth, 2005.
Skidmore, Max J. *After the White House: Former Presidents as Private Citizens.* New York: Palgrave-Macmillan, 2004.
Snowden, Yates, ed. *History of South Carolina,* vol. 5. Chicago: Lewis, 1920.
Stevens, William Oliver. *Old Williamsburg and Her Neighbors.* New York: Dodd, Mead, 1938.
Stiles, Kenneth L. *4th Virginia Cavalry.* Lynchburg, VA: H.E. Howard, 1985.
Stonebraker, J. Clarence. *The Unwritten South: Cause, Progress, and Result of the Civil War; Relics of Hidden Truth after Forty Years,* 4th ed. Hagerstown, MD: Hagerstown Bookbinding and Printing, 1903.
Symonds, Craig L. *Joseph E. Johnston: A Civil War Biography.* New York: W.W. Norton, 1992.

———. *Lincoln and His Admirals: Abraham Lincoln, the U.S. Navy, and the Civil War.* New York: Oxford University Press, 2008.
Taylor, Frank H. *Philadelphia in the Civil War 1861–1865.* Philadelphia: City of Philadelphia, 1913.
Thelin, John R. *A History of American Higher Education.* Baltimore: Johns Hopkins University Press, 2004.
Thwing, Charles F. *A History of Higher Education in America.* New York: D. Appleton, 1906.
Trimpi, Helen P. *Crimson Confederates: Harvard Men Who Fought for the South.* Knoxville: University of Tennessee Press, 2010.
Tyler, Lyon G., ed. *Encyclopedia of Virginia Biography,* vol. 4. New York: Lewis Historical, 1915.
———, ed. *Men of Mark in Virginia, Ideals of American Life: A Collection of Biographies of the Leading Men in the State,* vol. 1. Washington, D.C.: Men of Mark, 1906.
———, ed. *William and Mary Quarterly,* vol. 10. Richmond, VA: Whittet & Shepperdson, 1902.
———, ed. *William and Mary Quarterly,* vol. 11. Richmond, VA: Whittet & Shepperdson, 1903.
———. *Williamsburg: The Old Colonial Capital.* Richmond, VA: Whittet & Shepperdson, 1903.
Wallace, Lee A., Jr. *The Richmond Howitzers.* Lynchburg, VA: H.E. Howard, 1993.
Wallenstein, Peter. *Cradle of America: Four Centuries of Virginia History.* Lawrence: University of Kansas Press, 2007.
Warden, Page L. *The Kin Patch: A Path to the Past.* White Stone, VA: Brandylane, 1997.
Warner, Ezra J. *Generals in Blue: Lives of the Union Commanders.* Baton Rouge: Louisiana State University Press, 1964.
———. *Generals in Gray: Lives of the Confederate Commanders.* Baton Rouge: Louisiana State University Press, 1959.
Warren, Gordon H. *Fountain of Discontent: The Trent Affair and Freedom of the Seas.* Boston: Northeastern University Press, 1981.
Wertenbaker, Thomas Jefferson. *Princeton, 1746–1896.* Princeton: Princeton University Press, 1946.
Wills, Brian Steel. *The War Hits Home: The Civil War in Southeastern Virginia.* Charlottesville: University Press of Virginia, 2001.
Wilmer, L.A., J.H. Jarrett, and G.W.F. Vernon. *History and Roster of Maryland Volunteers, War of 1861–5,* vol. 1. Baltimore: Guggenheimer, Weil, 1898.
Wood, Gwen Y. *A Unique and Fortuitous Combination: An Administrative History of the University of Georgia School of Law.* Athens: University of Georgia Press, 1998.
Wyatt-Brown, Bertram. *Southern Honor: Ethics and Behavior in the Old South.* New York: Oxford, 1983.

Online Secondary Sources

"African Americans and the College: A Historical Timeline." The Lemon Project, College of William and Mary. http://www.wm.edu/sites/lemonproject/researchandresources/historicaltimeline/index.php (accessed November 11, 2012).
"Alexander T. Stewart." Picture History. http://www.picturehistory.com/product/id/18312 (accessed May 18, 2011).
"Alexander Turney Stewart." All Biographies, alexander_turney_stewart.htm (accessed May 18, 2011).
Baynes, Thomas Spencer. "Military Law." In *The Encyclopedia Britannica,* vol. 16. H.G. Allen, ed. 1888. k298. http://books.google.com/books?id=BZ0MAAAAYAAJ&pg=PA298&lpg=PA298&dq=cashiering+soldiers&source=bl&ots=PKPCN_8KIf&sig=mA0Pg-EQnrPlbJCbCCctDhScZcw&hl=en&ei=KCTgTY3yEOL10gHi86yoCg&sa=X&oi=book_result&ct=result&resnum=10&sqi=2&ved=0CFgQ6AEwCQ#v=onepage&q=cashiering%20soldiers&f=false (accessed May 27, 2011).
Biographical Directory of the United States Congress: 1771–Present. http://bioguide.congress.gov/biosearch/biosearch.asp
"Biographical Note," John Brown White Papers, Z. Smith Reynolds Library, Wake Forest University. http://zsr.wfu.edu/collections/special/archives/presidentspapers#white (accessed May 16, 2011).
"Biographical Note," Papers of Silas Totten, University of Iowa Libraries and Special Collections, Special Collections & University Archives. http://www.lib.uiowa.edu/spec-coll/archives/guides/RG05/RG05.01.02.htm (accessed May 16, 2011).
Brennan, Kelly, Ben Bromley, Zach Hilpert, Kim Lincoln, Maggie McDonald, Salar Mohandesi, Caroline Murray, Valerie Ponton, Cherie Seise, Constance Sisk, and Sam Walsh. "Integration at Work: The First Labor History of the College of William

and Mary." Unpublished paper. College of William and Mary, 2008, 13–14. https://digitalarchive.wm.edu/handle/10288/411 (accessed August 17, 2012).

Butler, Roseanne Thaiss. "The Man Who Said No." *Civil War Journal* (Autumn 2011). history.org/foundation/journal/autumn11/man.cfm (accessed August 17, 2012).

Clark, Burton. "The Organizational Saga in Higher Education." *Administrative Science Quarterly* 17:2 (June 1972): 178. http://www.wjh.harvard.edu/~dobbin/dobbin%20243%20readings/Clark1972.pdf (accessed November 23, 2012)

"College Cemetery." Special Collections, Swem Library, College of William and Mary. http://scdb.swem.wm.edu/wiki/index.php/College_Cemetery (accessed August 17, 2012).

"Cool Facts." William and Mary History and Traditions. http://www.wm.edu/about/history/coolfacts/index.php (accessed October 18, 2012).

"Copeland's name stricken from award." *Washington Times*, July 26, 2000. http://www.washingtontimes.com/news/2000/jul/26/20000726-011750-9948r/ (accessed July 10, 2011)

Daileda, Colin. "Powell Hall renamed." *The Tartan* (Radford University's student newspaper), September 7, 2010. https://php.radford.edu/~tartan/wp/?p=2389 (accessed July 12, 2011).

Freeman, Douglas Southall. *R.E. Lee: A Biography*. New York: Charles Scribner's Sons, 1934. http://penelope.uchicago.edu/Thayer/E/Gazetteer/People/Robert_E_Lee/FRREL/4/13*.html (accessed June 9, 2011).

Gabriele, Tony. "'To Perish in Its Purity': *Daily Press* editorial urged further racial separation in extreme terms," *Daily Press*, Newport News, Virginia. http://www.dailypress.com/news/black-history/dp-09955sy0may30,0,6566289.story (accessed July 10, 2011).

"George Washington Custis Lee," Arlington House, the Robert E. Lee Memorial (National Park Service, http://www.nps.gov/arho/historyculture/george-lee.htm (accessed June 21, 2011).

Green, Jennifer. "Virginia Military Institute in the Civil War," http://www.encyclopediavirginia.org/Virginia_Military_Institute_During_the_Civil_War," (accessed June 18, 2012).

"Historical Chronology of the College of William and Mary." The College of William and Mary. http://www.wm.edu/about/history/chronology/index.php (accessed May 11, 2011).

"Honorary Degree Recipients." The College of William and Mary. http://swem.wm.edu/departments/special-collections/exhibits/degrees.pdf (accessed June 11, 2011).

Hudson, Carson. "We Bow Our Heads to Yankee Despotism: Occupied Williamsburg in the War Between the States." In *The Colonial Williamsburg Journal* (Summer 2000). http://www.history.org/foundation/journal/summer00/yankee.cfm (accessed July 24, 2011).

"John," Image Archive on the American Eugenics Movement. http://www.eugenicsarchive.org/html/eugenics/essay7text.html (accessed July 15, 2011).

Jordan, Ervin L., Jr. "Charlottesville During the Civil War." *Encyclopedia Virginia*. http://www.encyclopediavirginia.org/Charlottesville_During_the_Civil_War (accessed June 9, 2011).

"Ku Klux Klan." Special Collections Database, Swem Library, College of William and Mary. http://scdb.swem.wm.edu/wiki/index.php/Ku_Klux_Klan (accessed August 17, 2012).

Lipscomb, Thomas. "'Two, Four, Six, Eight. We Want to Integrate.'" *William and Mary Alumni Magazine*, 75:2 (Winter 2009). William and Mary Alumni Association, http://www.wmalumni.com/?winter09_10 (accessed November 11, 2012).

Lombardo, Paul. "Eugenic Laws against Race Mixing During the Civil War." Historic Jamestowne, National Park Service. (accessed November 23, 2012).

"Lyon G. Tyler." Biographical Sketch, Swem Library Special Collections Research Center Wiki, College of William and Mary. http://scdb.swem.wm.edu/wiki/index.php/Lyon_Gardiner_Tyler (accessed November 17, 2012).

McClean, Joseph. "Archaeologists uncover the remains of a Civil War well." *William and Mary Ideation*, August 23, 2012. http://www.wm.edu/research/ideation/arts-and-humanities/life-during-wartime4258.php (accessed October 28, 2012).

Meyers, Terry L. "A First Look at the Worst: Slavery and Race Relations at the College of William and Mary." *William & Mary Bill of Rights Journal* 16:4 (2008): 1158. http://scholarship.law.wm.edu/wmborj/vol16/iss4/8/ (accessed November 10, 2012).

National Park Service, Civil War Soldiers and

Sailors Database: http://www.itd.nps.gov/cwss.

Riggs, David F. "Jamestown During the Civil War," Historic Jamestowne, National Park Service, http://www.nps.gov/jame/historyculture/jamestown-during-the-civil-war.htm (accessed November 23, 2012). "John Tyler," Biographical Sketch, Swem Library Special Collections Research Center Wiki, College of William and Mary. http://scdb.swem.wm.edu/wiki/index.php/John_Tyler (accessed November 17, 2012).

"Sunset Ceremony." Special Collections Wiki, Special Collections Research Center, Swem Library, College of William and Mary. http://scdb.swem.wm.edu/wiki/index.php/Sunset_Ceremony (accessed October 18, 2012)

"Traditions and Legends." Swem Special Collections Wiki, The College of William and Mary. (accessed October 18, 2012).

"University of Alabama Civil War, 1861–1865." The Historical Marker Database. (accessed May 16, 2011).

Vergakis, Brock. "William and Mary Civil War Remnants Discovered." *Huffington Post*, August 19, 2012. http://www.huffingtonpost.com/2012/08/10/william-and-mary-civil-wa_n_1765461.html (accessed August 17, 2012)

Zagursky, Erin. "Lemon Project wins Image award, gears up for events." *The William and Mary News*, April 26, 2011. http://www.wm.edu/news/stories/2011/lemon-project-wins-image-award,-gears-up-for-events-123.php (accessed July 15, 2011).

Index

Numbers in **_bold italics_** indicate pages with photographs.

Adams, Herbert 65, 155–156, 202*n*70, 203*n*94
"Alma Mater of a Nation" 7
Alumni Society 147, 160
American Revolution 1, 12, 15, 17, 20–21, 25, 33–34, 70, 83, 86, 90, 165, 188*n*9, 188*n*11
Anglo-Saxon 161–163, 165
Anglo-Saxon Club 163
Appleton & Co. 146
Armistead, Robert B. 179
Armistead, Robert T. 67, 170
Army of Northern Virginia 49, 67, 69, 71, 75, 96–97, 114, 119, 122

B. Westermann & Co. 43, 192*n*54
Baltimore, Maryland 16, 39, 43, 80, 145
Bardaglio, Peter 30
Barnard, Frederick 39, 146
Battle of Chancellorsville 68, 89, 119
Battle of Fredericksburg 63, 71–72, 74–76, 81, 91–92, 122, 125, 172, 185
Battle of Gettysburg 75, 119
Battle of Shiloh 49, 179
Battle of Williamsburg 11–12, 45, 47, 49–**_50_**, 71–72, 76, 95
Beatty, James 106, 169, 177
Belmont, August 145
Beverly, Robert 18, 187
Bidgood, Sgt. Maj. Joseph V. 76, **_77_**, 78, 81, 170, 195*n*28, 196*n*60
Bird, Hugh S. *see* Seven Wise Men
Bishop, Charles E. *see* Seven Wise Men
Blair, Rev. James 17–18, 154
Bledsoe, Albert T. 103
Board of Visitors (William and Mary): acknowledgment of slavery and racial intolerance 167; alumni in 105, 116, 128, 130–131, 133, 136–137, 143; attending Benjamin Ewell's funeral service 2; Benjamin Ewell's pre-war relations with 23–24, 143; Board actions in 1888 159; after Civil War 136, 156; Civil War activities of 43; Civil War tablet erected by 16; friction with President Ewell in 1850s 188*n*33; John Tyler as member 161; plans to remove College to Richmond by Thomas Jefferson 20–22; post-war attempts to save college 145, 152–153; President Ewell's last report to 158; pre-war political views 37; vote to repair Wren Building after 1859 fire 34
Bonner, Robert 145
Botetourt, Lord 34
Brafferton Historic Campus 15; Federal headquarters 45–46; Indian school 19; 19th century 34, 43–44; post–Civil War 138; restoration 165
Bragg, Gen. Braxton 97–98
Brown, Capt. E.V. 63
Brown University 39
Bruton Parish Church 49
Buchanan, John L. 159
Buckley, Charles W. 150
Busteed, Brig. Gen. Richard 62
Butler, Maj. Gen. Benjamin 130, 149
Buttz, Lt. Charles 45

Cabell, Joseph 22
Cameron Dragoons *see* 5th Pennsylvania Cavalry
Campbell, Col. David 46, 51, 53–55, 59–60, 193*n*11
Carmichael, Peter 7, 31, 162

215

Carter, Robert "King" 70, 118
cashiering 193*n*16
Chambliss, Brig. Gen. John R., Jr. 113, 176
Chambliss, John R., Sr. 113, 176
Chandler, Alvin Duke 164
Chandler, J.A.C. 163, 168
Charles, John 58
Charter Day 10
A Chronicle: A Weekly Insurance Journal 151
Civil War Trail 11
Civil War Trust 12
Clark, Burton 7, 9, 10
Clemson University (Clemson Agricultural College) 142
Cohen, Michael, D. 7, 12, 26
Coleman, Cynthia B. Tucker Washington 70, 73, 81, 88, 137, 195*n*21, 195*n*42–44, 196*n*49, 196*n*75, 197*n*11–12, 201*n*26
College bell 3, 22, 35, 121
College Corner 164
College Hotel 34, 44, 137
College library 25, 34, 37, 40–41, 43, 62, 145
College of Henricus 17
Colonial Williamsburg Foundation 6, 11, 15, 28
Columbia University (Columbia College) 21, 39, 43
A Confederate Catechism: The War of 1861–1865 162
Cooke, John E. 151
Copeland, Walter S. 163, 167
Corcoran, W.W. 145–146
Corse, Brig. Gen. Montgomery D. 77–78, 87
Cranstone, Lefevre James 28
Crittenden, John J. 8, 10, 106, **110**, 111, 113, 131–132, 174
Cronin, Maj. David E., descriptions: of Shingler's Raid 55, 61; of Union vandalism 63–64, 192*n*71; of war 53, 147–148; of wartime Williamsburg 49, 51, **52**, 64
Crump, William W. 157, 177
Custer, Maj. Gen. George A. 122, 133

Dabney, George M. 143
The Daily Press 163
Dartmouth College 158
Davis, Jefferson 62–63, 73, 88, 95, 97–98, 102, 112, 121, 144, 198
Dawson, H.N.R. 157
Dew, Thomas Roderick 23
Dix, Maj. Gen. John A. 51, 53–54, 60, 62
Dodge, W.E. 145
Dubbs, Carol K. 6

Duke of Gloucester Street (Main Street) 42, 51

Earl Gregg Swem Library Special Collections 166–167
Early, Lt. Gen. Jubal 73, 83, 114, 119, 172, 176
Eastern State Mental Hospital (Eastern Lunatic Asylum) 49, 135
Elzey, Maj. Gen. Arnold 62
Emory and Henry College 35, 103
English, Thomas Dunn 145
eugenics 162–163
Ewell, Col. Benjamin S. **23**, **94**; advocate of post-war conciliation 138; attempts to cross Federal lines 134; "bell-ringer" 155; College acting president 23; Commander of 32nd Virginia Infantry 72, 120; criticisms by Rev. Silas Totten 38, 142–143; death of 161; education at West Point 92–93, 154, 197; 1859 fire 25–26; election as College president 38; establishing teacher training at the College 155, 158; faculty member at West Point 93; family of 24, 27, 172; grave in College Cemetery 11, 16; Honorary Fellow of Historical Society of Great Britain 155; lobbying at Congress for compensation 57, 65–66, 147–149, 150, 152, 156; marriage to Julia McIlvaine Ewell 24, 142–143; military service of 85–86, 92–93, 144, 173; "Old Buck" 44; opposing secession 27–29, 37; papers of 6, 166; plan for Peninsula defensive lines 42, 89, 94–95; post-war funding issues 135–136, 138; as president *emeritus* 160; preventing removal of College 137–138, 140, 152, 156, 188*n*33; pre-war protection of College 41, 61; promoting the College's historical significance 6, 13, 139, 141, 154; raising funds for College 139–140, 145–147, 151, 153, 157; rebuilding after war 134; relations with John Tyler 199*n*32; resignation of 144, 159; reviving Phi Beta Kappa chapter 3, 11, 158, 160; significance to College 3, 8, 12, 17; sister's death 144, 146; staff officer 95–96, 98–99, 102–103; support from higher education leaders 157; teaching at other institutions 23; teaching at the College 2, 23, 36, 39; tenure at the College 102, 158, 188*n*32, 192*n*48; work with Board of Visitors 43, 135, 143
Ewell, Elizabeth (Mrs.) 24
Ewell, Julia McIlvaine 24, 142, 143
Ewell, Rebecca 24, 146
Ewell, Lt. Gen. Richard S. 11, 96, 99, 136, 142–144, 173

Index

Ewell Hall (Benjamin Ewell's farm) 143
Ewell Hall (William and Mary building) 16

Faculty Minutes 37, 43, 166
Female Academy 42
5th Pennsylvania Cavalry 46–47, 49, 51, 53–55, 58–59, 62, 152
1st New York Mounted Rifles 52
The Flat Hat 163
Fort Pocahontas 12
Fort Magruder 12, 44, 49–51, 63, 94, 197*n*29
Fort Monroe: diary of Elisha Rhodes 47; Maj. Gen. Benjamin Butler commands 130, 149; military correspondence to 53, 58; 65th Pennsylvania Regiment at 46; Union-held 27, 42, 44, 58, 94

Gardiner, Malachi 3, 155
Garland, William H. 22, 175
Garrett, Dr. R.M. 60
Garrett, Van F. *see* Seven Wise Men
Gee, Capt. Sterling H. 68, 76, 171, 194*n*7
Geiger, Roger 13
Gilman, D.C. 157
Gilmer, Maj. Gen. J.F. 89
Godson, Susan H. 6
Goodrich, Milo 150
Goodwin, Rev. W.A.R. 6, 165
Grant, Madison 162
Grant, Lt. Gen. Ulysses S. 40, 49, 59, *139*, 148, 150, 199*n*18
Greenhow, George 167
Greenspan, Anders 164
Griffin, James 55, 58
Grigsby, Hugh Blair *135*, 138

Haight, Rev. B.L. 146
Hall, John L. *see* Seven Wise Men
Halleck, Maj. Gen. Henry W. 51, 53–54
Hampden-Sydney College 29, 35, 93, 133, 138
Hampton Military Institute (Hampton Male and Female Academy) 130
Hannahs, Capt. Diodate C. 55–58, 64–65, 152; *see also* Yale Class of 1861
Harding, Warren G. 3, 168
Harris, A.W. 157
Harvard University 9, 35, 36, 41, 124, 146
Harvie, E.J. 2
Hawley, H.R. 150
Hill, Lt. Gen. A.P. 71, 83
Hill, Lt. Gen. Daniel H. 89
Hoar, George F. 141, *149*, 150–151
Holmes, George F. 23
Hood, Lt. Gen. John B. 98

Hudson, Carson O. 7
Hughes, Judge Robert W. 149

Jackson, Lt. Gen. Thomas J. "Stonewall": alumni service under 89, 102, 114, 173, 178; Lt. Gen. Richard S. Ewell service under 96; Maj. Gen. William B. Taliaferro's interactions with 124–125; Virginian 27, 73, 83; VMI faculty member 85
James I, King of England 17
James City County 64, 78, 82, 109, 143
James River–York River peninsula 12
Jamestown 10, 15, 18
Jamestown Island 12
Jamestown Road (Mill Road) 49, 164
Jefferson, Thomas 2, 9, 20, 21–22, 63–64, 70, 73, 116, 136, 188, 195
Jefferson Hall 44
Jim Crow laws 163
Johns Hopkins University 155, 157
Johnson, Philip A. 106, 169, 181
Johnston, Gen. Joseph E.: alumni serving under 52, 75, 93–94, 102, 125–126; Benjamin Ewell and 95, 97–*98*, 144, 173; at Bull Run 108; honorary degree awarded 105, 141; Virginian 27; in Williamsburg 45
Jones, Lt. Henley T. 59, 81–82, 171
Jones, Judge Warner T. 157, 177
Joynes, Edward S.: in Confederate service 87, 103, 173, 192*n*48; Eastern Shore native 89; as educator after Civil War 99, 101; professor at William and Mary 11, 36, 41, 43, 85–*86*
Junkin, Rev. George 101

Kale, Wilford 6
Keyes, Maj. Gen. Erasmus D. 56, 58–59
Kilpatrick, Maj. Gen. Judson 62
King, Dr. John C. 44
Ku Klux Klan 163–164

Lamb, Col. William 2, *120*, 121, 123, 130–131, 182
Lawton, Brig. Gen. Alexander R. 11, 87, 173
Lee, Brig. Gen. Edwin Gray 118, 121, *122*, 124–125, 131, 181, 200*n*49
Lee, Maj. Gen. George Washington Custis 144, 201*n*51
Lee, Gen. Robert E.: commander, Army of Northern Virginia 49, 67, 87, 93, 94, 97–99, 102, 114, 118, 122–123, 131, 137, 144, 170, 181; joining Confederate Army 27; at West Point 197*n*25, 198*n*33
Lee, Victoria King 44
Lemon Project 164, 167, 212
Lincoln, Abraham 26, 40, 117

Lincoln, Mary T. 40
Lincoln, Robert T. 40, 191
Longstreet, Lt. Gen. James 95
Lord Botetourt 34
Lyons, James 113, 121, 175

Macfarland, William H. 113, 175
Mackall, Brig. Gen. William W. 97
Madison, Bishop James 158
Magruder, Maj. Gen. John B. 12, 49, 52, 82, 87, 93–95, 130, 177, 197*n*29
Marshall, John 3, 118, 185
Marshall-Wythe Law School 164
Mary II, Queen of England 18–19
Mason, James M. 8, 175
Mason-Dixon Line 10, 36, 42
Massey, Mary E. 189*n*43
Massive Resistance 164
Mayo, William C. 136
McCandlish, Capt. Thomas P. 39, 85, 87, 173, 184
McClaws, Maj. Gen. Lafayette 11, 71, 83, 87–88, 91–92, 118, 172–173, 197*n*11
McClellan, Maj. Gen. George B. 42, 45–47, 49, 51–52, 61, 63, 94, 108, 110, 148
McClelland, Maj. George C. 59–60
McKinney, Maj. Edward P. 56–58, 64, 152, 194*n*29; *see also Life in Tent and Field, 1861–1865*; Yale Class of 1861
McPherson, James 7, 27, 189*n*46, 192*n*53
Meade, Maj. Gen. George G. 69, 83, 148
Mercer, Brig. Gen. Hugh 71
Mercer, Lt. Thomas H. "Tommy" 67, 71, 73, 76, 81, 171
Meyers, Terry 164, 204*n*24
Middle Plantation 18–19
Minor, Charles L.C. 141
Missouri Compromise 109
Monroe, James 3, 9, 70, 109
Montague, Col. Edgar B. 77–78, 95, 120, 183, 196*n*58
Morison, Samuel E. 35, 190*n*10, 191*n*41, 191*n*42
Morpurgo, J.E. 6, 187*ch*1*n*2, 187*ch*1*n*6
Morrill Land Grant Act 35, 146
Morris, Maj. Charles 39, 43, 85, 87, 99, 101, 103, 173, 197*n*7, 197*n*8, 198*n*53
Morrison, Capt. Robert J.: college war protection 41–43; and 1859 fire 25, 36, 139, 189*n*36; military and academic career 85, 88, 173, 192*n*48
Morton, Jackson 113, 131, 175
Mosby, Col. John S. 62
Myers, Lt. John D. 41, 72, 80, 171, 195*n*28

New York (state): alumni connections to 80; Silas Totten from 38

New York City: alumni connections to 80, 177, 192*n*71; Capt. Diodate Hannahs from 56, 65; Columbia University in 39; donors based in 33, 37, 43, 145–146, 151, 191*n*24, 192*n*54; Maj. Edward P. McKinney from 57
New-York Historical Society 52, 61, 192*n*71
The New York Times 50, 55–56, 145, 193*n*1, 194*n*32, 196*n*65, 196*n*78, 202*n*57
Newman, J.J.H. 106, 169, 185
Nicholas, Wilson Cary 136
Nicholson, Frances 18

Old Buck *see* Ewell, Col. Benjamin S.
Old Steward's House 44

Pace, Robert M. 7, 13 189*n*50, 189*n*58, 189*n*60–62, 200*n*2–3, 200*n*7
Page, John 63, 70, 195*n*15
Page, Mann 70
Page, Maj. Peyton 69–70, 73, 75, 78, 171
Palace Green (Courthouse Green) 166
Palmer House *see* Vest Mansion
Paschall, Dr. Davis Y. 11
The Passing of the Great Race see Grant, Madison
Peabody, George 153
Peabody Education Fund 153
Peachy, William S. 43
Perce, Legrand 141, 149, 192*n*70
Peyton, Maria T. 60, 152
Phi Beta Kappa Society 3, 11, 20, 24, 158, 160, 203*n*103
Philadelphia, Pennsylvania 43, 47, 53, 55, 69, 151, 193*n*72
Pierpont, Francis H. 140
Poe, Edgar Allan 145
Pomfret, Edward 164
Powder magazine 49
Powell, John 163, 167
presentism 167
President's House: as Benjamin Ewell's office 155; Capt. Robert Morrison in 25; Ewell family in 24, 143; historic campus 15, 34, 44; post-war repair 137; restoration of 165; Revolutionary War use and damage 33–34, 42, 151; Southall family in 45; Union occupation of 134; use as laboratory space 138
Princeton University 21, 36, 40–41, 151, 164, 190n20, 191n43
Putnam, Sam 64

Quarterpath Road 12

racial purity 162–163
Randolph, Jefferson 136

Index 219

Randolph-Macon College 35, 101, 163, 190*n*68
Ransom, Maj. Gen. Robert 68
Redoubt Park 12
Reynolds, William: career 80; military service 169, 172, 195*n*39; as possible deserter 194*n*2–3; as Unionist student 28–29, 32, 67–68
Rhode Island College 151
Rhode Island Historical Society 63
Rhodes, Elisha Hunt 47, 193*n*74
Richmond Daily Dispatch 37, 191*n*25
Richmond Examiner 38, 191*n*26
Richmond Road (Stage Road) 16, 44, 49, 59
Riggs, David F. 12, 195*n*35, 187*ch*Intro*n*7, 196*n*72
Rives, Capt. Alfred Landon 94
Rives, William Cabell 113, 131, 174
Roanoke College 29, 103
Robert Carter-Saunders House 63
Robertson, James I., Jr. 27, 189*n*48–49, 192*n*51
Robertson, Wyndham 129, 131–132, 175, 200*n*67
Rockefeller, John D., Jr. 6, 164–165
Rouse, Parke 6, 193*n*3, 199*n*15, 199*n*19, 201*n*50
Ruffin, Edmund 10, 131, 174, 200*n*73

Saunders, Robert Jr. 23, 63
Scott, Beverly 143
Scott, Elizabeth "Lizzy" Ewell 24, 142, 202*n*56
Scott, Lt. Gen. Winfield 1, 8, 10, 106, ***107***, 131, 169, 174, 188*n*18, 198*n*6
Scribner's Monthly 151, 202*n*79
Seddon, James 90, 178
Semple, Judge James 109
Seven Days' Battles 47, 76, 91, 96, 110, 122
Seven Wise Men 160
Sheridan, Gen. Philip 57, 133
Shingler, Lt. Col. William P. 51, 55–56, 59
65th Pennsylvania Regiment *see* 5th Pennsylvania Cavalry
Slater, James 55–56, 58, 194*n*27
Smith, Col. Frances H. 142
Snead, Capt. Thomas T.L. 36, 39, 85, 89, 99, 173, 184, 197*n*15
Southall, Mary T. 152
Southall, Virginia 45
Southern Association for the Benefit of Widows and Orphans 147
Southern Orphans Educational Association 147

Stage Road 44, 51, 59
Staples, Waller R. 113, 179
Stetar, Joseph 13, 202*n*62
Stewart, Alexander T. 37, 145, 191*n*24
Stoddert, Benjamin 27
Strode, Henry A. 141
Stuart, Maj. Gen. J.E.B. 12, 27, 69, 82, 111, 119, 122, 184, 199*n*20
Stubbs, James N. 157
Stubbs, Thomas J. 82, 160, 172, 186
Sugrue, Michael 13, 30, 189*n*64–65
Sunset Ceremony (Sunset Parade) 11, 187*n*6

Taliaferro, Maj. Edwin 36, 39, 85, 89–***90***, 99, 102, 173, 192*n*52, 197*n*17, 197*n*19, 197*n*21, 198*n*46
Taliaferro, Maj. Gen. William B.: alumni serving under 70; Board of Visitor member 2, 130, 157; brother of P.A. Taliaferro 180; House of Delegates 129–13, 178; military service 85, 121, ***124***–125, 131, 178, 200*n*57
Taylor, James 46
Taylor, Tazewell 43
"Their Majesties' Royall Colledge" 8, 15, 187*ch*1*n*2
Thelin, John 7, 13, 35, 164, 190*n*11, 204*n*31–32
32nd Virginia Infantry: alumni in 117, 120, 128, 130, 176–186; Benjamin Ewell association with 93, 95, 173; faculty in 173; students in 71–72, 76–77, 81, 87–88, 91, 170–172
Thwing, Charles E. 190*n*12–13, 190*n*20
Totten, Rev. Silas 24, 34–37, ***38***, 39, 142–143, 190*n*8, 190*n*19, 191*n*26–27
Tucker, Cynthia B. *see* Coleman, Cynthia B. Tucker Washington
Tucker, Lt. Thomas S. Beverly 70–71, 73–76, 81, 88, 90, 172, 195*n*21, 195*n*42–44, 196*n*49
Tyler, John ***116***; alumnus 9; arguing against moving college 22, 188*n*17; chancellor 26, 41, 188*n*34; in Confederate Congress 27, 115–116, 131; death of 43; family 69, 114, 161, 176, 180; supporter 12, 39; U.S. president 3, 117, 121
Tyler, Lyon G.: attending the University of Virginia 162; college president 6, 64, 159; department of history named for 167; as historian 22, 64, 82; lobbying for College 157, 159, 161

United Daughters of the Confederacy 12, 166
United States Military Academy at West Point: Benjamin Ewell as faculty mem-

ber 192, 198*n*40; Benjamin Ewell as graduate 23, 38, 92–93, 148, 154, 197*n*25; donates to College 43; other graduates of 59, 96, 119, 144
University of Alabama 35, 41
University of Iowa 38, 142, 191*n*27
University of Knoxville 100, 103
University of Mississippi 35, 39, 142
University of Richmond (Richmond College) 35, 103, 133
University of South Carolina (South Carolina College) 100–101, 103
University of Virginia: alumni of 80, 87–88, 90, 111, 113, 131, 162, 203*n*11; alumni wartime service of 106; Anglo-Saxon Club at 163; bequest to 156; establishment of 21–22, 136, 188*n*17, 188*n*22; faculty wartime service 85; growth of 35–36; in relation to the college 33, 68, 147; stays open in wartime 133–134; student militia company 29, 133; students at 190*n*68

Vanderbilt University 100, 103
Vest, William T. 37
Vest Mansion 51–52, 54, 192*n*71
The Virginia Gazette 165
Virginia Military Institute (Virginia Military Academy): alumni service 106; Col. Frances H. Smith, first superintendent of 142, 144; Corps of Cadets 111; faculty military service 85; lobbying by 147; Maj. Gen. William B. Taliaferro, Board of Visitors member 130; student secessionists at 29, 72; wartime destruction at 41, 133–134
Virginia Polytechnic Institute and State University (Virginia Agricultural and Mechanical Institute) 141, 147
Virginia State University (Virginia Normal and Collegiate Institute) 153

Wallenstein, Peter 189*n*57, 196*n*1, 198*n*54–56, 198*n*4, 202*n*63, 203*n*17
Washington, George 3, 19, 25, 27–28, 70–71, 107, 134, 188*n*9, 188*n*34, 198*n*6
Washington & Lee University (Washington College) 23; alumni of 122; Benjamin Ewell teaching at 93; Edward Joynes teaching at 99–100; Gen. Robert E. Lee as president of 114, 137, 139, 143–144; lobbying by 147; student secessionists at 29; students at 72; Unionists at 103; wartime destruction at 133–134
Watts, J. Allen 160, 203*n*11
The Weekly Gazette 141, 190*n*6, 190*n*8, 201*n*34
B. Westermann & Co. 43, 192*n*54

Wharton, Lyman B. *see* Seven Wise Men
William and Mary Center for Archaeological Research 167
William and Mary College Quarterly Historical Papers 160–161
William and Mary NAACP Chapter 167
William III, King of England *see* Mary II, Queen of England
Williams, John G. 5, 67, 73, 80, 196*n*72
Williamsburg Bicentennial Park 166
Williamsburg, Virginia **59, 65**; after Battle of Williamsburg 46; Anglo-Saxon Club in 162; capital moved to Richmond 21; capital of Virginia colony 20, 22, 32; climate 39; Confederate occupation of 42, 45; Confederate possession of (Shingler's raid) 53–55; Confederate raids on 61; Confederate sympathizers in 28, 50, 62; contested zone during Civil War 46, 49, 50, 51; federal martial law in 52; federal outpost 45; Lemuel Bowden in 109–110; local college students 36, 68, 70–72, 80–82, 87, 128; Lyon G. Tyler history of 64, 162; Maj. David Cronin history of 52–53, 63, 147; Masonic Lodge 90; renamed from Middle Plantation 19; research by Colonial Williamsburg Foundation 6, 64, 166; restoration of 13, 15, 164–165, 187*n*1; Revolutionary War occupation 33; strategic location 27, 49, 62; Victoria Lee King 1861 description of 44; *see also* Battle of Williamsburg
Williamsburg Junior Guard 72, 76, 195*n*28
Williamsburg Masonic Lodge 90
Winthrop College 101, 103, 197*n*5
Wise, Brig. Gen. Henry A.: Board of Visitors member 37; college supporter 3, 138, 149; family of 118, 181; military service 46, 51–53, 62, 89, 96, 110; military strikes against Federals in Williamsburg 46, 51–53, 62, **69**, 96; speech by 121; Virginia governor 83
Wise, John Sargent 136
Wise, Capt. Richard A.: college lobbyist 157; college student militia 28, 69; medical career 78, **79**, 80; military service 70, 73, 75, 118, 172, 195*n*38; Republican 82
Wren, Sir Christopher 187*ch*1*n*1
Wren Building (main building): archaeology 167; Civil War damages cost 135; Civil War memorial tablet 4, **16**, 170; colonial history 9, 15, 33, **34**; Italianate style 35, 141; military use 9, 33, 42, 44–45, **46**; plans for addition ca. 1772 188*n*11; post–Civil War repairs 137, 140, 145; renamed for Sir Christopher Wren 187*ch*1*n*1; restoration 165; September 8,

1862, fire 10, 41, 51; September 9, 1862, fire 53, 57–58, 60, 64–65, 96, 147–148, 150, 152; skirmish outside of *61*
Wren Chapel 2, 149
Wyatt-Brown, Bertram 30, 189*n*62
Wythe, George 3, 20, 25, 70, 195*n*19

Yale Class of 1861 *see* Hannahs, Capt. Diodate C.; McKinney, Maj. Edward P.
Yale University 3, 35–36, 39, 55–57, 190*n*20, 194*n*31, 194*n*34

Yeardley, Sir George 17
York, Pennsylvania 24, 142
Yorktown, Virginia: college regiment 72, 94; federal occupation of 62; historic triangle 12; Maj. Edward P. McKinney at 58; Peninsula Campaign 42, 46–47, 51, 53–54, 56, 94; Revolutionary War siege of 151; students from 36; Yorktown Centennial 153

www.ingramcontent.com/pod-product-compliance
Lightning Source LLC
Chambersburg PA
CBHW032052300426
44116CB00007B/702